Business English

"A Complete Reference Manual for Effective Business Communication"

Prem P. Bhalla

Published by:

F-2/16, Ansari road, Daryaganj, New Delhi-110002
23240026, 23240027 • *Fax:* 011-23240028
Email: info@vspublishers.com • *Website:* www.vspublishers.com

Regional Office : Hyderabad
5-1-707/1, Brij Bhawan (Beside Central Bank of India Lane)
Bank Street, Koti, Hyderabad - 500 095
040-24737290
E-mail: vspublishershyd@gmail.com

Branch Office : Mumbai
Jaywant Industrial Estate, 2nd Floor–222, Tardeo Road
Opposite Sobo Central Mall, Mumbai – 400 034
022-23510736
E-mail: vspublishersmum@gmail.com

Follow us on:

All books available at **www.vspublishers.com**

© **Copyright:** *V&S Publishers*
ISBN 978-93-505717-3-6
Edition 2016

The Copyright of this book, as well as all matter contained herein (including illustrations) rests with the Publishers. No person shall copy the name of the book, its title design, matter and illustrations in any form and in any language, totally or partially or in any distorted form. Anybody doing so shall face legal action and will be responsible for damages.

Printed at : Param Offseters, Okhla, New Delhi-110020

Publishers Note

V&S Publishers has published a number of books in the **English Improvement** category by the name of **EXC-EL Series**, such as *English Grammar and Usage*, *English Vocabulary Made Easy*, *Improve Your Vocabulary and Spoken English*. This book, **Business English** is a valuable addition to this exclusive series of books that helps readers to improve one's both Spoken and Written English which has though emerged from England but has been Indianised to suit our needs. However, *there are certain words and phrases in English* that are commonly used in *official and business transactions* across the globe, particularly in India as English is primarily used in offices as well as schools as a medium of instruction.

Business English is not just an offshoot of a popular language used to communicate with each other. It is much more. *Business involves buying and selling of products and services*. From this has emerged several professions, many of them highly specialised in the modern world. Each of the specialisations has adopted or developed words from within the language, making Business English, yet more complex.

The main objective and motto of publishing this book is to equip a person to know the *polished and highly refined English language* that is generally used in big companies, offices, MNCs, etc., and to make it easy for the person to understand and communicate in the English language that is used in professional and business circles in India and throughout the world.

Business English is therefore very important, or rather indispensable for people pursuing any kind of business or profession and also for building good professional relationships. To be able to be proficient in English and to understand the language well, as well as the various facets of human behaviour, one has to learn Business English thoroughly. Learning this language also becomes necessary to understand the many factors that influence success in business and professional life. This makes the study of the subject more complex than learning just another language.

Basically, ***Spoken and Written Business English*** bridges the gap between the elementary knowledge of the language which is usually taught in schools and colleges to the complex requirements of the language to succeed in one's professional and business career.

The book is a treasure trove of the vast knowledge accumulated by the author in English language, its varied uses over centuries of observations of human behaviour, development of business and professional activities in and outside India, and most important, the gradual development and modernisation of this vast, rich and diverse language.

Hope the book serves its purpose well in educating and enlightening its esteemed readers!

Contents

Publisher's Note 3
Preface 7

Section 1 – Communication Basics 11
1. Business is People 13
2. Communicating Effectively 14
3. Communication Skills 17
4. Body Language 19
5. Developing Self-confidence 31
6. Etiquette and Manners 33
7. Communicating through Silence 39

Section 2 – Spoken Business English 42
8. The English Language 43
9. English as a Second Language 45
10. Speaking English 47
11. Learning to Speak 49
12. Be A Good Listener 51
13. Learning Some Essentials 53
14. Making a Conversation 54
15. Asking Questions 55
16. An Effective Vocabulary 58
17. Speaking on the Telephone 59
18. Speaking on the Mobile Phone 61
19. The Magic of Words 63
20. A Difficult Word to Use 65
21. Speaking about Yourself 66
22. Mind What You Speak 67
23. At an Interview 69
24. A Telephonic Interview 71
25. A Luncheon Interview 72
26. Learning Negotiating Skills 73

27. Handling Conflict at the Workplace 77
28. Group Discussion 79
29. Speaking to Sell 83
30. Speaking at Meetings 91
31. Speaking in Public 98
32. Self-development as a Speaker 101
33. Conveying an Effective Message 106
34. Delivering an Effective Speech 111
35. Reading a Speech 114
36. Mistakes to Avoid When Speaking 115
37. Understanding the Audience 117
38. Aids for Effective Speaking 120
39. Telephonic and Video-conferencing 123

Section 3 – Written Business English 126
40. Why is Written English Important? 127
41. Written Business English 129
42. Clarity in Writing 131
43. Writing Concisely 140
44. Courtesy in Writing 144
45. Writing Convincingly 145
46. Writing a Complete Message 147
47. ABC of Writing 148
48. Using Punctuation Marks 149
49. Effective Writing Tools 152
50. Developing a Personal Writing Style 154
51. Polishing A Written Document 156
52. Writing about Yourself 158
53. Writing A Letter 171

54. Addressing the Envelope 176
55. Writing a Personal Letter 178
56. Writing a Cover Letter 180
57. Writing Business Letters 185
58. Writing a Follow-up Letter 188
59. Writing Persuasive Letters 191
60. Writing Letters of Complaint 193
61. Writing to Convey Unpleasant News 195
62. Writing Meeting-Related Documents 200
63. Communicating Within the Office 203
64. Filling Forms, Records and Returns 208
65. Writing Business Reports 210
66. Writing a Technical Report 215
67. Writing a Project Feasibility Report 218
68. Writing a Business Plan 223
69. Writing A White Paper 228
70. Understanding Audit Reports 230
71. Writing a Legal Document 233
72. Publishing an In-house Newsletter 247
73. Writing a Press Note 251
74. Writing An Advertisement 253
75. Using Electronic Mail 255
76. Using SMS 261

Section 4 – Reference Section 265

Preface

English emerged as the spoken language of England. The people of England were adventurous and outgoing. This took them to faraway places in search for *fortunes that Mother Nature had showered on mankind*. Their language travelled with them; and they shared it wherever they went. Many countries gradually accepted it as the *first language*. Today, *besides England*, English is the *mother tongue in U.S.A., Australia, New Zealand* and several other countries around the world. However, several nations have accepted it as a *second or business language*.

The language spread just as their influence grew in trading all over the world. The need for effective communication in trading led to the gradual emergence of what is known as *Business English* today.

Business English is not just an offshoot of a popular language used to communicate with each other. It is much more. *Business involves buying and selling of products and services*. From this has emerged several professions, many of them highly specialised in the modern world. Each of the specialisations has adopted or developed words from within the language, making *Business English*, yet more complex.

A language is a living entity. It is forever growing. New words are adopted from other languages or created through popular use. *While the English language is growing so is Business English*. An important aspect of any language is that there are words that touch human feelings and emotions, and influence behaviour and relationships. Since all businesses and professions are based upon the concept that these fulfill human needs, it becomes necessary for all of them to develop good relationships to attain success in their field of activity.

Business English is, therefore, a medium of communication, pursuing a business or profession and also building good relationships. To be able to do this, a person needs to know the language well and also understand human behaviour. It also becomes necessary to understand the many factors that influence success in business and professional life. This makes the study of the subject more complex than learning just another language.

Spoken and Written Business English bridges the gap between the elementary knowledge of the English language taught in schools and colleges to the complex requirements of succeeding in a career by understanding human behaviour, and knowing what to speak and write on different occasions.

Since modern businesses and professions require complex handling at different times and on special occasions, the subject has been broadly covered in simple easy-to-understand language. To make it easier for the reader, the book has been planned in **four distinct sections**. While the *first section* deals with *Communication Basics* explaining the involuntary and voluntary use of body gestures to communicate with each other, the *second section* deals with *Verbal Communication* and the *third* with *Communicating through the Written Word*. An elaborate *fourth section* has been compiled to include *Reference Materials* that can help broaden one's knowledge and use of Business English in everyday life.

A person learns by seeing and understanding how others do it in different situations. To enable this, elaborate examples have been included throughout the book explaining the use of concepts and principles one must remember at the workplace. These examples can be easily adapted for use in businesses and professions. A person could do so until such time that one can handle the situation independently. *This makes this book a ready reference guide that every businessman or professional needs to keep in his/her workplace.*

I am grateful to *Graphic Impressions, Mumbai,* for the use of the *caricatures* to illustrate the use of *body gestures in communicating with each other.*

The book is based upon the vast knowledge accumulated over centuries of observation of human behaviour, development of business and professional activities, and most important, the gradual development of the English language. I offer my salutations to all those unknown people who have contributed to the *development of Business English* we use today at our workplaces around the world.

Happy Reading and Learning!

–**Prem P. Bhalla**

Section 1

Communication Basics

Mutual interaction is a basic necessity of all mankind. One can hardly live without it. Ask any prisoner punished with solitary confinement. Knowledge of a language is no limitation to interact with each other. *A baby cannot speak and can yet interact with the mother.* The mother and child communicate through touch, through love and care. Who has not seen a child running to a mother waiting for him with open arms and a welcome smile on the face?

Just as a person can express love without speaking a word, it is equally possible to convey feelings of anger, jealousy and hatred without speaking a word. We see it in our homes, at the workplace and society each day. Without a word said or written, feelings are communicated easily.

There are innumerable languages and dialects used to communicate with each other. The written languages further strengthen communication ability. Mankind could be using several languages for mutual interaction. *Of these, English is a very important link language among the people spread all over the world.* Yet we cannot overlook the significance of *mutual interaction* and *communication through facial expressions and body gestures*, which sometimes convey much more than spoken words.

Irrespective of the language one speaks or writes, communication through facial expressions and body gestures is common to all mankind. People love and hate, laugh and cry, and do many other things without a word. We must understand these gestures before we can speak or write well.

This section of the book is dedicated to understand human reactions and behaviour that make it possible to understand our own body language and also that of the people we interact with. It is equally important to understand that when we live in a civilised world and are involved in a variety of businesses and professions, we must observe certain etiquettes and manners so as not to hurt someone's sensitivities. *It is also important to understand how mankind uses silence to introspect and also use it as a communication method to please or to punish others.*

Success in business and professional activities depends greatly upon human relationships, which are closely related to communication basics. Only after a person has understood the communication basics, it becomes easier to learn how to speak and write a language well. We will discuss these in greater detail in later sections.

Chapter 1

Business is people. So is every profession. Success at the workplace in every business and profession comes from good relationships with the people one deals with every day. *The greater the harmony a person can develop with the people, the better the performance and greater the attainment of success.*

Sallust suggested, "Harmony makes small things grow; lack of it makes great things decay." Harmony between people comes from trust, from agreement of thoughts and actions. This, in turn, is possible only when people communicate freely, leaving nothing to doubt. It is the doubt that sows the seeds of suspicion, leading to distrust and disharmony. *Effective communication ensures that there is a*

Just as effective communication is the lifeblood of a successful organisation, it is also the stepping stone to success for all people. Everyone needs to communicate effectively – at home, at the workplace and in the society. All relationships are built upon a person's ability to communicate with others. The human body is sending out messages at all times. We need to understand them better. *Using the faculty of speech, mankind has evolved almost 5,000 languages and dialects to communicate with each other.* Written languages followed later. *A spoken language is the most popular way to communicate between people; other methods followed later out of human necessity.*

One form of communication that must have emerged even before the development of the faculty of speech would be body language whereby every person is continuously sending out messages through body gestures without even being aware about it. Have you ever observed how much a smile can

to others. What about the eyes? There is so much that two lovers convey without uttering a word. The parents and the children communicate all the time through the eyes. When the face conveys so much, the different parts of the body cannot be far behind.

Every person is continuously observing others for the messages they are conveying through the spoken words, *the body language* and in many cases, through the written word. Of the 5,000 spoken languages and dialects used by people around the world, the English language has a special position in that it is not restricted to a particular part of the world. The circumstances and situations have made it a universal means of connecting people in different countries and regions, promoting the development of better relationships, business and trade around the world.

Business is People

Chapter 2

All relationships are built by communicating effectively with each other. This need begins at birth and continues throughout life. At every stage and at all levels, relationships are sustained through effective communication.

Communication is an act or process of sharing or exchanging thoughts, opinions or information. It also refers to something *imparted, interchanged or transmitted. Generally, it refers to the use of speech or written words and is done through speech or messages from one person to another, as through conversation, speaking on the telephone or conveying a written message through a SMS, a memo, a letter or through Internet.* The changing world has made it possible to communicate in many ways. The real purpose is to communicate one's feelings, sentiments and emotions that are the foundation of all relationships.

This is achieved not only through the spoken or written words, but many times, even through one's presence on a particular occasion. Strangely, much can also be communicated through silence when the method is used to introspect or talk to oneself. Many use silence as a potent tool to punish another person. This is common amongst couples, or between parents and children.

Have you observed how people communicate through their dress, make-up and personal mannerisms and habits? Even the fragrances used by men and women communicate much about them. In religious *positive vibrations* that are unknowingly communicated to them. In the same way, the negative vibrations in some places make people alert to the lurking dangers. The *positive* and the *negative vibrations* emerge from the positive or negative thoughts in the minds of people.

Communication is instinctive initially. Have you ever observed a woman who realises for the

communicate with the mother and a strong bond of love and attachment develops between the two. At birth, a baby cannot speak or write. Yet it has the ability to communicate his/her needs to the mother and father.

baby learns other sounds related to various needs and objects around the house. Learning is made easy by using *colourful objects, pictures, rhythm and music.* It has been observed that children respond well to the *rhythm of poems* rather than to *plain words. Music enables use of rhythm and scale and through repetition, the information gradually sinks into the sub-conscious mind gradually building up the child's vocabulary.* This is the beginning of learning in an individual. *Communication skills are built gradually upon this simple learning.*

. Information is growing steadily and one begins to sort out what is useful and what is not. No two individuals are alike. Therefore, it becomes necessary to understand how others react to particular situations and circumstances. This is important for communicating effectively in everyday life.

Next to parents, it is the responsibility of teachers to provide knowledge to children. If a teacher cannot communicate effectively to a student, he or she has no business to be in the teaching profession.

teaching only. Here are a few common examples that make effective communication necessary for everyone:

Medicine – Can a doctor treat a patient effectively until the patient is able to communicate effectively about his or her problem? The doctor must be clear about what treatment would be best in a particular situation. Besides a physical examination, doctors maintain a complete record about the patient at all levels of treatment.

Law – Can a lawyer represent a client effectively without knowing the exact problem? In the same way, is it possible for the lawyer to explain his client's side of the case without knowing it well? Besides knowing the circumstances of the case well, the lawyer also needs to effectively communicate the legal angle of the situation to the judge.

Business – Can a business succeed without everyone involved in it knowing what is to be done? Everyone must be sure about what is to be done, how it is to be done and when it must be done. This is possible only through effective communication at all levels irrespective of the size of the business.

Science and Technology
technology. This progress is of no use unless it can reach those people who can translate this

at each stage and at every level?

Selling–Is it possible for a salesperson to sell anything without convincing a prospective

the quality of the product, and then to convey the same to the prospective customer.

Government – The government serves mankind in a variety of ways offering the necessary services through many departments. From the lowest to the highest level wherein new laws are enacted, every person serving in the government needs to communicate effectively. At all times, information is passed on from the lowest level to higher levels and vice versa.

work suffers. We see it happening every day.

Home – All businesses and services are targeted to serve the common man. His home is the primary institution that contributes to form a community, a village, a town or a city. Within this home, there is a family. Even within this family the need for effective communication cannot be overlooked. *A happy married life depends upon two-way effective communication between the husband and wife.* In the same way,

happy family and a good society.

lives. We need it everywhere. We know how important it is to all of us, yet each day, we see how easily we face defeat because of lack of it. *Charles E. Kettering* explains, "*We can communicate an idea around the world in seven seconds, but it sometimes takes years for an idea to get through one-fourth inch of the human skull.*"

Effective communication is a skill. It is the responsibility of all parents and teachers to teach it to all children. When they fail to do so, it is for the individuals to learn it. A successful life depends upon it.

Chapter 3

The ability to communicate well is a skill that all people desiring success must learn. A few are extremely that lead to effective communication. An important thing that everyone must understand is that like all other skills, one can learn communication skills by understanding the different aspects of the subject and putting them to use in everyday life at home, at the workplace and in the society where we live.

A newborn baby is able to communicate instinctively with the mother because of the bonds that develop between the mother and the unborn baby. As the baby grows up, the communication is restricted to the parents and the immediate family. At school, the teachers try to develop skills in all the children, but since each one is unique in his or her own way, their perception of looking at the same thing varies sharply based upon what their parents have taught them and how their genetic characteristics have reacted to the situations they have come across in life.

Effective communication skills appear to be very simple and easy. But unfortunately, they are not. Most skills depend upon the ability and perseverance of the person who has acquired the skill. Communication skills are different.

Effective communication depends not only upon the person who is trying to communicate a message, but equally so upon the person or persons at whom the message is targeted. *A minimum of two persons are involved in an effective communication.* While it is the responsibility of the person trying to communicate the message to ensure that the message conveys what he or she desires to communicate, it shall remain ineffective unless the targeted person receives the message in the same sense and spirit that the message is communicated. Since two persons can look at the same thing with different perceptions, there is the likelihood of the message becoming weak. When more than two persons are involved, the message could weaken further with everyone interpreting it in his or her own way.

To be effective, the message must be clear and conveyed in a form that the targeted person can receive and understand it without any misinterpretation. *This means that an effective communication is possible only when there is a clear two-way understanding between the sender and the receiver, and again a feedback from the receiver to the sender.* **In any situation, the following factors would of a message:**

The sender – He or she must be clear about what is to be conveyed and to whom.

The message – It must be clear so that it cannot be misinterpreted.

Appropriate method to convey the message – It could be verbal, written or by some other way.

The recipient – He or she must receive the message appropriately, understanding what it intends to convey.

Communication Skills

A feedback – When the recipient gives a response on the message to the sender, the level of effectiveness of the message can be gauged. And this is called a *feedback*.

effectiveness of a communication. Since each person is unique and has a distinct personality and of course, a way of looking at things, it becomes imperative that the sender must have a personality and ability so that the recipients can accept the message. At the same time, it would be necessary for the sender to understand what makes the recipients receptive to the message. In both the cases, a person needs to learn skills that promote good human relationships. Some learn these skills quickly. *Most people struggle with hit-and-miss methods throughout life.*

The message could be verbal, written or in any other form, but it must attract the attention of the recipients and must be simple to be understood. Each situation would be different from the other and therefore, the sender would need to develop skills to convey verbal messages through effective speaking in different circumstances. It would also be necessary to learn skills to write a variety of messages to

Advances in technology have made it possible to convey messages effectively through different means, but that has simultaneously increased the responsibility of understanding and using modern technology.

Few understand it in depth that every person conveys much through *body language*. We are being observed by others all the time and our gestures are conveying messages that could make or mar our image in the eyes of the people, who would be the recipients of our messages. This requires that a

make others attractive to what is spoken to individuals or groups and also written to individuals or to the society in general. *Personality development is a continuous process, which is best started early but would go on throughout one's life.*

Chapter 4

Irrespective of the language a person uses to communicate with others, everyone is continuously communicating even without uttering or writing a word. Messages are being communicated through the body without a person being conscious about it.

Take a look at the *ten caricatures of the same person made in different situations*. Without he saying a word, you can see a variety of emotions in different pictures - *surprise, shock, doubt, confusion, anger, happiness, smugness, fear, shame* and *"I couldn't care less"* attitude. Every person behaves differently on particular occasions and the face immediately sends out signals that can be understood by those who are conscious about them and use the information to their personal advantage.

. When you become aware of individual reactions in certain situations, you begin to appreciate how little things can convey a complete message without a word spoken. *The facial expression is a combination of the reactions of the eyebrows, the*

livid, or folds to frown. Dimples can be expressive also. All kinds of emotions ranging from love to fear can be seen on the face. You can also see *anger, greed and hatred. The expressions change with the feelings and emotions*.

People who understand body language can immediately understand how the other person is feeling by observing the facial reactions and act accordingly. In an appropriate situation a businessman would negotiate a deal, a salesman would close the sale, and a person making a presentation would deliver the punch-line to drive home his point. When the other person does not react in a desired manner it would

Body Language

The caricatures in the last page depict expressions in men. In comparison, how do the women react? Are they as expressive as men? *The truth is that men try to control their feelings and emotions more than women.* They are able to hide their reactions. *Women are very expressive.* You will appreciate this fact when you see the caricatures of a woman expressing a variety of emotions. Look at each caricature for a moment and try to understand what feelings are expressed through the facial expression.

Watch the *eyebrows, the eyes, the nose, the lips and the chin*. Watch how the expression changes with the each little part of the face   . In real

are conveyed to the onlooker.

It is useful to observe the whole face because the position of the head when tilted forward indicates an interest in the other person, a head held casually and eyes shifting from one point to another indicates lack of interest. *Since the facial expression is a combination of the reaction of several distinct parts, it would be useful to consider each separately.*

The Eyebrows: The eyebrows are very expressive of a person's feelings. Raised eyebrows express surprise and mild disapproval. They also express *envy and disbelief.*

The Forehead: It is natural for sweat to break out on the forehead when a person is nervous or afraid. The skin on the forehead folds when a person frowns or is angry. The forehead also

The Eyes: The eyes are the most expressive of all on the face. The size of the pupils is

pupils to dilate. Fear shows immediately in the eyes. Eye contact is important in expressing feelings when building relationships. When a mother and child look at each other, or when two lovers are deeply interested in each other, the pupils dilate making the contact intense. In well-knit families, it is common for much to be communicated amongst each other only through eye contact.

Generally, during conversation, people look at each other for 30 to 60 percent of the time. When it exceeds 60 per cent, it is apparent that the individual is more interested in the other person rather than in the conversation. It has also been observed that a person makes a longer eye contact when listening rather than when talking. *Longer eye contact when listening facilitates the process of learning.*

Eye contact is interpreted differently in cultures around the world. For example, in many cultures, the younger persons are expected to look down when addressing elder or superior people. In the same way in some cultures, the women must not look directly when talking to in-laws and senior members of the family. Long eye contact in such instances could be interpreted as an aggressive act. At other times, lack of eye contact could be interpreted as lack of trustworthiness. People who make eye contact easily

. A look into the eyes expresses mutual interest.

person, love, frustration and fear, threat or anger. *Celebrities are often seen to hide their eyes behind dark glasses.*

the use of innumerable phrases that literally speak for themselves. They are useful in appreciating the

life:

Look down upon a person, meaning to have a poor opinion about a person.

Look up to a person, meaning to seek guidance and help from a person with a greater ability or higher position.

Look away from someone or something, meaning to avoid a person or situation.

Steal a quick look at someone or something, meaning to assess a person or situation quickly.

Steal an eye, meaning to take a quick look at someone or soothing without anyone getting to know about it.

He gave him an 'eyeful', meaning a long steady look.

Give someone the eye, meaning looking at someone with interest.

cherish.

Tears well up in the eyes when a person is in pain, which could be real or perceived. It would be natural for people to cry when sad, lonely or when ignored. Tears could also be just a ploy to persuade someone to do something. It is also common for the eyes to get wet when a person is moved emotionally out of joy and happiness.

Spectacles: Everybody does not wear spectacles. They are also not like dark glasses that enable a person to hide their reactions. People who wear spectacles unconsciously use them

his spectacles, put them on the table or clean the lenses and wear them again. This suggests that the person is seeking time to think and decide on what the other person might have said.

Body Language

Many people let the spectacles slip down to the lower bridge of the nose and close the eyes. This expresses that the person is trying to concentrate on the proposal, the other person might have given. It could also mean that he is searching for a solution to a problem. These gestures are common amongst highly educated people like business executives, doctors and lawyers trying to seriously understand a problem.

Some people use the spectacles as a weapon when holding it in the hand pointing it towards the door to convey to a person to leave. Taking off the spectacles and aggressively placing them on the table would express a threatening gesture. It is common to see judges and lawyers doing this in the courtroom expressing, "You're going beyond limits." This could also be an expression of resistance. This would require a change in strategy immediately.

The Nose: *A person breathes and smells through the nose. Breathing means life. The moment it stops, life ends. The nose appreciates certain fragrances, but also detests certain odours.* Watch a child's reaction to food. His nose will tell it all. Observe people at a party. Just by observing the reaction of the nose, you will understand what a person likes or disapproves. *Turning up the nose universally means dislike and rejection.* The nostrils and short breathing immediately express anger. *When it is accompanied with scratching of the back of the head, it would express frustration. Deep breathing and slow exhaling express disgust and frustration.* . Some people pinch the bridge of the nose with the eyes closed. This means that the person is thinking and trying to come to a conclusion. Rubbing the nose with the eyes open is an expression of doubt. When negotiating a deal, one could make a counter offer to close a deal.

The Lips: The shape and the size of the lips is an inherited characteristic. However, like the eyes the lips express the most particularly because they are used to smile. To smile means to form the lips to express pleasure, happiness and friendliness. A smile is the bread and butter of the people in the hospitality industry. It helps earn millions of dollars each year.

friends. A smile expresses joy. Accompanied with appropriate eye contact it communicates a greeting to a friend or acquaintance. Both victory and happiness are conveyed with a big broad smile.

All smiles are not the same. A smile could also express sarcasm, an effort to ridicule another person.

in amusement.

Smoking: Just as the use of spectacles is closely linked with the eyes, smoking is related to the lips. Despite worldwide warnings against smoking people continue to smoke cigarettes, *biris* and the pipe. Smoking is addictive. It gives a great inner feeling of relaxation. Since a smoker

In between deep puffs, people keep looking at the cigarette as though to read what is written on it. Sometimes they keep looking into nothing. Others close their eyes as they puff, using a cigarette as a tranquillizer to soothe the nerves. When relaxed they might make smoke rings. Whenever there is a greater need to concentrate the smoker tends to take deeper puffs. After some smoking the person makes a decision. Those who smoke pipes take longer to make decisions. They keep playing hide and seek as they light the tobacco repeatedly in the pipe.

The Chin

cheerful" when things get tough. Since the chin is the hard part of the face, some would say, "Take it on the chin", meaning "accept the situation without complaining". When a person rubs the chin during a conversation it means that he is trying to evaluate facts. Stroking the beard during a conversation also has a similar meaning. Tightening of the jaw muscles and

students it is common for physical trainers to shout, "Hold your heads up, chins out and the stomach in."

The Hands: Next to the face, it is the hands that are involved in conveying a message. The most popular use of hands in inter-personal relationships is to convey greetings.

Some raise the hand and say, "Hi" or "Hello". A handshake is a common form of greeting in many parts of the world. The custom of shaking hands varies from one nation to another and also from one culture to another. Women working in a man's world also shake hands, but not the same way as men do. When two women meet, they may not shake hands but exchange greetings by holding hands with a facial expression of joy.

hands indicate a nervous temperament. Politicians and public people shake hands with the right hand and cup it with the left hand to convey expression of being close and concerned. Those who are close shake hands with the right hand and also hold the shoulder with the left hand. Some embrace. Along with

In India, the customary greetings is conveyed by raising the arms and putting the palms together to say, "Namaste" or "Namaskar" meaning "Welcome!" I bow to the divinity in you". It is also customary for younger people to greet elders and senior people by touching their feet to seek their blessings. The hands of a couple put together express deep feelings of love, loyalty and commitment for each other.

Quintilian explained, "Other parts of the body assist the speaker but the hands speak for themselves. By them we ask, promise, invoke, dismiss, threaten, entreat, deprecate. By them, we express fear, joy, grief, our doubts, assent or penitence; we show moderation or profusion, and mark number and time."

Besides the face, the hands too convey the most through a variety of gestures. To express the universal gesture of complete

not armed and mean no harm.

It is common for people to fold their arms across the chest. Women fold their hands at a lower level because of the structure of the upper torso. This position expresses a position of defence, or closing up. The person desires to check everything before accepting it. The younger generation uses this posture to defy their parents. Teachers, doctors and other professionals use it against their colleagues. Through this gesture, each expresses, "I know best. Why should I move?"

person is rigid and is of the extreme view.

extreme option, the discussion would be futile. In such situations, they are "turned off". Some things can be achieved only when people are open-minded. Therefore, when holding discussions or negotiating a deal, it is essential to observe the other person closely and ensure that he or she remains open-minded. If it is suspected that the person is gradually closing away, it would be appropriate to change one's strategy or even postpone the negotiations for another day.

A common sight particularly during interviews is one of a person holding tight

A person who holds his hands on the hips is conveying readiness to get into action. It is common

plans to attain them stand like that to instruct the team to follow him. The younger generation uses these gestures to face their parents.

When an individual faces another person standing beside a table has the two arms widespread it is an expression of an ultimatum. It is common to see this when young people do not approve the parents' demands, or when a subordinate wants to tell the boss that "enough is enough". In such circumstances a person must use patience and tact to diffuse the feeling of anger and frustration, and also reassure the other person that perhaps all the facts are not known to him or her.

This is a common gesture to be seen amongst policewomen. Generally, the girls are taught not to have their hands in the back because it emphasises the bosom, which is not approved in some cultures.

Public speakers are well known for gesticulating movements with their hands to emphasise what

When a person suddenly covers the mouth with the hand it expresses astonishment. However, when in conversation with elbows resting in the table a person covers the mouth with the hand it means that he or she is trying to withhold some information. It could also express self-doubt and lying. It could also be that the person is trying to hold back for the conversation to come to a conclusion.

Though children use the gesture most adults also place the palm at the back of the neck. Women do it deceptively pretending to do up their hair. This is a defensive gesture and is popularly referred to

pendant.

or even clutching the chair before sitting on it. These people seek to be reassured through help and cooperation.

Another example of people seeking reassurance is when we see people drumming on a tabletop or

of a mother reassuring the unborn baby. The beat of the drumming could also express boredom. When the beat slows down it expresses the possibility of a reconsideration of the issue and making a decision.

and proud. Showmen, businessmen, lawyers and teachers use this gesture frequently. These people have a feeling of self-importance particularly when they are face to face with someone on a negotiating table.

When you see people scribbling thoughtlessly or making drawings absentmindedly during a conversation or discussion it is an indication that the person is bored and not interested in what is being done.

Couples or friends who hold hands, lean close to each other or place their arm around the waist or shoulder express the right of possession or ownership.

Sitting Gestures: People convey a lot even when they are sitting. Observe how they behave. People choose a chair that is in harmony with their temperament. Those who are in an important position seek a chair that is so placed that overlooks others. Sitting on a high chair, particularly

positions. This puts them in a position of advantage. In many games the umpires occupy high seats. Where all the chairs are the same size and level, people seek positions from where they can overlook others.

Everyone does not sit the same way on a chair. When a conversation is going on across the table some prefer to sit on the edge of the chair, bending forward, supporting the chin with the hand with the elbow on the table. Some sit relaxed occupying the whole chair with the back resting on the chairback.

completely relaxed. Some would sit leaning forward resting the elbows on the

eyes on the person sitting across.

Sitting postures could be positive or negative. Those with a positive attitude prefer to talk, communicate their viewpoint and complete the job at hand. However, those with a negative attitude 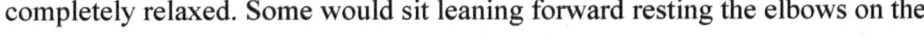 are suspicious and secretive. They will have their arms and legs crossed in a defensive gesture. They would have the head or body tilted forward trying

with a negative attitude repeatedly look at the door probably waiting to

avoid others.

Positive people holding high positions evaluate the situation with greater maturity and understanding and come to logical decisions. They could be critical but would be positive and come to realistic conclusions. Generally, people with average intelligence adopt a wait-and-see attitude. They wait for a consensus to build up.

The Legs: It is not common to give as much attention to the legs as one would give to the gestures of the hands and the arms. However, the gestures conveyed by the legs are also important.

Like the arms, crossed legs also express a defensive posture. People adopt different styles for crossing legs. Generally, people have the right leg crossing over the left leg. Some, particularly the Americans,

A common sight at airports and railway stations is to see persons sitting alone with their legs

legs crossed out of boredom.

A person sitting with his leg on the armrest appears comfortable, but through this gesture, he is expressing an unco-operative temperament with a lack of interest in what is being discussed. His indifference to the situation is clearly visible. Sometimes purchase managers use this gesture against salesmen, who need to change their outlook.

on the table, or another chair. In another variation, the person could be sitting backwards, using the back of the chair as a shield. These gestures express dominance and an aggressive attitude.

Walking Gestures

friends and acquaintances. *Despite this unconsciously, a person's walking style changes in different situations*.

People who adopt and work to goals sincerely walk rapidly with a swing in their arms. On the other hand, those who walk with their hands in the pockets are secretive by temperament and have a tendency to criticise and run down others.

When you observe a person walking with his head down looking up sometimes, it means that he or she is dejected and frustrated. These people have stooping shoulders and have their hands in their pockets. In another variation, when a person walks with the head down but the hands behind the back, it means that he or she is pre-occupied with some problems and trying to come out of it.

, *taking calculated steps, walking at an impressive pace with a swing in the arms.*

It is a common sight to see people pacing up and and down with the head held down

a problem. It is best not to disturb such people because it can interrupt their chain of thoughts leaving them disturbed and irritated.

When you see two people walking close to each other with one's hand on the

to dominate the person being spoken to.

When walking, kicking the ground or an imaginary object expresses irritation, anger and frustration. Another variation of this gesture is kicking at the door rather than opening it slowly.

The Skin: The skin covers and protects the skeleton, muscles and the organs of the body.

it also expresses body language. For example, everyone is aware how the skin reacts to the atmospheric temperature. It sweats profusely when it is hot, and shrinks to conserve body heat

the hairs erect prompted by cold weather and fear? In a state of fear the skin turns livid and

red with the heart beating faster. The skin is sensitive to touch and could in certain situations convey feelings of both pleasure and pain. Since it is also sensitive to the weather people make great efforts to keep it soft, elastic and glowing by using moisturisers and cosmetics.

Moving Closer: People tend to move closer when walking and talking together. This is a common sight among dating couples. Even in business it is common for people to move closer

the two is growing. However, if the other person moves away, it is an expression of being "turned off" and a refusal to a closer relationship.

Special Gestures: There are some gestures that pertain to a combination of other gestures. In

when he needs to stay longer and is familiar with the people and the situation, he would take off his coat expressing informality and closeness. In a home the person could take off the coat, loosen or take off the necktie as an expression of informality. In many homes people take off

the hair' as an expression of informality and closeness.

common amongst children. It is an expression that the person is not interested in what is going on.

one could make an effort to comfort the other person. This would require patience and tact.

People are usually nervous during an interview. This is a temporary phase and has nothing to do with a person's ability. The interviewers would do well to comfort the person before asking him or her

It is common for the mucous to choke the throat when a person is anxious or under stress. This women. Some prefer to drink a little water before they begin to speak. A hot cup of tea or coffee taken a little earlier is useful. Many singers drink warm water to soothe the throat before a performance.

Every human being is unique. Since the human body reacts as a whole to one's feelings and emotions it has been observed that when a person is anxious, stressed or under pressure, one needs to visit the washroom more frequently.

Giving Body Language A Meaning

A person cannot begin to understand the body language immediately. It takes a long time in observing people, connecting the clusters of gestures that come from different part of the body, analysing them and then drawing conclusions. One learns it slowly. Here are a few suggestions that would be useful:

Observe. Make it a habit to observe. Watch children playing. Observe how they behave. Watch people at a bus terminus or a railway station. You could also observe people waiting for

Compare individuals with groups. It has been observed that those in groups would be more relaxed and enthusiastic than individuals.

Observe people in a hospital waiting room
would be very anxious and stressed because of an ailing relative. You can see such people

walking out of the hospital carrying a newborn baby, or a patient who has recovered.

Observe how people dress. Try to connect and compare different personalities. See how they dress and feel about it. Watch them sit, stand, talk and walk about. Even without a word, you will begin to understand the situation they are in.

Analyse body gestures. One cannot base an analysis on a single gesture. It has been observed that gestures come in clusters. Observe and analyse them as a group of gestures. Give meaning to each gesture, but analyse the whole cluster of gestures together. Since each person is unique, everyone reacts to a situation in a different way.

Observe your own behaviour. If you are a part of the situation, you must observe your own

face could make all the difference.

Different situations arouse different reactions. People behave in harmony with a situation. An otherwise reasonable person could behave illogically in a mob. The husband-wife or parent-child reactions could be different at home or in the society. The differences could be confusing.

Observe positive restraint. Do not be hasty in evaluating and giving meaning to the gestures. The analysis might not be correct. One learns over a period through hit-and-miss methods. During the process of analysis also, consider possible motives for a particular behaviour.

Differentiate between voluntary and involuntary gestures. All the gestures that one observes are not involuntary.

Voluntary and Involuntary Gestures

All the gestures that one observes may not be involuntary. They could be voluntary. The study of body language is based upon giving meaning to the involuntary gestures. To a certain degree everyone is

to personal advantage. We have all seen how a child purposely pretends to have a painful tummy by making obvious gestures when he does not want to eat something or not go to school. We have also seen

branches of commerce and business people play games to send out wrong messages to deceive others. One needs to be careful about such situations.

Who has not come across con-men who could cheat you to buy something that is of poor quality or not worth the money? People always look at salespersons suspiciously because they could make you buy what you don't really need. This is happening everyday at almost all places. These people are not only glib talkers but are equally good actors who can easily convince people and get their way through.

Actors working in theatres, on television and in movies create real life situations through voluntary body gestures and language. They are so realistic in the art that they can make the audience laugh or cry with equal ease. A person might not think much of this because it is not real life. However, when we come across people and situations in everyday life we see people using acting techniques to get their way through in business, in different professions and even within the home. Many children are capable of getting their way through with the parents. Even brothers and sisters and friends use these techniques to convince each other. Married couples are always playing games with each other with a similar purpose. It is far too common to not to be noticed.

to gain personally. A good public speaker not only desires to be heard, but also uses gestures to convince audiences about his or her convictions. Politicians specialise in using body language in persuading the masses to support them.

A person needs to understand that the knowledge of body language can be useful in appreciating what is being conveyed to him or her by others, and also in using some of the techniques ethically to persuade others to one's way of thinking. It is necessary to be ethical because unethical behaviour could be useful, as it is with con-men, but such people are always looked at with suspicion. It is not long before they lose credibility. Many a businessperson or professional has over a period lost everything that was attained through unethical means.

Body Language and Sign Language

It is necessary to appreciate that body language and sign language are not the same thing. Whereas body language pertains to the involuntary gestures made by a person in particular situations, sign language uses hands, arms or the body or facial expressions to convey a message instead of using sound or written words. We see deaf and dumb people communicating through sign language.

The use of sign language is not restricted to the deaf and dumb only. We see it being used on the

out. In the same way there are signs to communicate when a bowler throws a wideball or a noball. In other games like football and hockey the umpire also uses sign language.

In everyday life sign language is common to say "hi" by raising the hand, or conveying "bye-bye" by waving the right hand. When driving the hand is also used to communicate whether a person is turning right or left, or could signal the following vehicle to slow down, or to communicate that the driver is going to stop his vehicle. In the recent past many of these signals have been replaced by blinking lights indicating a right or left turn, of caution or even a red light to indicate that the vehicle is coming to a halt. However, hand signals continue to be used around the world. In contrast, you can observe the body language of the person following you when you stop suddenly without a signal and

Maintaining Self-control

When observing body language in others it is necessary for a person to observe self-control. One must observe quietly and patiently without coming to hasty conclusions, which could be counter-productive.

It is important to observe whether the gestures are voluntary or involuntary. During negotiations a person a position of importance. This is to be seen every day in business and professional life.

listen to those who are better placed than them. Some importance comes from knowledge and position.

just as one would learn any new skill.

Chapter 5

. It is self-assurance in one's abilities to achieve something. Why do people lack it? Why would people not believe in their own abilities?

person's mind when faced with the ever-increasing competitiveness in everyday life. Every young person makes the best of whatever knowledge and facilities that are available in school and college and ensures that he or she is well prepared. However, with a lack of experience a person feels disillusioned in a world that is very different from the ideologies taught in educational institutions. When doubts

It is common for young people to seek comfort through reassuring parents and friends rather than seek a solution within oneself. This might make facing doubts easier, but it is only at the cost of a person relying more upon others than upon one's own ability to discern between good and bad. It soon

We need to understand the situation in a little greater detail.

trust the person has in these abilities, one's assumption and levels of belief.

With lack of trust in one's capabilities a person considers oneself to be of low worth, and experiences low self-esteem. If the person just lacks trust in one's capabilities, then it can be said that

arrogance, which is not liked by people. Arrogance comes from the assumption that the person has the divine gift to succeed always. This is only an assumption and cannot be the truth. Nobody can succeed at everything and at all times. God has endowed everyone with special capabilities. These can be enhanced by gaining knowledge and making an appropriate effort. Both trust and belief in oneself and in one's abilities is important.

ensure maturity of thought, which is necessary to take a realistic view of life and the world we live in.

one cannot continue to live under the shadow of their protective love and affection. It is your life. You must take responsibility and move forward to the best of your ability.

A person can be said to have taken responsibility over one's life when he or she accepts responsibility for personal successes and failures. Defeat and failure are as much a part of life as success, fame and

success. At the same time it also grows when one is able to differentiate the productive efforts from those that lead nowhere. One must learn to repeat those activities that lead to success.

Success in life comes from a variety of activities that together provide happiness at the workplace,

Take control over your life. It is your life. It will be what you make of it.

Begin from where you are
a single step.

Do not give in to self-doubt. God made you unique. The truth is that God has provided you as many opportunities to succeed as anyone else.

Live for today. Do not live in the past or in the future. The past is gone. The future has yet to come. Live well today. God intends everyone to live well every day. Make today the best day of your life.

You are the most important person in the world. Place trust and belief in your ability to get ahead in life. You can do it.

All your abilities depend upon will-power. Develop will-power. It converts ordinary people into extraordinary leaders.

. The moment goals are set the body and the environment unleashes power to attain them.

Learn to live healthy. To be healthy means to have a sound body governed by a sound mind. God intends everyone to be healthy. We become sick by placing a greater burden on the body than what it can cope with.

Develop health consciousness. It is the key to develop good habits that contribute to living a healthy life.

Avoid stressful situations
stressed. Develop an environment of harmony and peace around you.

Seek complete relaxation. Never compromise on rest and good sleep.

Chapter 6

Etiquette and good manners are an essential requisite to ensure effective communication. In any situation irrespective of how appropriately a message is worded, spoken or written, unless it comes

purpose.

The society has over a period evolved certain guidelines through trial and error method to ensure that the relationships between people at home, at the workplace and in the society are cordial. Every

to the expected behaviour when functioning to pursue a particular business or profession. It is these guidelines that are referred to as etiquette and manners. Since the needs of each situation could be different the guidelines that have been developed would vary with it.

Etiquette and good manners are not instinctive. They need to be learnt. A few conscientious parents teach them to the children at an early stage. Many fail to do so because of personal ignorance and lack of sensitivity. Children that grow up in joint families have a better opportunity to learn these within the home. The majority learn etiquette and good manners partly at home and partly at school. Much is learnt later at college and through experience. Since the society is a dynamic entity and is forever

Etiquette and good manners help smooth out the little wrinkles or points of friction that develop in the process of two or more people interacting with each other. Just like a little drop of oil stops a rusty door-hinge from creaking, etiquette and good manners help remove the friction that develops through familiarity and anxiety that emerges from human interactions. It is good manners to be thoughtful about others' feelings and sensitivities. Everyone must be accepted as a unique person and given due respect.

People from different regions and cultures around the world perceive etiquette and manners in different ways. What might be relevant in one culture or region might not be so in another region. For example, the method of greeting each other when you meet varies in different places. Some greet by waving a hand, others through a handshake and still others by joining the hands to say, "*Namaskar*". In some cultures it might be all right to kiss each other on meeting, and yet it might be taboo in another culture or region.

With the world shrinking very rapidly with fast modes of travel, and people's businesses and professions taking them to faraway places around the world, it becomes necessary to understand and

It is common to come across a variety of people and situations in everyday life. One must know how to conduct oneself in these situations. Much of this knowledge would come from what a person has learnt from the parents, at the school and college, and through experience. One must appreciate the

Etiquette and Manners

needs as prescribed in one's culture and way of life. That will enable effective communication and a smooth journey through life.

Dress Etiquette

Clothes play an important role in projecting an image of a person. Here are a few common observations about dress etiquette:

Clothes speak loudly of a person's tastes, disposition, likes and dislikes.

Clothes help to draw immediate attention. Like personal charm clothes must be comfortable to wear and must delight the eyes and the mind.

Salwar-kamiz or a sari is best for ladies. If used to wearing slacks, the tops must be long. Low necklines and backless blouses must be avoided. Jewellery should be restricted to the minimum. Avoid heavy makeup and strong fragrances. In winter the sweaters and pullovers must be sober.

can wear heavier saris or *salwar-kamiz* with jewellery to match. Footwear and accessories are important. Match them well.

Ensure that at all times the clothes are attractive and not garish.

Greeting Etiquette

All over the world it is common for people to greet each other appropriately when they meet. Some say, "Good morning" or "Hello", others may say "*Namaste*" or "*Namaskar*". Others prefer to say "*Ram Ramji*" or "*Jai Hari Krishna*". Sikhs greet by saying "*Sat Shri Akal*". Muslims say "*Aadabarz*". Here are a few common observations about greeting etiquette:

Irrespective of the way people greet each other, it immediately removes barriers between people. It creates a feeling of belonging and oneness amongst them.

Waving a hand, shaking hands or joining them to say, "*Namaskar*" depends upon individual cultures and situations. Follow the prevalent norms in a particular situation and place.

preferable to be conservative rather than be liberal.

Greetings motivate. They inspire. They set a conversation going. They help develop better relationships.

Learn to perfect the art of greeting people wherever you go. It will help you to be welcome everywhere.

Making Introductions

It is good manners to introduce two or more people who are known to you, but not to each other.

would be appropriate to introduce one to the other. Here are a few common observations about making introductions:

Making introductions helps put everyone to ease. It helps make people talk to each other.

When making introductions, introduce a younger person to an elder person, gent to a lady, a subordinate to a senior person, an immediate relative to an outsider. Different occasions might require some variations.

Never hurry when making an introduction. Do it slowly. Announce the names clearly so that the other person can pick them easily. Sometimes it would be useful to add special positions

with…" Such small remarks open opportunities for conversation.

A well-worded introduction helps promote friendships. People will appreciate you for it.

When you are introduced to another person, you could say, "How do you do?" or "Pleased to meet you". If you feel interested you could start a conversation. An introduction could or could not lead into long-lasting friendships. It would depend upon mutual interest between two people.

Dealing with Important People

It is desirable that people who are important by age and position must be accorded respect and honour.

dealing with important people:

In some cultures the elders are given special respect by greeting them by touching their feet and seeking their blessings.

Sahib

Sharma Sahib.

The President of India and the governors of the states are addressed by using the words: His Excellency. This is another inheritance from the British.

Justice of the Supreme Court of India would be addressed as the Honourable Chief Justice of India, followed by his name. The judges would be addressed as Honourable Justice followed by the name. The chief justice and judges of the High Courts of various states would also be addressed in the same manner. At the district level the head of the judiciary is the District and Sessions Judge.

The Prime Minister is addressed as the Honourable Prime Minister. The ministers would be addressed as Honourable Minister of… Similarly, at the state level the Chief Minister is addressed as Honourable Chief Minister and the ministers as Honourable Minister for…

When dealing with diplomats, the ambassadors and High Commissioners from various countries, they are addressed as His Excellency, the Ambassador of…

Every religious organisation would have people in important positions. When you need to

In Hindu temples the persons conducting the ceremonies are addressed as *Pujaris* or *Pandits*. Those who have renounced worldly life and wear white, yellow or saffron clothes are addressed as *Swami* or *Swamiji*. Some address them as *Maharajji* instead of *Swamiji*. The head of a sect is addressed as *Mahantji*. A senior *Mahant* could have the title *Mandaleshwar* or *Mahamandaleshwar*.

Shri 108… or Shri 1008…depending upon the position.
In everyday life when interacting with people in important positions it would be all right to address them by the position one holds. The Mayor of a city could be addressed as Honourable Mayor…

within certain discipline. Some rules are written. Many are not. Those which are not come within the working style or custom developed over a working

person works diligently during the working hours. One must reach

The midday tea or coffee is intended only as refreshment. Do not leave your table or use this

when you want to use it.

individual responsibility well. A single lapse can break the chain and ruin things for everyone.
Deal appropriately with the senior management, the colleagues and the subordinates. Everyone is a unique person. Learn to accept them as they are and not as you would want them to be.

situations. Do not argue. Your progress depends upon how well your boss accepts your work.

in employees is the desire to learn new skills and take on additional responsibility.
Always share praise and success with colleagues and subordinates who support you in your responsibilities.
Always treat subordinates well. When things go wrong give them an opportunity to explain their viewpoint. If you need to reprimand them do it in private. Do not insult them before others.

management and ensure that it does not repeat.

stationary.
Always ensure that the morale of the workers is high. Let them look up to you as a leader, not as one who represents authority only. Be fair to everyone. Nothing is more demotivating than a person who is partial to some.

rules about this.
With men and women working together sexual harassment is a much greater problem than what many would imagine it to be. Both men and women could be equally responsible for it.

time arrangements for their safe return home must be made.

receptionist. How she behaves with the visitors is important. It is really the responsibility of every employee to project a good image of the organization by treating everyone well. Make

Etiquette with Foreign Guests

With swift modes of travel it is now possible for people to travel all over the world. Since cultures vary greatly from one region to another it becomes necessary for people to appreciate the need for etiquette when one travels abroad, or when people from other countries come as guests. All guests are worthy of special attention. People generally have different living standards, customs and eating habits. We must be able to make them comfortable to build goodwill and better relationships. Here are some observations about etiquette with foreign guests:

People are sensitive about the timing of appointments. When you tell a person that you will meet him or her at 10.00 a.m., it should mean 10.00 a.m. and not around 10.00 a.m. You should be there at 5 minutes to 10. In the event of a delay it is simple courtesy to inform the person on phone about the delay.

When you invite foreign guests do tell them about the occasion. They would then dress appropriately. Otherwise they could be dressed casually, which could embarrass them if it is a formal function.

items that they do not like to try. Also, do not pile their plates with food. Wasting it would embarrass them.

Foreign guests are sensitive to normal water. Offer mineral water or cold drinks.

When offering home hospitality offer them accommodation where they can have comfort and privacy. The bed linen must be clean and fresh. They are used to western style toilets. Have toilet paper available.

When they desire hotel accommodation check the hotel tariff they can afford.

When taking them for sight-seeing do not overload the vehicle. If the car can accommodate four persons comfortably seat only four. Do not make it hectic for them. Restrict it to whatever is comfortable. Fatigue builds fast in warm weather.

When taking them to shopping take them only to reliable shops where they get value for money. It is common for people to get cheated.

In many cultures it is common to hold hands, embrace or even kiss on the cheek or forehead. Do not interpret it in any other way.

Do not ask for any favour from your guests. Good etiquette does not permit you to desire it. If they offer a gift in response to your hospitality it is their choice.

Let your guests take home happy memories. When they acknowledge it through mail tell them know how much you enjoyed having them.

Chapter 2

Everything is not always said through words. Sometimes silence conveys a message emphatically. We have all observed when a mother or father turns away in silence from a child to convey a message or to enforce discipline. No mother or father would want to hurt a child, but sometimes when words are ignored silence works. Even in a married couple of many years silence is a tool that either partner might

We have already observed how every little body gesture quietly conveys a message through body language. Good etiquette and manners convey much about a person's personality and behaviour.

People use silence as a communication medium both in business and professional life. We have all seen how a doctor refuses to answer some questions about a patient's condition when he is uncertain. He prefers silence to being misunderstood. We have also observed how a lawyer might not answer a question, or might prefer to keep silent about a situation that might affect the client's interests. In the same way all business and professional people prefer to observe silence because that would be a more

Blair explained, "Silence is one of the great arts of conversation, as allowed by Cicero himself who says, "There is not only an art, but eloquence in it." A well-bred woman may easily and effectually promote the most useful and elegant conversation without speaking a word. The modes of speech

restrain the tongue; he approaches nearest to the gods who knows how to be silent, even though he is in the right."

tongue, he is much mistaken; for it is a point to be silent when occasion requires, and better than to

without charity."

Silence always has a loud message to convey. Irrespective of whether it is at home within a family, amongst friends or at the workplace with many colleagues, silence is never ignored. Shenstone explains, "A person that would secure to himself great deference will, perhaps, gain his point by silence as

expresses everything, and proclaims more loudly than the tongue is able to do so." Theodore Parker

It requires discipline and great inner strength to use silence as an effective tool of communication. R.W. Emerson explains, "What a strange power there is in silence! How many resolutions are formed, how many sublime conquests effected, during that pause when lips are closed, and the soul secretly feels the eye of her Maker upon her! They are the strong one's of earth who know how to keep silence when it is a pain and grief unto them, and who give time to their own souls to wax strong against temptation."

If use of silence was not effective in business or professions, it would have since long been given up. However, mankind has continued to use it effectively since thousands of years. Bulwer explains, "The

which proverbially belongs to the unknown; and, secondly, because silence provokes no man's envy,

Here are a few things a person must remember in using silence as a means of communication in everyday life:

    Use silence judiciously. When it is used too frequently it becomes a habit and no longer remains a method of communicating a message.

    Highlight the positive qualities. A positive attitude conveys well of a person. When a person

    Take a stand against the negative. In many situations a person is compelled to accept the negative. Avoid it. If words fail you, use silence.

    Use silence to emphasize your point. Observe how debaters and public speakers use silence to pause and give the audience a moment to think.

    Use short spells of silence. A long period of silence would be misunderstood.

    Never use silence to hurt or insult a person. That would be counter-productive.

Shakespeare has rightly suggested, *"The silence, often, of pure innocence, persuades when speaking fails." Try it at the workplace.*

Section 2

All languages of the world emerged as spoken languages. Only with time and the necessity to record what was worthy of repetition did the written language evolve gradually. English is no different. Over

but also in many important countries and parts of the world.

Spoken English is a popular form of communication in business and professional activities. Even

as a second language. A very large percentage of business and professional transactions across different countries are conducted in English.

Spoken English is not restricted within the precincts of schools, colleges and universities as a medium of academic communication. It is not restricted to common conversations in everyday life. From within it, *Business English has evolved by using words and phrases that are suitable in a trade or profession. These are popularly used in a variety of ways in all business and professional activities.* These link people and vocational activities together.

The common everyday conversation has led to speaking to groups and larger audiences. It has become a means to interview prospective employees, gauge their skills and abilities and also become a tool to negotiate important agreements at local, national and international levels. Capable use of speech

Good speaking skills have moved millions both in the direction of good and bad. We are aware how

of Americans through his brief speech at Gettysburg. Equally well known are speeches of Hitler that led to war or those of terrorist leaders leading to the death of innocent citizens.

In business and professional life, we need good speaking skills to serve our customers better by providing the best of products and services. We need to speak to train the workforce and develop leadership at all levels in business and professional life. We need to speak the language of love and concern, creating better relationships with people who are a part of our life. May God guide us to do so!

Chapter 8

The English language is one amongst the many that are used around the world to communicate with each other. Like all other languages, it started as a spoken language. *Though it is the principal language in U.S.A., Canada, Australia, New Zealand and the United Kingdom, there are many variations in the way it is spoken in each of these countries* home of Queen's English, the *accents and dialects of the spoken language vary from one place to another.*

. It has grown out of the necessity to record what is said. The written language also makes it possible to reach many more people than could be reached through the spoken word. *Of course, the radio and the television have brought about far-reaching changes in communication.*

Different means are used to develop a written language. *For example, the alphabet used to write English is also used to write languages like French, Spanish and German, using the alphabets to convey the sounds of the spoken language.* Though Hindi and other related languages are written in the *Devanagari* script *or varnamala*, it can also be written in the *Roman script* using the *English alphabet*. *This has helped English-knowing people to learn Hindi faster.*

Like all other languages, the English language is a living entity. It is undergoing change all the time. *Depending upon the needs, people create new sounds and words to convey what they desire to say.* New words are adapted from other languages. Just as Hindi has adapted words like *engine, rail or ticket* from the English language, words like *guru and mantra* have been adapted from Hindi into English. *The dictionaries are periodically updated to include new words and phrases explaining the changing concepts and meanings.*

It is interesting to observe that just as the accent and dialect used to speak English varies in different regions and countries, the spellings of some of the words also vary in different countries. The *pronunciation, spelling and sometimes the meaning of the same words* vary from one region to another and it is common to have them listed as such in the dictionaries published in respective regions and countries.

The spoken language is the real language. Children learn it from their parents and the family. Different regions adapt their own pronunciation, grammar and style. It could be very different from the

form. This is used in the day-to-day written communications.

estimated 500,000 words expressing varying shades of meaning. Some assert that there would be twice this number of words in the language. These may be of importance only to the academicians. To the common person it is the personal vocabulary that is important as a means of using the language. Some

The English Language

people have a vocabulary of a few thousand words. Most people go through life with a vocabulary of only a few hundred words.

Every person has two kinds of vocabulary – receptive vocabulary and an active vocabulary. The receptive vocabulary includes words, which a person can understand on hearing or reading them. The active vocabulary includes words, which a person uses to express oneself through the spoken and the

effort the active vocabulary is invariably much smaller than the receptive vocabulary.

O.W. Homes exhorts, "Language is a solemn thing: it grows out of life – out of its agonies and ecstasies, its wants and its weariness. Every language is a temple in which the soul of those who speak it is enshrined." H.W. Beecher asserts, "Thinking cannot be clear till it has had expression. We must write, or speak, or act our thoughts, or they will remain in a half torpid form. Our feelings must have

So it is with all the inward feelings; expression gives them development. Thought is the blossom; language the opening bud, action the fruit behind it."

A language is a medium of expression of one's thoughts and ideas that need to be turned into reality. The popularity of the English language as a global medium of interaction has made it a vital tool in the hand of those involved in business and professional life, giving it a new name: Business English,

human interaction in the world of business and professions. Develop a love for the language and move onwards towards success.

Chapter 9

Except for a few countries where English is the primary language, it is learnt as a second language in most parts of the world. With the world becoming a global village where a person can move from one place to another swiftly, it is a necessity to learn English to communicate effectively. Besides, it has become a universal medium of communication in the world of business and professions.

It is common to look at learning a second language with some apprehension and anxiety. When it is not the mother tongue learnt from the parents, the pace of learning is slower. Personal doubts make

to use it later in the world of business. However, it has repeatedly been observed that those who make

their professional life and in society.

must learn the basics of speaking and writing. This is not possible without understanding grammar, vocabulary, spelling, word division, punctuation and writing or revising sentences. The written work can be corrected but not the spoken language.

Nobody was born learned. Everyone had to make the effort to learn various skills. Learning to communicate well in the English language is also a skill. Through effort everyone can learn it. Those

use the language freely in everyday life.

What exactly are you trying to attain? Have you a goal for yourself? For most people the goal is as simple as to have the ability to speak the language effectively to get ahead in their professional life. After one can speak it writing it becomes a little easier, but to most people it is not that important because people are really judging you the way you speak. Very few see what you write, which in most professions is very limited.

Here are a few guidelines that can help you learn English faster:

Know your goals. The moment a person sets goals a success mechanism begins to operate within. One begins to move towards success.

Understand your strengths and weaknesses. Every area of strength is an opportunity to grow; every weakness is a threat that can let you down.

Develop a plan of action. Based upon where you are today you should develop a plan of action to enhance your English speaking and writing skills.

Allot some learning time every day. It wouldn't be right to devote longer periods twice a week. Instead have thirty minutes learning period every day.

Speaking and writing is not the same thing. You will need to practise both. The spoken language that will take longer to master.

Be patient with yourself. Learning anything is a slow process. The beginning is the most it is to write small words? Once the basics are learnt it becomes easier to progress further.

Observe others speak. The best way to learn a new thing is to observe how others do it. A child learns speaking just by observing his mother and father. Later, he learns new words from the teacher. Sometimes when a child hears someone repeat an abusive word, without knowing the meaning, he learns to repeat it with ease.

Don't be shy to use new words. People are afraid of ridicule lest they use a word in the wrong context. Turn every mistake into an occasion to learn. Mankind has done it for thousands of years. Why should you be shy to do it?

Never be afraid of making mistakes. The more the mistakes you make, the sooner you will learn. Before a child can run, he crawls, then stands up, takes a few faltering steps, learns to walk and ultimately run. It takes time to do it.

. Those who master the art of writing Business English rise swiftly in their professional life.

Practise regularly. Whether it is writing or speaking practice is the key to learning a skill quickly. Business English is no different.

Reward yourself. When you do well and are complimented reward yourself by taking a longer leisure time. When you make mistakes, think about them.

Never give in. Winners never give in. The little defeats or setbacks prepare them for greater successes yet to come.

Everyone can learn to speak English. The secret lies in being committed to master it as an important means of communication in business and professional life. Others have done it successfully. So can you!

Chapter 10

Speaking a language is the primary form of communication. Amongst the English-speaking people the

baby and through repetition of the words pleases both the parents and the baby.

At this stage, the baby speaks instinctively. In several languages the words for mother and father are similar to "ma" and "pa". However, the baby learns new words gradually by listening to the parents and family members. Children who have impaired hearing cannot speak. A child learns to speak just like a parrot that repeats what it hears. It is interesting to observe that a child uses a similar pronunciation as used by the parents. Even amongst English speaking people there are differences in pronunciation and dialect.

A child learns simple words usually associated with the family and everyday life. Soon he begins to construct short sentences. A little later, when the child goes to playschool and nursery and interacts with other children, one learns new words and also names of other children. At this stage it has been observed that the children learn faster when rhyming and rhythm are used to make learning fun. Nursery rhymes, little poems and songs presented with colourful images are enjoyed by all children.

environment where everyone speaks gently and everyone observes etiquette and good manners the child repeats the same. If the same child is exposed to a rustic environment where the family is accustomed to crude language and lacks etiquette the child talks and behaves in the same way. The child is like an echo. You hear whatever and however you say it.

Like all other languages English also emerged as a spoken language. A spoken language is the use of words spoken through the mouth by a person to convey a message to another person. Through use of similar words used by many the spoken language develops. With time, with changing lifestyles and needs new sounds and words evolve. The language grows gradually.

The spoken language is the real language. It is the mother tongue. It is the authentic language. It has its own grammar and style. One learns it initially from the parents and later in school. With the need to interact with many people to promote and develop businesses and professions around the world, people are compelled to learn and master more than one language. It is likely that a person might not learn speaking English from birth, but learn it as an additional language in school and college.

will discuss its effective use later.

Effective speaking is a useful tool used to build good relationships and get ahead in life. Adolf Hitler emphasized, "All epoch-making revolutionary events have been produced not by the written but

Speaking English

To speak means to convey a message orally. This is possible with the use of the vocal cords and the vocal apparatus situated in the lower part of the neck in human beings. The study of speech sounds

quality of sound, the tone and rhythm, besides the way the message to be communicated is presented.

The tone of the voice refers to the musical effect with reference to the pitch, quality and strength of the voice expressing a feeling, emotion or mood. The pitch describes the extent of the sound or tone as high or low. The sound is said to be rhythmic when it follows a strong, regular and repeated musical

taught to speak English or any other language.

The tone of the voice is important. The meaning of words can be misinterpreted with the change in tone. This fact is widely used in debates and declamation contests. Lawyers are known to vary the tone to place special emphasis on some facts and underplay others to impress the judge. Politicians use the skill to sway the feelings and emotions of the public. Public speakers use these skills to touch the feelings and emotions of the audience and persuade them to accept new ideas. These skills are widely used to inform, to educate and to entertain audiences.

Religious gurus are known to use a variety of methods including music, rhythmic speaking alternated with singing to move the feelings of huge audiences acknowledging many of them as charismatic speakers. *Singing is a rhythmic presentation of words accompanied with music and is known not only to entertain people, but devotional singing is known to move huge audiences emotionally touching the hearts of everyone.*

Chapter

Children begin to speak early in life. They are taught to spell and pronounce words correctly. English has a lot of words that sound similar, but have different meanings and also spelt differently. One begins to appreciate them gradually. In school, the children are taught elocution, the skill of clear and expressive speech.

speaking skills. *Declamation refers to the act or art of speaking or reciting in a dramatic or passionate way.* The spoken matter would usually not be written by the child who is speaking. *The emphasis is on speaking clearly, and to control the pitch and the tone of the voice that the subject creates an impact on the audience.*

Teaching the art of speaking is not new. It dates back to the times of Aristotle and Quintilian.

been useful in private, professional and public life.

Speaking good English is taught in almost all public schools. However, it receives only limited attention from the students because school assessments are made on the basis of written exercises. Learning speaking skills are restricted to the few who participate in elocution and declamation contests, or in debates within the school. It is only in later professional and public life that people realise the utility of good speaking skills. A person who can speak convincingly is considered to be intellectually superior.

A step ahead of narration is the art of debate, which aims at formal discussion, where opposing views are presented and argued. The discussion aims at taking decisive action on important issues that affect everyday life. Debates prepare a person not only to make good presentations, but to think, learn and argue logically. These qualities prepare young people for important professional positions at the workplace and in public.

Initially most young debaters carry a written speech, but with practise most of them develop

situations. In professional life it is common to have group discussions, negotiations and making

us consider some of the methods to acquire and develop special speaking skills for use in different situations and places.

Read the English newspaper loudly. All English newspapers are written well in a language that is easily understood by the common man. Read the headlines. Read the sensational items.

Read the games pages. They help hold the interest of the reader, exposing him or her to good Business English.

Read from a magazine loudly. They are also written in a language that appeals to the common man. Most of them carry interesting articles. Read loudly. Don't let it worry you if the family laughs at you. Reading helps you get a feel of the words and develop a good pronunciation of each word.

Read a page from a book. Most people are not fond of reading books. Reading will help you develop a liking for them. Read short stories, mystery novels or humorous books. They will encourage a love for the language.

Hear TV news in English. Observe how the news reader pronounces each word clearly. That will give you a good idea how to pronounce words clearly. The language you hear is common everyday English easily understood by people.

Hear debates in English. All news channels feature debates in English, Hindi and the regional languages. Observe how the discussion leader moves from one person to another, asks them leading questions and how each participant responds with brief remarks that lead to conclusions. Sometimes when the discussions get too "hot" or off the mark, observe how the discussion leader intervenes and brings the discussion on track.

Watch an English movie. All the movies do not serve the purpose well because when they are made in different countries the accents and dialects are local and could sometimes be misleading. The dialogue in humorous movies is slow and arouses greater interest. Observe how punch lines are used to arouse interest and laughter in the audience.

Record your own voice. This wasn't easy earlier because it required complicated tape recorders. However, now many of the mobile phones have recording facilities and one could record one's voice when you read a passage from a book and then hear how it sounds. By analyzing your own mistakes you will learn to use emphasis on the correct words and phrases.

Always remember that children learn to speak what they listen from the parents and teachers. Adults

Chapter 12

This is not true. The reality is that people are ineffective speakers because they are not good listeners. Effective communication does require an appropriate message that is effectively spoken, but if the audience is constituted of people who are not listening, of what use is the message? This is a serious problem. It is as important to be a good listener, as it is to speak well.

Good listening begins with an understanding of how the listening process functions. It is a complex process that could be better understood in smaller segments. These are:

Sensing. The person hears the message.

Interpreting. The person then tries to understand what has been heard.

Evaluating. The person then evaluates and forms an opinion about what has been said and understood.

Remembering. The person then tries to recall past memories in relation to the message and also considers whether the message is worthy of being stored in the memory for future use.

Responding. The person then gives an appropriate response to the message.

When seen as small segments the listening process might appear complex and slow, but in reality it is very swift. The effectiveness of listening is adversely affected by other factors. Let us try to understand them also. In general, they are:

Noise. When there is noise the message has to compete with it before it can reach the person for whom it is intended.

Boredom. When a person is overtaken by boredom the message becomes unattractive with the person losing interest in it.

Mental block. Many persons have rigid mindsets about people and situations and it is common for them to "turn a deaf ear" to certain messages.

Restlessness. When a person is restless, rather than listen, the person likes to interrupt the speaker and contradict him.

Fatigue. When a person suffers from physical or emotional fatigue the process of listening takes a back seat.

Everybody can become an effective listener. It is an acquired skill. If you can understand the complexities of listening and what could affect its effectiveness, you have made a good beginning. To listen well follow these simple rules:

Sit up and listen. When you have your back straight you listen better.

Establish eye contact. Look directly into the eyes of the person speaking to you. You will be able to understand what is being said better.

Concentrate on the message. Do not let distractions take your mind elsewhere.

Evaluate the usefulness. Every message has a certain amount of usefulness. If you can appreciate the usefulness the message will impact you better.

Avoid extraneous thoughts. Do not let stray thoughts reduce your concentration on what is being said.

Do not interrupt. It is common for listeners to interrupt and begin speaking. Avoid it. Let the

Sum up at the end
up in your own words. The speaker will appreciate it.
. If you are a large group your nodding the head would

up at the end of the session.

Take notes. When the message conveyed to you is important note it down immediately. It will not need to compete with other messages in the memory.

and is as essential to all true conversation." An African proverb simply asserts, "The one who listens is the one who understands." It has been further emphasized, "To listen is to learn; to learn is to make

times that of human speaking ability. With such a wide gap between speaking and listening speeds the mind drifts to think of other extraneous thoughts disconnected with the subject. This lowers the level of concentration and ultimately that of understanding the subject. Poor listening results in ineffective communication.

It is a personal choice how effectively a person desires to communicate verbally with others. Good speaking skills encourage lively conversation at the workplace and in the society. Atwell reiterates, "The art of conversation consists as much in listening politely, as in talking agreeably. The efforts would eventually be rewarded."

Chapter 13

essentially be well remembered. Their importance is still greater when a person is involved in business and professional life. These words would be used both in the spoken and the written language.

Here are some of the essentials that you must know well:

Months of the year. January, February, March, April, May, June, July, August, September, October, November and December.

Days of the week. Monday, Tuesday, Wednesday, Thursday, Friday, Saturday and Sunday.

Seasons of the year. Winter, spring, summer and autumn. In India, we have the monsoon season between summer and autumn.

The four directions. North, south, east and west.

How to tell time? Every watch, time-piece or clock has two hands – the hour hand and the minute hand. Some also have the second hand.

Common sporting events. Cricket, hockey, football, basketball, volley ball, throw ball, swimming, running, sprint, long jump, high jump, pole vault, javelin throw, shot put and others.

Common medical systems
medicine and others.

Common medical specialties. Physician, surgeon, gynaecologist, obstetrician, orthopaedics, ophthalmologist, dermatologist, urologist, cardiologist, psychiatrist, hepatology, hematology, radiology, pathology and many more.

Common weights and measures. Ton, quintal, kilogram, gram, microgram; hectare, kilometre, metre, centimeter, millimeter; acre, mile, yard, foot, inch; pounds, ounces; gallon, quart; cc, litre.

Measure of temperature. Degrees Celsius, Degrees Fahrenheit.

Zodiac signs. *Aries, Taurus, Gemini, Cancer, Leo, Virgo, Libra, Scorpio, Sagittarius, Capricorn, Aquarius and Pisces.*

Common fruits. Apples, bananas, plums, peaches, pears, mangoes, oranges, grapes, grape-fruit, strawberry, raspberry and cherries.

Common vegetables
pumpkin, gourds, radish, turnips and broccoli.

Chapter 14

An informal spoken exchange between two or more people is referred to as a conversation. This is the most common interaction between people. It could be at the home amongst family members, at the workplace between co-workers or in the society on a variety of occasions. Much can be achieved or lost through effective or ineffective communication at this level. Many people share their experience for common good.

According to a Chinese proverb, "A single conversation across the table with a wise man is worth a month's study of books." Emerson warns, "Conversation is an art in which a man has all mankind for competitors." Steele advises, "It is a secret known to but few, yet of no small use in the conduct of

he has a greater inclination to hear you, or that you should hear him." Atwell suggests, "Great talent for conversation should be accompanied with great politeness. He who eclipses others owes them great civilities; and whatever mistaken vanity may tell us, it is better to please in conversation than to shine in it." To become a successful conversationalist take advantage of these observations:

Talk less, listen more. You will get to know more about the other person.

Encourage the other person to talk. He will like you for it.

Ask questions. This will keep the conversation alive. The other person will like it because you are giving an opportunity to express his or her views.

Ask open-ended questions. These begin with who, what, when, why, where and how. Close-ended questions kill the conversation.

. This gives the other person an opportunity to elaborate further on a subject.

Re-check information
been listening. It will delight the other person.

Do not interrupt. It is common to be tempted to interrupt the other person. This breaks the chain of thought bringing the conversation to a halt.

Encourage the person

Rousseau suggests, "The tone of good conversation is brilliant and natural. It is neither tedious nor frivolous. It is instructive without pedantry; gay, without tumultuousness; polished without affectation; gallant without insipidity; waggish, without equivocation."

Chapter 15

The foundation of all knowledge is information. This comes from asking questions. It is the questioning mind that helps collect information about people, places and situations. In every business and profession, it is only through questioning the other person that one makes progress and attains his/her goal.

It is the goal of every doctor to help and treat his patient to live healthy. Can he do it without asking questions? Before the doctor can treat the patient, he would want more than a dozen questions, many of them personal and answered. This is part of his work.

It is the duty of every lawyer to provide legal guidance and advice to his clients. Can he do it unless he gets to the bottom of what is true and real? To do so, he asks innumerable questions, sorts out the facts, relates them to legal provisions and then only he is able to serve the client satisfactorily.

It is the responsibility of the police force to maintain law and order. When something goes wrong, do they judge the situation only by looking at the scene of the incident? No! They seek answers to questions they ask all those who were present at that time.

Businesses and professions are based upon all kinds of questions. The manufacturer asks what the that would satisfy the needs of the consumers. The salesman asks how he can reach the products to the consumer. The consumer enquires whether the products would suit him. At every step, there is a doubt, and to dispel the doubt, there are questions.

The questioning mind begins to ask questions early in life. The type of questions change when a person moves from one stage to another, but the questioning does not stop. It is a part of life. It begins and ends with it.

To speak well, every person would need to know how to ask questions and also answer them. This is a simple conversation. The purpose of asking questions is to know the other person better, to know more about one's business or profession and also to know how one can live well in the society.

Beginning at the most primary level, a person would want to know more about the other person through these simple questions.

    What is your name?
    Where do you live?
    Is it your own home?
    Were you born here?
    How long have you lived here?
    What school did you go to?
    In which college did you study?

Where did you complete your higher education?
What are you doing presently?
Do you have a scooter/motorcycle/car?
Are you married?
How long have you been married?
Do you have any children?
Where does your family live?
Do you have any special interests/hobbies?
How long have you been collecting stamps?
Are you fond of reading?
What kind of books do you like?
Is there a library close to your home?
Could I have your phone number?

These are very simple questions that anyone can ask. The answers would tell you what the other

speech improves. Soon a person is able to ask these questions effortlessly.

Let us look at another situation. You wish to buy some clothes and visit a store. There is much

shirts?" He will guide you to the counter and ask someone to attend to your needs if he is already busy. The salesman would ask: "Can I help you, Sir?" This would lead to new questions:

What colours are available?
What material is it?
Is the fabric satisfactory?
Can it be machine-washed?
Are the fabric colours fast?
What is the price?
Does the price include taxes?
Do you accept credit cards?
Could I have these two, please?
Where do I pay?

You will observe that these are simple questions that we ask when we visit a store in everyday life. When we use these questions, we get to know more about the products we use and are also able to speak

People do it every day, each helping the other.

Here are some common questions we hear in the marketplace:

Could you tell me the time?
Is there an ATM nearby?

What is the name of this street?
What is the number of this house? I'm looking for number 72.
Is there a fast-food store nearby?

Some people are cooperative and answer them helpfully, others might think that they are an interruption on their time.

Chapter 16

A person's ability to speak effectively depends upon his or her vocabulary of the language. *A person has two kinds of vocabulary – receptive vocabulary and an active vocabulary.* The receptive vocabulary includes words, which you can understand when you hear or read them. The active vocabulary includes words, which a person uses to express oneself through the spoken and the written language. Generally,

smaller than the receptive vocabulary.

strengthening one's vocabulary, both receptive and active. The next step should be to reduce the gap

To strengthen your vocabulary you must learn to enjoy words. Learn new words. Be clear about their meaning. Make the dictionary your constant companion. Select a dictionary that displays the words attractively. Make it a habit to browse through it to learn new words. Read the newspaper,

books. Get yourself a thesaurus and a book of synonyms and antonyms. You will be surprised at the range of words that have a similar meaning, and yet the shade of meaning varies for each word.

Make a deliberate effort to learn a new word every day. By the end of the month you would have learnt 30 new words. In a year you would have added 365 words to your vocabulary. Wouldn't that be some achievement? A person who is passionate to get ahead maintains a personal notebook to note

meaning of the word has been correctly understood the person writes one or two sentences using the word. A step further the person tries to use the word in everyday conversation. The more a word is repeated the deeper it goes into the subconscious and one begins to understand and use it regularly.

The best way to increase the vocabulary is to read the newspaper, magazines and books in English. Whenever there is a new word that you cannot understand check it in the dictionary. This way a person can build the vocabulary very fast. In the Reference Section of this book in the Glossary of Business

would have added substantially to your vocabulary.

Chapter 12

telephones have connected every room and every working table. Telephones have made it possible to send documents, pictures and movies from one end of the world to another. The telephone has opened the world to us.

The popularity of the telephone to communicate has raised new issues. A conversation on the telephone can be very refreshing on one occasion, and yet on another it could arouse anger and hostility. The fault is with how and when we use it. Learn all you can about it to make it an effective tool of communication. Here are a few observations on the use of the telephone:

Know your instrument

and redial. Many phones have incoming call display and also store telephone numbers. Be well acquainted with the instrument.

Know all about numbers. Every telephone has a number, which is a combination of the exchange and the customer number. Every city too has a number. For example, Delhi is 011,

India the number is 91.

Use a telephone directory

special occasions. Create your own edition with numbers you require along with emergency

Use the phone judiciously. Every call is charged for. There is great misuse of the telephone

. You must know the purpose of your call and also who you would like to talk to. That would make your call effective.

Dial the correct number

the number. When you hear "Hello" from the other side, identify yourself by saying, "I am Satish Chopra calling. Could I speak to…?" If the person is available he will come on phone, or you will get an appropriate response. In the event of dialing a wrong number, say "Sorry" and hang up.

Business Numbers. When you dial a business number the call will be responded by the receptionist saying, "Good morning. This is ABC Ltd. What can I do for you?" You should respond by saying, "I am Satish Chopra speaking from…Could I please speak to Mr. Roy?" or "Could you please connect me to the Service Department?"

Be patient. When the receptionist connects you to the appropriate department she will put you on hold with music playing. Be patient while this is being done.

No response. If there is no response and the bell keeps ringing it means that there is no one at the other end. You could call again later.

Answering machine. When an answering machine is installed at the other end you could

message?" At this point you could respond, "I am Satish Chopra calling from 271 2692." You can then expect a return call later.

Personal exchanges. When you dial from a hotel or a residence where a personal exchange

can then dial the desired number.

Computer-connected numbers. When you connect to computer-connected number it will automatically give instructions, which you need to comply with by dialing appropriate numbers. You will get the required information.

Home-service on phone. Many suppliers offer home service for food and other services. When you place an order on such a number identify your name and the telephone number you

International calls. International dialing is not available on all numbers.

city code and then the number. Do check the country time. It could be midnight in another country when it is daytime elsewhere.

Speak politely. On the phone it is your voice that makes or mars your image. Speak courteously. Be gentle and polite. Never use harsh language. Do not speak on the phone and with others simultaneously. Telephone instruments are sensitive. They can pick up sound from a distance and cause misunderstandings.

Receptionists at business houses attend to phone calls throughput the day. They must

a smiling face. There should be an air of helpfulness in connecting people to speak. The image you project on the phone lingers a long time.

Chapter 18

The mobile phone has outdone the telephone because of convenience of use and low cost. Almost everyone carries a mobile phone, which means that it is now possible to connect with everyone on dialing a number. People have got so used to it that if they forget to carry it or are travelling in an area that is out of range they feel they are incomplete and cannot deliver. The rapid advances in technology has converted the mobile phone into a digital diary, an address book, a camera, a music and video call all the time.

The high-end mobile phones are limited to those who can afford them, but the average phones are reasonably priced and within the means of every person. Both skilled and unskilled workers are using them to stay connected in their profession and also with their families. At the click of a button people can speak to others. This is a great convenience to an average person but at the same time it has become necessary to be careful that one does not impose upon other people's privacy and time. Here are a few observations about use of mobile phones:

A mobile phone is for personal convenience. Just because a person has a mobile phone does not mean that one should respond to a call whenever called.

Make business calls only during business hours. You should preferably use landline

Don't call persistently. If the other person does not pick up the phone that keeps ringing it could be that the phone is in mute mode and the person is busy with work or is in an urgent meeting. Call later.

Send a message. If you need to communicate something urgent and the person is not picking the phone a message will prompt him to call back soon.

Be short and to the point. Convey the message in as few words as possible. If the person is traveling or in a different territory he would be charged extra.

Talking to a busy person. If the person is busy offer to call again later. The person could also call you back.

Use FAX or Internet. Business messages can easily be sent through FAX or through Internet. These messages are precise, convey the exact meaning and are proof of communication.

Switch off the ringer. Many people are guilty of not switching off the ringer when in a meeting, a cinema hall, restaurant or in a public place where the ringing of the phone could disturb a lot of people, particularly when the environment is very quiet, as in a cinema hall or a meeting.

Seek a quiet corner. If you wish to take a phone call in a public place you should move outside or to a quiet corner where you would not disturb others when you speak.

Switch off your phone. When you attend a meeting as an important part of it and are either seated on the head-table or in the front row, irrespective of how important you are, switch off your phone. If you cannot switch it off for whatever reason give your phone to another person who is at a little distance from you to receive calls, if any.

Do not indulge children. Many parents are guilty of giving mobile phones to children more to play games than use it as a communication tool.

Do not drive and speak on the phone. It is unfortunate to see people speaking on a mobile phone when riding a bicycle, a motorcycle or a car. Even drivers of commercial vehicles are known to speak on the mobile when driving. These people endanger not only their own lives, but also of many more on the road. If it is urgent, stop the vehicle and speak.

It is undeniable that mobile phones have helped enhance human productivity. However, a tool is useful only when it is appropriately used. Public attention has repeatedly been drawn to the possible harmful effects of the waves emerging from mobile towers installed by service providers and also to the risk to a person from the mobile instrument. The subject is debatable, but one must observe restraint in being carried overboard through excessive use even of a good thing.

Chapter 19

There is magic in words. When spoken sincerely they touch our feelings and emotions. There are four would strengthen your relationships with them forever.

we say, "Can I have it?" We get the usual reaction of average service. When you change it to, "Can I politeness to our request. Politeness is a symbol of goodwill. It becomes natural to attract good service.

Montaigne said, "Courtesy is a science of the highest importance. It is like grace and beauty in "Small kindnesses, small courtesies, small considerations, habitually practised in our social intercourse, give a greater charm to the character than the display of great talents and accomplishments."

it to your wife when she brings a glass of water for you when you return from work.

have given them a feeling of appreciation. Their effort has been acknowledged by the gratitude you have expressed through these words. They will enjoy serving you.

appreciated the self-esteem grows and makes them happy. They serve again to seek this happiness repeatedly. Every day we receive innumerable services from people in our lives and a sincere

At the same time we receive better service and a ready welcome the next time.

are very hesitant to use these two words. When it is time to use them we become tongue-tied and fail

that these two words will not only make others happy but would also help us build better relationships. The next time whenever things go wrong and there is the slightest chance that it could partly be due to you just step forward and say, "I'm sorry". The problem will be sorted out immediately. It might hurt your ego momentarily, but you will soon realise that you have gained much more than what you perceive you have lost. To accept one's fault is a sign of maturity, of having grown up to the realities of life. It is human to make mistakes. Why pretend to be God? An apology in time spares a person of much hardship later.

becomes clear once again.

uses the magical powers of these words every day at home, at the workplace and in the society. Colton explains, "To know a man, observe how he wins his object, rather than how he loses it; for when we fail, our pride supports; when we succeed, it betrays us."

Just as good food becomes additionally attractive through garnishing and presentation these words become more powerful when they are spoken with sincerity and a smile on the face. They are simple

same.

Chapter 20

denies or disagrees with another person about something, it is bound to create some hurt in the mind of the other person.

child who experiments by crawling into strange corners, touching things that could break or harm him, goes towards the stairs where he could fall and a hundred other things the parents want to protect him

them it is an exercise in teaching the child what is right or wrong.

Adult life is different, particularly when you are in business or a profession. It is common for

ways. Those who give in are usually seen to repent later for having parted with their time, effort or

situation both for the person who seeks the favour and for the one who denies it.

To seek favours people will call at odd times; they will ask for rebates. They could seek credit of which they might not be worthy. As a close associate, one could pass on his or her responsibilities to you. You have to make the choice. Do you want to suffer quietly within, or would you want to end the

honestly, but do not let others take advantage of your goodness. Tell them in clear terms why you need to say "no" to their request.

Elbert Hubbard said, "I believe in freedom – social, economic, domestic, political, mental and spiritual." Everyone who seeks such freedom must learn when to say "yes" and when to say "no". It is not intended to turn down all favours. Many requests could come from friends who would return them some day. Randolph S. Bourne warned, "Friendships are fragile things, and require as much care in handling as any other fragile and precious thing."

Chapter 21

It is generally believed that speaking about oneself is the easiest thing to do. The reality is that it is not. It might be true that nobody knows you better than yourself. But when it comes to talking about

do something as simple as that, can we expect him or her to speak about other people and situations?

Speaking about you becomes important when a person is seeking to get an admission in a school, a college or seeking a job. It is common for institutions to interview prospective candidates when admitting them to an organisation.

organized thoughts and, second, it the anxiety that a person experiences when speaking to new people. When a person makes the effort to organise thoughts and know what must be spoken the anxiety gradually fades away.

and father, brothers and sisters, family members, friends, your school and college, your teachers, your

might have attained. Withdraw your thoughts from all else; concentrate on your own past life. There

the negative and bring forth the positive. This is your life. Build it on a positive platform.

Nobody knows you better than you do. You should be aware of your own strengths and weaknesses.

strengths predominate a person moves steadily towards success.

The purpose to speak about oneself is to be accepted as a person in one's own right, and not as someone's son or daughter, a nephew or relative. People accept others on the basis of how useful they are. Therefore, when speaking about your attributes emphasize those that make you useful to your family, enhance productivity at the workplace or help support causes for the society. Discover your own

Chapter 22

Everything that a person speaks is not taken well. Many things are usually misunderstood, as we see in everyday life. This is equally true in business and professional life. Irrespective of the language that a person uses everyone involved in business and professional life must choose the correct words and

deal of nothing: his reasons are as two grains of wheat hid in two bushels of chaff; you shall seek all day to hear himself talk, and will speak more in a minute than he will stand to in a month."

Socrates did not hesitate to remind us, "Nature has given us two ears, two eyes, but one tongue, to the end that we should hear and see more than we speak." He goes on further to add, "The tongue of a fool is the key of his counsel, which, in a wise man, wisdom hath in keeping."

In business and professional life it is essential that a person must speak moderately, giving every word and sentence due meaning. At the workplace, particularly in the corporate world, the stakes are always high. Success always favours those who know when to speak what and also how they should behave with each other.

Have you observed that unconsciously we prefer to go to a store where the salesmen speak courteously; we choose a family doctor and dentist who speaks with a smile and convinces us that we are well? We join clubs where the members are friendly. Our children like to go to a school where the teachers are gentle, kind and speak softly, and the students are friendly. The key to good relationships is positive interaction amongst each other in every sphere of life.

The English language has a vast vocabulary. In contrast you could have a very small vocabulary of one to two thousand words, but that should not restrain you from choosing the correct words when you interact with people at the workplace. When writing, you have the option of thinking, looking up the dictionary or a thesaurus, but when you speak it is your own wisdom you have to rely upon to choose the correct words in a given situation or the prevalent circumstances.

Here are a few things everyone must be careful about when speaking to each other:

Always be courteous. It does not cost anything, nor does one need to make an extra effort.

unpleasant word is used.

Speak with a smile. When you smile the other person cannot help smiling back at you. You have a friend listening to you.

Choose the words carefully. Many English words are similar in spelling and pronunciation, but they have different meanings. We will discuss them later.

Be cautious about personal sensitivities. Everyone is sensitive about something or another. It could be one's personality, colour of the skin, height or attachment to one's family. Honour these sensitivities. Never talk about them.

Do not gossip. It is human nature to gossip about each other, about the boss, or the management. It is in everyone's interest to avoid gossip. It might appear harmless, but it is not. It comes back with a wrong slant.

Do not criticize. You could have a hundred reasons to criticise your subordinates, colleagues, the boss and the management. If you want to be happy at the workplace just remind yourself

Do not retaliate to criticism. If you do not criticize others it does not mean that you will not be criticized. Accept criticism from a positive angle. Ask yourself if the person who has criticized you is right? If he is, be grateful to him quietly and make amends. If he is wrong, still be grateful because he has reminded you through jealousy that you are on the right path.

Always highlight the positive. Every situation can be looked at from both the positive and the negative angles. Always highlight the positive. It will keep you enthusiastic and will also generate enthusiasm in the other person.

Underplay the negative. It is common for people to highlight the negative to show down others. Respond by underplaying it. Tell them how every cloud has a silver lining.

Never lose your cool. People can be unreasonable. Situations can be explosive. Very often it

Just end the conversation, "We'll talk some other time. Bye!"

Chapter 23

It is commonplace for everyone to be a part of an interview. Children are interviewed at school, young people in college and again when seeking a job. In everyday life one needs to meet and speak to many

attain success.

from one's own perception, hoping that both will get what they are seeking through the exchange of views and facts.

For success at an interview a person must be aware of certain essentials. Here are a few observations that would be useful:

Acknowledge the call for an interview. When you get a call the venue, date and time of the interview.

Arrive on time. You could have a valid excuse for being late, but that won't be of any use to the prospective employer.

Be appropriately dressed for the occasion. If it is a job interview wear business clothes, not casual wear. Ensure that your face and hair is well groomed.

. If the interviewer desires it you could leave the copies after comparing them with the originals.

Observe etiquette and good manners. Don't act over-friendly. Speak conservatively. Listen carefully. Remain seated in the waiting hall.

Interacting with other candidates. There would be other candidates waiting for the interview. Remember that they are your competitors. Be cordial, not familiar.

Are you aware of the job requirements? If not, don't expect to achieve much during the interview. You must collect as much information as possible about your prospective employer and the job.

The face-to-face meeting between the interviewer and the candidate decides the outcome of the meeting. Although a prospective employer seeks to hire people with appropriate skills these can often be

desires to check up personality traits of the person. The obvious questions in the mind of the employer are: Does the personality of the candidate match with the company's image and job requirements? Does

goals for the organisation? Can the person be depended upon to give steady results over a long period? Employers are never happy with workers who jump from one job to another to seek new pastures.

Candidates who are aware of employer needs are always well prepared to seek success in an interview. Here are a few observations a candidate must know when proceeding for the actual interview:

Always enter the meeting room after taking a deep breath. Have a pleasant smile on the face.

Sit down only when asked to. Do not talk unless asked to. Try to build eye contact with the interviewers.

The interviewers would initially ask questions for which they already have the answers. That would be to put your mind at ease. They would want to know about you, about your achievements and failures. Be brief and to the point.

The pertinent questions would follow the simpler pleasantries. The interviewer would now like to hear you speak and he would listen. Do not take liberties and speak thoughtlessly. Answer the questions point-to-point. Do not use slang or crude language. Do not take a rigid

aggressive. Never interrupt the interviewer when he is speaking.

Do not accept a cigarette from an interviewer even if you smoke. Refuse courteously by saying, "Thank you."

The interviewer could ask provocative questions to see how you react. Do not take offence or

The interviewer could ask about certain areas of life when you did not do well. Do not tell lies. Be honest and positive about such things. Do not blame others for your failures. Instead tell about the lessons you learnt from failures.

Some interviewers could have whims and fancies. That is their business. Do not let these

Throughout the interview be brief and to the point. When over, thank the interviewers to have given you an opportunity to speak to them.

To save on time and effort many prospective employers are now using the telephone to interview

the applicant's point of view also because it saves time and effort, and also anxiety. The prospective employer would inform the applicant about the proposed time for the call. The applicant must ensure that the telephone is in good working order and he or she should be present close to the phone.

For a successful interview on the telephone a person must be careful about several important issues. It has been observed that the applicant must be careful about the following issues:

- The telephone must be in a place where there is no noise. Switch off the television or radio. If you are using a mobile phone ensure a quiet place in the house to receive the call.
- Have a copy of your application and the resume sent to the prospective employer handy. He could ask you about something on your resume. Be ready to answer it without hesitation.
- Have a pencil and a pad ready to jot down any enquiries or details that the interviewer might ask for. If necessary, these could be mailed through post.
- Be prepared for giving a short introduction about yourself. He could ask you about your strengths, and sometimes weaknesses, as apparent from the resume.
- Listen to the interviewer carefully. Try to understand what he wants to know. Speak in

- Speak slowly and clearly. The interviewer cannot see you. Therefore, your dress is not important. At this time your image is being conveyed through your voice. Give him the impression of a smile on your face, as you speak.
- When he talks or makes a mention of the proposed job let him feel your enthusiasm for it through your voice.
- Do not be eager to tell more than what the interviewer wants to know about you. If there is something special just make a hint and let him ask you about it.
- Do not convey negative or strong judgments about issues and events. He should not feel that you have a rigid mindset.
- At the end of the interview thank the interviewer.

Chapter 25

Several companies now conduct an interview with a prospective employee over lunch. This provides an altogether different environment both to the interviewer and the interviewee, making it somewhat informal. It can still not be overlooked that the interviewer is representing the employer and the applicant has offered to serve the organization. The purpose of the lunch is not to enjoy a meal together,

employer desires of him or her.

Despite the informal environment it is still necessary for the applicant to observe proper etiquette and manners throughout the interview. The interviewer will not evaluate only on the basis of the verbal interaction during lunch, but also evaluate the applicant on the basis of body language, personality,

would do well to keep the following in mind to create the right impression during the interview:

- Be appropriately dressed for the occasion. Arrive on time. Check the venue in advance so that you do not get confused at the last moment.
- Let the interviewer be seated before you take a chair. Sit straight. Smile. Build eye contact with the interviewer.
- Choose food that is easy to eat and talk at the same time. If the interviewer asks you to choose

talking.
- Do not accept to drink even if the interviewer insists that you join him for a glass of beer. Agree to take a soft drink.
- All the conditions that one needs to remember for a conventional interview must be followed during a luncheon interview.
- To be able to eat and speak take small bites of food. Never have your mouth full.
- To avoid any interruptions keep your mobile switched off.
- When speaking be honest and sincere. Answer the questions truthfully.
- Though the interviewer will pay for the meal, as he has invited you, it would be good manners to ask if you could pay for the meal.
- Thank the interviewer before leaving. Follow with a written "thank you" note.

Chapter 26

To negotiate means to reach an agreement through discussion. We are doing it all the time every day at home, at the workplace and in society. Sometimes we come to agreement quickly, particularly when one is in a commanding position. When a person discusses on an equal plane, one with better negotiating skills has the balance tilted in his or her favour.

We see it every day. The housewife bargains with the vegetable vendor to negotiate the best price. Once successful she bargains for other necessities using the best of her negotiating skills. At the workplace every worker has two important things in mind – a little less responsibility, meaning a little

obtained through negotiations, or discussions leading to logical results.

All of business works on the concept of selling products and negotiating skills. It is a specialized subject that would be discussed in greater detail at a later stage.

Negotiating skills could be useful like the housewife bargaining for a special price with the vegetable vendor, but could also include high level negotiating to buy land or property for a residence, a factory or a business house. It could even involve two countries holding discussions between representatives to reach agreement on doing business or settling a boundary dispute.

Negotiations involve two parties. Both desire to come to a mutual agreement. The problem

advantage when coming to agreement. Since the agreement is arrived at through mutual verbal

be well acquainted with the circumstances of the matter and also possess good speaking and debating skills.

claims of the other party. Objections would have to be countered through logical arguments.

not misinterpreted. They must be understood correctly.

the parties are involved emotionally in the matter. The negotiations could be about the division of a property. One of the parties could be emotionally involved with it because of having worked or lived there and developing an attachment for it. Discussions on such issues require a skilled person to convince the parties appropriately.

Learning Negotiating Skills

Negotiating is a skill everyone must possess. It begins with learning to organize one's thoughts methodically and be able to speak convincingly. Here are a few common observations on learning these skills:

and can discuss without interruptions.

party to keep speaking. This way you will get to know the party's strengths and weaknesses. Do not interrupt. Speak only when the other party has exhausted arguments in support of their claim.

called strengths of the party are only illusory. Explain that they are not real but only a creation of the mind. Also explain how each of the weaknesses of the party is a possible threat that

taking advantage in any way, that you seek a mutually agreeable settlement suitable to both the parties.

Making negotiations is a game of patience and tact. Sometimes you need to blow hot and at other times you need to blow cold. Always be well acquainted with the facts of the situation. Also be aware of what is at stake. The greater the stake more careful you would have to be.

Never stretch a situation too far. Many negotiations fail when one of the parties is adamant and rigid on its stand. A good negotiator knows when the situation has been stretched far enough. Just then clinch the deal. You have achieved whatever is possible.

Once a verbal agreement becomes a document it has legal sanctity.

Ramcharitmanas when Sri Ram asks Angad to go to Ravan as his ambassador to tell him to either send back Sita or face war.

When Angad enquired as to what attitude he should adopt while negotiating, Sri Ram said, "You should aim that our purpose is achieved. This would be possible only when you keep our purpose and also the interest of the other party in mind simultaneously."

To ensure success when negotiating, it is important that the interests of both the parties must be kept in mind to ensure a reasonable settlement where nobody loses face. It is equally important that a person must enter into negotiation from a superior position.

Only a few days earlier Hanuman had wrecked and burnt Lanka. The demons feared the sight of a monkey. Taking advantage of the situation, Angad walked boldly through the streets of Lanka. When Prahast confronted him, an argument started. In anger, Prahast kicked him. Angad held Prahast by the leg, gave him a spin, and threw him on the ground. He died on the spot. In fear the demons ran away. When he reached Ravan's assembly, he was immediately ushered in. Everybody stood up as though in

Ravan was very knowledgeable and knew the ways of the world. He feigned surprise and ignorance of what was going on.

Ravan asked him who he was, and what was the purpose of his visit? Angad spoke gently, telling him that he was Sri Ram's ambassador. He also said that his father and Ravan had been friends. Angad desired that negotiations must be peaceful. He even went on to use praise as a way to disarm and pacify Ravan. Talking of his goodness he suggested that he should return Sita to Sri Ram and seek his refuge.

Ravan was lost to pride and arrogance. Rather than accept negotiation as a medium of conciliation, he behaved as though it was a one-sided surrender.

Ravan provoked Angad, pretending that he did not know his father, Vali. As usual, he talked of his own prowess. He would never tire of praising himself.

To counteract his claims Angad talked of those who had defeated him. His father, Vali was one of them.

He said, "I know of another Ravan who was held tight under Vali's arm. Tell me the truth. Which one of these are you?"

When Ravan casually admitted that a monkey had visited Lanka, once again Angad caught him on the wrong note.

"Fool! You call Hanuman an ordinary monkey? Did he not crush your army and your pride? He guard. He warned him about his pride and delusions. He used sarcasm and insult. He did not hesitate to even talk of his own strength and threaten him.

"Fool! Throwing you on the ground, killing your troops and ruining your city, I can take away Sita along with your wives."

Ravan's pride and arrogance were the biggest hurdles. They always are. Besides, Ravan was obsessed with war. He wanted to show that he was strong, valiant and invincible.

He said, "Which hero can be like me? With my own hands I cut off my heads repeatedly

Throughout the negotiation Ravan was repeatedly trying to provoke Angad. Angad too was trying to provoke Ravan. The purpose of the provocation was to arouse anger in the other. Once a person loses personal calm and becomes angry, one loses reasoning. This is a shortcut to defeat. Whereas Ravan did get provoked, Angad maintained his cool.

Angad responded with a smile. He remained calm. He was quick to respond and make comparisons.

was lost to pride and arrogance and wanted a trial of strength he struck both his hands on the ground with great force. The earth shook as though there was an earthquake. The seats moved. Fear struck the hearts of all present. Even Ravan toppled over. Angad quickly snatched his crowns and tossed them over towards the camp.

monkeys and bears. Catch the two hermits and bring them to me alive."

Angad responded with an equally loud voice, "Are you not ashamed of what you boast? Are you out to destroy your race? Can you not see strength? You abduct women and speak senselessly? Death awaits you, wretched demon! I could pick the whole of Lanka and throw it into the ocean. I restrain

Learning Negotiating Skills

myself because I have no permission from my master to do so."

When Ravan provoked Angad again by calling him a liar, as show of strength Angad placed his foot

He said, "Fool, if you can, I challenge you to move my foot. If anyone of you succeeds to do it, Sri Ram will return without Sita."

Ravan asked his soldiers to hold the monkey by the foot and crush him. One by one the demon warriors came, but none could move Angad's foot. Even Meghnad could not. Each returned with the head hanging in shame. When everyone failed, Ravan rose to move Angad's foot.

Before Ravan could reach it, Angad said, "You cannot be saved by holding my foot, fool! If you must hold somebody's feet, it must be Sri Ram's."

Ravan felt ashamed to hear Angad, who had put the whole assembly to shame.

"What good is my talking to you, fool?" Angad said. "I will kill you in battle." Throwing the challenge Angad returned as the demons watched quietly.

Did you observe how Angad used friendliness, praise, patience, tact, knowledge, provocation and also strength to negotiate a peaceful settlement with Ravan? He used all the techniques to get his way,

glimpse of his strength. Such skills take a long time to develop, but it can be done when one makes an effort persistently.

Chapter 22

they lead to anger, frustration and even stress. In such situations a person can say things that one would repent later.

explained as a lack of agreement between opinions and principles of two or

principal causes of stress.

Every person is unique. There has never been one like him or her earlier, nor there will be one in the future. Every person grows up in his or her own special and unique way. Considering the genetic make-up and

thing everyone needs to understand is that when everyone is unique, opinions on issues are likely to be different and rather than adopting an attitude of confrontation it would be sensible to adopt an attitude of understanding and acceptance. That would lead to harmony instead of

it grows. When exposed both parties try to resolve it quickly. Even when the problem is resolved it

different situations leading to a mature handling of situations later.

Do you use abusive language to give vent to your anger? Or do you use authority to tell the other person who you are? In other situations there are people who avoid the unpleasantness of the situation and divert their attention to other things. Some give in to the other person's point of view. Many women

upon the situation and suggests appropriate steps to maintain peace and harmony.

to handle the situation. Maintain complete self-restraint by not speaking abusively or unreasonably.

a spirit of mutual understanding, and not by giving in to others' whims and fancies. To be effective everyone must work in harmony.

would need to give up some of these. Through some effort it is possible to rid oneself of a bad habit. Many have done it successfully to attain important positions in business and professional activities.

possible to maintain harmony at the workplace by following these simple suggestions to keep it free of

. It would come suddenly. When it does accept it as a part of everyday life at the workplace.

Maintain self-restraint. Do not respond with anger and foul language. That would only confound the situation.

What caused it? Look for reasons within you and also the other person. If you are at fault, apologize and move on. Do not sleep over it.

Use patience and tact. If the other person is at fault use patience and tact to explain it to him. Seek support from others, if necessary.

. Ensure that the same faults do not repeat in the future.

Chapter 28

When a business organisation has a choice of several young people to choose from for employment a group discussion is an easy format where several persons can be evaluated simultaneously and only a few selected for a personal interview.

The usual procedure followed is to have six to a maximum of ten people seated around a round table or in a circle, give them a topic to discuss and ask them to come to a consensus to settle the particular issue. Everyone must be given an opportunity to speak and nobody should speak excessively. Time permitting the discussion between the participants could continue for the allocated time, which could be up to 20 to 25 minutes. The evaluator does not intervene. He observes each candidate and marks them appropriately.

On what basis do the evaluators judge different candidates? If the participants would have the answer to this question they could be better prepared. The need of every employer would be different.

The common observations are that the prospective employers look for the following qualities in the candidates:

. These can be immediately evaluated on the basis of a person's body language, the way the person dresses, stands, sits and speaks.

Leadership qualities
on the basis of the person's initiative, patient hearing, an understanding of other people's opinions, a positive attitude and good speaking skills to put forward reasonable arguments.

Good speaking skills. A person with good speaking skills is courteous, maintains eye contact with colleagues and speaks to the point on relevant issues only. The person is unconsciously persuasive and carries others along.

Good knowledge. This would require a person to have good knowledge not only about the

general knowledge can speak effectively about different issues and problems, and suggest appropriate solutions.

Organised thinking. In any discussion it is necessary to have organized thinking because that only will ensure a reasoned presentation and a logical conclusion to the discussion.

Besides a complete understanding of what the prospective employer is looking for it would be essential that the participant must be well prepared in advance for the group discussion. The participant must also know how to conduct oneself during the group discussion and impress the evaluator to be selected for a personal interview.

Some of the common observations about conducting oneself during a group discussion are as follows:

Arrive on time. There is no excuse for not reaching the venue of the group discussion at the prescribed time. If you arrive late, you have lost even before the discussion has begun.

Be appropriately dressed. A group discussion is a formal evaluation of prospective candidates for a job. You cannot afford to be casually dressed.

Carry a pen and pad. It is not possible to remember too many points presented during the discussion. You should jot down points so as to arrive at a conclusion logically in the end.

Know the subject clearly. When the subject is given to the group, jot it down. Ensure that you begins. Don't do it later.

Be natural. Don't try to be what you are not. Even if you pretend for a short while it would be of no use. You can't pose to be someone else all the time.

Build eye contact. Look around at all the participants to build eye contact with them. You don't need to look at the evaluators. Let them do their job.

Initiate the discussion. The person who initiates a discussion has an advantage over others. This is not easy. To do so a person must be knowledgeable about the subject, have structured thinking and possess good speaking skills.

Listen patiently. Try to understand how other participants look at the subject. Think of in what other ways the subject can be perceived.

with someone, raise an objection. Do not be aggressive or rude. Look at the subject from the positive angle; underplay the negative. Try to sort out objections and contradictions.

Step in when necessary. If some of the participants speak too long or interrupt repeatedly remind them that the time is limited and everyone must put forward their opinion. Such an intervention will highlight your leadership qualities.

Be brief and to the point. The purpose of a group discussion is not to speak often and long, but to be precise and clear about the subject. The aim should be to reach a consensus.

Lead to a consensus. A person who can gradually convince the participants to come to a consensus has leadership qualities, which are appreciated by all employers.

Do not feel guilty. Even if you make an effort to bring everyone to a consensus but fail to do so let it not make you feel guilty. A group is formed of all kinds of people and building consensus is not easy.

Put in your best effort. Leave the rest to the evaluator's judgment.

What subjects are usually given for group discussion? The truth is that the prospective employer can ask for a discussion on almost anything. It would depend upon his attitude towards the subject. It is common to have a subject that is in popular discussion at that time, and everyone would have something to say about it. The subject could pertain to personal life, the society, country or even humanity. Here are a few common subjects that would arouse discussion amongst most people:

Sex education is a must in schools.	There should be greater control on NGOs.
Religion and politics must not be mixed.	We must stop commercialization of healthcare.
We must stop brain drain.	
Women are as good workers as men.	Is India a soft state?
	The MBA bubble has burst.
better than family-run businesses.	Privatization of education has created new problems.
Prosperity leads to lifestyle diseases.	
Love marriages are better than arranged marriages in modern times.	Women empowerment is the need of the day.
Indian culture is decaying.	Economic reforms must continue.
Globalization is a necessity.	Beauty and brans don't go together.
We must change to change the world.	India needs a good dictator.
Life is a life-long duty.	
Change is a part of life.	Politics must be value-based.

This is only a small representation of the subjects that can be discussed. The list can go on

In a debate a person knows the subject in advance and can plan to speak after advance preparation.

few ideas that can be elaborated when speaking. In a group discussion the person is completely at test. How do the evaluators look at different participants after the group discussion? Here are a few common observations about their role in a discussion:

Leaders. These are the participants who take the initiative to speak, to keep control over others and try to build a consensus on the subject. They look at others as team members and try to carry them along.

Debaters. These are the participants who take a rigid stand and love to argue. This type are excitable, speak aggressively and often. They make the discussion lively. Since they take a

Spoilsports. These are the participants who have a rigid mindset. They feel their viewpoint is the only right one. They have a one-track mind. They block discussion, and have to be silenced frequently.

Silent observers. These participants are the quiet observers who listen more than they speak. They are temperamentally shy. They could have a lot of good ideas but have to be goaded to present them. A good leader gets the best out of them.

Objectors. These participants can raise an objection to everything. They love to counter others' views. They stimulate discussion. However, they take on an obstinate attitude and would present their views aggressively.

Accommodators. These participants maintain a balance between listening and speaking.

and seek a consensus on the subject.

In corporate training group discussions are popular to acquaint the participants on new techniques and also to inform them of the latest developments. For this form of group discussion the ideal number

sitting in the centre from where they have an eye contact with every participant. The leader would ask a leading question, which would be answered by the participants. After the brief discussion the leader would sum up the answers, adding additional views that might not have been covered. He then moves on to the next question. This keeps the discussion alive giving everyone an opportunity to speak. When

keeps everyone involved. Here are a few common observations about this form of group discussions:

    The group discussion leader must pre-plan key questions in advance, maintaining continuity from one point to another.

    All the participants must speak out their views on different aspects of the subject. Be brief and to the point. The leader should not let the subject drag.

    Begin and end the subject on time, making appropriate conclusions at the end.

Chapter 29

Everyone is a salesperson. Generally, to sell means to exchange a product or service for money; in reality, to sell would also include persuading someone to the merits of an idea. Everyone is doing this at all time.

Mothers are forever trying to sell the idea of what to eat and what to avoid, or how to dress up and how not to. Fathers are forever trying to sell the idea about being frugal and careful with money. In response the children are also trying to persuade the parents on how they need to change with the times.

At the workplace every employee is trying to sell his or her ability to the employer, forever making an effort to convey the message: "I'm the best!" In the society also everyone is continuously selling new ideas and concepts to gain recognition and position. Although everyone is a salesperson in his or

held in excess for those that one did not have.

In selling as a profession a person needs to communicate or speak well and be persuasive to convince others to accept an idea, a product or service. Persuasion is the art to make the other person believe what you believe. This, in turn, would mean that you sell a belief that the idea, product or service that you offer is good value for money. A belief is only a strongly held opinion and is not easy to sell because others too would have their own beliefs. Selling a belief becomes easier when the prospective customer is known and places trust upon you. This leads a person to the obvious – build good relationships and you can sell well.

Building good relationships require positive body language, etiquette and good manners and most important good speaking skills and knowledge of the prospective customer's mindset.

The most popular way of selling is still the one-to-one method where the seller sells a product directly to the customer at home or at a retail store. As long as there is no product variations the seller passes on the needs of the customer without much conversation, but when a large variety is available the seller could have inclination towards certain brands and would then need to use persuasive skills to sell them. Selling is no longer what it was to begin with. In the current time it requires specialized knowledge and special skills to succeed at selling.

The ever-continuing addition of new products and variants has provided opportunities to sell and service them. New showrooms are coming up every day in every city and town to sell them, and the need for service centres to maintain them. Selling is no longer restricted to local areas or even within a state or country. People all over the world are looking for new and better products in countries thousands of miles away. The complexity of selling over large areas has made it necessary to involve

many forms. Some of the popular methods are:

One-to-one selling	Mail order selling
Retail selling	Telemarketing
Selling in bulk	Selling on the Internet
Direct selling	Export marketing
Redistribution stockists	Providing services

Irrespective of the selling method used to move products and services from the manufacturer to process better. These stages are:

1. **The person who has something to sell.** He could have the product ready in stock, or could manufacture or procure it for the consumer.
2. **Finding a person who needs the product.** There could be many people interested in the product. There could also be many different brands or variants available and each could have differences in quality and price. At this point the element of competition takes over. The seller would need to use persuasive skills.
3. **Negotiation between the seller and buyer.** If the buyer feels that the product quality offered by the seller is suitable for his need, it would be necessary to negotiate the price. While the seller would seek the best price, the purchaser would seek the most competitive price in relation to other competing brands. At this point both the seller and the purchaser would require good negotiation skills.
4. **Delivery of the product.** The purchaser would desire an early delivery, but the seller could have production constraints. A sale would be completed when the product is delivered and the seller has received the price. The purchaser could desire credit or delayed payment. This is again an issue of negotiation between the seller and the purchaser. Delayed payment could be received through a post-dated cheque.
5. **Servicing the product, if necessary.** It might be necessary to install the product such as an air-conditioner, a refrigerator or a television or something similar. Some products like motor cycles, scooters and cars require after sales service also. This is a very important stage of a sale because without it many products would not sell at all. Effective servicing is an important selling point.

and skills. A salesperson in a store could succeed with etiquette and good manners along with some speaking and persuasive skills, but a sales manager of a big company could be leading a large skilled sales-force and would sell through a network of distributors and retailers making it a complex operation.

At every stage the salesperson needs to speak and persuade the purchaser. To be successful the salesperson would need to possess certain qualities. It has been observed that all good salespersons ensure the following:

      They are kind and courteous.
      They observe etiquette and good manners.
      They are good communicators. They speak well.
      They get along well with people.
      They remember the names of their clients.

They are well acquainted with the products that they sell.
They are well acquainted with competitor products and competitive pricing.
They are enthusiastic and always take the initiative to serve others.

when they are travelling away from home.

Customer is the King

To the salesperson the customer should always be "king". He is the key person to be kept pleased and happy. The product or the service that you offer must satisfy him. If it does not he will feel cheated.

take the customer for granted. This is not right. It is this lapse that makes most customers suspicious of salespersons.

A good salesperson makes efforts to build long-term selling relationships with prospective customers. This ensures steady growth. It sounds good but is not easy to attain. Salespersons are always over enthusiastic to sell and customers are always suspicious of the motives of the salespersons. Initially, the interactions begin with high tension and low levels of trust. It is for the salesperson to convert the low-trust high-tension situation to a high-trust low-tension situation. When the level of trust increases the resistance by the customer diminishes. People who trust the salesperson become lifetime customers. A good salesperson does not only sell products to the customer, but also serves as a trusted guide and provides service beyond the call of responsibility.

Know Your Products

A good salesperson knows the products like the back of the hand. People often wonder what is there to know about the products. They come packaged from the factory to be sold to the consumer. The salesperson is only a facilitator to help the product reach the customer. This is not true. A salesperson is a key person who makes things happen. If it were not for him or her the entire manufacturing trade would come down crumbling.

What constitutes good knowledge of a product? The answer could vary for different products. Here are a few common questions that must be answered to know all that there is about a product:

Origin of the product. What was the origin of the product? When did it happen? Who made it possible? What research and development followed the original product? What improvements were made? Who gave the brand name to the product? What makes the brand special?

Variants of the product. How many variants of our products are available? What are the sizes and weights? What are the models, colours or designs that are available? What is the standard packing? Can it be altered, if desired? What is the minimum order we can entertain?

Quality of the product. Do we have reliable quality control? Is our quality superior to that of our competitors?

Use of the product. What is the most popular use of the product? What kind and class of people use it the most? What are the unique selling points of the product? Does the product have any limitations? What has been done to eliminate them? Are there alternative products?

Pricing of the product. How do our prices compare with the competitor products? Do we offer any discounts? What is the basis of discounts? sAre the discounts based upon the quantity purchased or is it based upon the value of the order?

Competitive products. What competitive products are available in the market? What is their placement like? What is their market share? How does the quality and pricing compare with our product? If they are cheaper, how does the manufacturer make it possible?

Advertising and publicity. What is the advertising support given to the product? Is it advertised on the television? In newspapers and magazines? Is local publicity done through hoardings and displays in stores? What support is provided to retailers for providing display space?

Delivery of the product. How would the delivery be made? Would it be through road, rail or courier? Who would pay the charges? When would the delivery be made? What happens if we are unable to deliver on time? Would the consignment be insured in transit? Who pays the insurance charges?

Service facilities. Some of the products would require installation and servicing. What is the company policy about these? How close are these facilities available to the customer? What are the standard charges prescribed by the company? How soon would the service be provided to the customer?

Credit facilities. Does the company have a credit policy? If so, what are the criteria for selling on credit? What is the possible limit of credit? Do we take a post-dated cheque? What happens if the customer fails to pay on time?

Have you observed how much there is to know about a product when you set out to sell it? These are only sample questions of different possibilities. When the salesperson is face to face with the customer many more questions would be asked and the salesperson would need to answer them spontaneously or lose the sale. It is imperative that the salesperson must know all that there is to know about the product.

Know the Prospective Customer

A sale can go through only when the prospective customer buys the product. While the salesperson is always enthusiastic about what he or she is selling, the purchaser is always suspicious about the quality of the product, the price and also about the person who is selling the product. The level of this suspicion goes down only through experience, but that takes time. The salesperson would do well to get to know the prospective person as well as possible.

All products don't sell the same way. Every customer too has his own whims and fancies. It is, therefore, common for salespersons to collect and tabulate prospective customer information into

The larger organisations sell through wholesalers and redistributors who might function from small

the salesperson representing the manufacturer needs to develop a good relationship with the wholesaler or the redistributing stockists, and also with the retailers who are the principal customers.

Only a few products are sold directly to the customers and these would require a very special handling by the salesperson. Irrespective of the kind of product one is selling or the method adopted to market it, at every stage the key person is the prospective customer. It is imperative that the salesperson must know all that is possible about the customer, keep in touch with him, and also update information about him periodically. This way the salesperson can expect a steady relationship with the customers and also ensure the movement of the products that are being sold.

Salesperson's Talking Points

Salespersons use a variety of methods to talk about the products that they sell. Each group of products would require different kinds of presentation, but there are some common talking points that all salespersons must be well acquainted with. These are:

Success story about the product. The salesperson would like to talk about how and why the product is a success in the market.

Market share of the product. Every reputed manufacturer or known brand would command an important share in the market. All salespersons take pride in this fact and make it a part of the presentation story.

An edge over competitor products. All successful salespersons acknowledge the presence and importance of competitor products, but like to explain how their product has an edge over them.

Unique usage of the product. Many products have multiple uses, which can be of great advantage. This information should feature in a sales presentation.

Experts' views about the product. All manufacturers seek reviews of their products from the

Use by celebrities. All manufacturers seek endorsement of their products by celebrities.

mention the endorsement in the sales talk.

Advertising on television. Products that are advertised on television sell nationally and internationally. This creates a psychological impact on the mind of the prospective customers. As a measure of popularity of the product the salesperson likes to mention it in the sales presentation.

Warranty backup. When customers are wary about the quality of a product the warranty provides an assurance that the manufacturer assures the desired quality in his product. The sales person would like to talk about it too.

Service backup. Many products need installation and after sales service. The salesperson would like to highlight the same in the sales talk.

What's in it for them? When the salesperson is talking to wholesalers and retailers who buy

margin that ensures a fair return on investment and effort to them.

The salesperson must write down all the talking points, prioritize them according to their importance and have a ready presentation for the prospective customers. All customers are not generous in giving

ask the person to hold on until he has spoken, and then he would answer all the questions. A well prepared sales talk goes a long way in closing the sale.

Persuading the Customer

The immediate purpose of every sales presentation is to persuade the prospective customer to buy the products on offer. One persuades another through reasoning and argument. A person learns this skill through understanding of human behaviour and by communicating effectively. The salesperson's presentation will have to be persuasive without appearing to be so. How does one do that? Successful salespersons use these simple methods to do so:

> **Use reason.** It is presumed that all people are reasonable in looking at a situation. To reason, one uses logic and reasoning.
>
> **Appeal to the emotions.** All advertising takes advantage by connecting a product to an
>
> **Use propaganda.**
> unconsciously through a message that is repeated frequently.
>
> **Body language.** Have you observed how people use body language as a tool of persuasion? Salespersons use it too.
>
> **Effective communication skills.** All successful salespersons are known for the "gift of the gab". They speak their way through a situation.

It would be appropriate to point out that some salespersons use position, coercion and deception to attain sales targets. This might appear reasonable in given circumstances. In the long-term this is the wrong thing to do. Never use unethical methods as a tool to persuade people to buy something. Selling

How Persuasion Works?

Whereas every salesperson desires to close a sale as fast as possible, in reality it is not possible because a customer would have many needs. With limited money to spend it is not easy to decide what should

salesperson makes a presentation to the prospect, persuasion goes through several stages. These would be:

1. The prospect is not interested in making a purchase.

3. The prospect resists the salesperson's offer through objections, offering new ideas and opinions on the product.
4. The salesperson hears patiently because by speaking freely the prospect is indirectly telling what he expects from the product.
5. The salesperson uses persuasion techniques to match product features with the prospect's expectations, reviving the interest of the prospect for the product.

sale.

Approaching the Customer

to decide whether a standard approach would work for all customers, or should there be a tailor-made approach for each customer? A standard approach works in selling popular items of use, but when it comes to selling specialized products, particularly those of high value, there would be the need for a tailor-made approach to convince the prospective customer.

When approaching the customer the salesperson must follow certain principles that have been

upon the situation. These principles are:

Know the customer. Collect as much information about the customer as is possible. The customer could be a company, a group of people or an individual. The more you know about them the easier it will be to close the sale.

Have a reason to call. Most people are very busy and interruptions on their time are looked

Verify the exact needs.
best person to decide what it is. Verify it tactfully.

Take a positive approach. Customers are human beings. They like positive people who are enthusiastic and optimistic. When the salesperson has these qualities the prospective customer

Maintain self-control. Enthusiasm is good. One can easily pass it to another. But when the salesperson is over-enthusiastic it can be counter-productive. In dealing with a customer be patient and tactful.

Keep on track. When making a presentation never go off-track. It creates the impression of an unprofessional approach towards one's work.

Make the customer feel important. When the customer feels that he is important to you he would look at you kindly and give preference to your product.

Give more than what is expected. Nothing makes a customer feel happier than to receive more than his own expectations. This little extra could be in the form of additional service or

A salesperson needs to make consistent effort to gradually build a long-term selling relationship with the customers. The initial efforts made go a long way in helping salesperson perfect good persuasion techniques.

The Sales Presentation

Therefore, it is for the salesperson to make a presentation that informs, motivates, persuades, convinces and arouses the desire in the prospect to buy. The presentation should make a promise to the customer that the product would provide him satisfaction that he seeks. The presentation should be realistic, present the correct facts, and must be pleasant to hear. Many salespersons use illustrations, charts, visual aids, and brochures to effectively present the facts, ideas and thoughts to convince the prospective customer. Many presentations are a two-way interaction between the salesperson and the prospective customer.

A good sales interview has several elements that together result in making a sale. All salespersons must understand these. They are:

1. **Draw the attention of the prospect.** Customers are busy people. Even when a sales interview

    His mind would be pre-occupied with something of importance to him. Therefore, drawing the attention of the customer is very important.

2. **Get the prospect interested in the product.** When the customer continues to hear the salesperson it would mean that he is interested in the product. A common technique used by sales-

persons to arouse the interest of the customer is to link the product to the customer's hopes and aspirations, problems, accomplishments, family and other interests.

3. **Create a desire for the product.** The presentation should aim at making the customer aware of the need for the product. The need would gradually convert into a want, and the want would convert into a desire. The desire would gradually intensify to unconsciously compel him to make the purchase.

4. **The desire becomes a conviction.** When the intensity of the desire converts it into a conviction to buy, the customer begins to look at the price, competitor brands, evaluates the products and thinks in terms of buying it.

5. **Agrees to buy the product.**
of the product and agrees to buy it. This attains the purpose of the sales presentation.

Closing A Sale

Every salesperson has only one aim: to close a sale. This is the last part of a sales presentation and provides the maximum delight and satisfaction to the salesperson. Though this is the last part of the

product. At this stage the salesperson needs to re-assure the customer that he has made the best choice and would gain much from the use of the product.

Everyone needs to attend meetings that come in all shapes and sizes. From a one-to-one meeting in an

where you live. It could also be a larger meeting like a felicitation function in honour of a newly-elected representative in the municipal corporation or a condolence meeting in the memory of a relative or an important citizen.

Some public meetings can be very big. Politicians love them. Most meetings are small with a limited

in our lives. It would surprise most people that millions of meetings are conducted all over the world

these meetings were not required. Somebody decided to have the meeting to pass on his or her responsibility to a group. The second reason is that most of the people who participate in these meetings do not know how to conduct themselves or to conduct the meeting correctly. If we could learn how to make meetings effective we would achieve much more not only in business or a profession, but also in every sphere of life.

Every meeting begins with one person, one who feels that a mutual discussion amongst those involved would help resolve a particular issue. This person could be involved in the meeting as the leader, or could appoint another person as a representative with similar authority. The leader of the meeting must understand that he or she:

      is not just a member of a group; he or she is the leader.

      is responsible for the success or failure of the meeting.

      knows best as to what is to be achieved through the meeting.

      must be in complete control of the meeting in terms of time and the discussions.

      must hear everyone with an open mind, accepting the positive suggestions and explaining why the negative suggestions would harm the interests of the group.

      must conclude the discussions at the appropriate time to ensure that the purpose of the meeting is attained.

Successful meetings are not just a matter of chance. To ensure a successful meeting it must be planned like any other important activity and be conducted by a person who has learnt the necessary

attain what is desired.

A person skilled in conducting good meetings does not rush into calling a meeting. One must consider several issues before calling a meeting. Several observations have been made about conducting effective meetings. Let us consider some of them.

Is a meeting necessary? The unfortunate truth is that most of them are not necessary. A person in authority could easily give instructions that would eliminate the need for the meeting. A

Is it the appropriate time for the meeting? The correct timing of a meeting is important to attain success. Some people are very impulsive and call a meeting on the slightest pretext. This does not work. Call the meeting only when you feel it is the right time for it.

What purpose would the meeting achieve?
the purpose of the meeting it should not be called. A person must premeditate on the purpose of the meeting and call it only when the purpose is clear to everyone.

Is it the appropriate place to call a meeting? All business meetings are conducted within the premises of the business-house, but the place of meeting could affect results. Politicians are aware about appropriate places because they seek support from others. Meetings are best conducted in common places where everyone can speak and discuss the issues freely. Avoid places that would be objectionable to some of the participants for whatever cause.

Have all the concerned persons been informed of the meeting? This is a common problem with meetings and people. Many complain that they were not informed, or informed too late

participant in a meeting has to be informed about the meeting.

Do the participants know what the meeting is about? Most people confess ignorance. It is essential that the agenda of the meeting should be sent to all the participants in advance. This ensures that they come prepared for discussion, and the issue is resolved one way or the other.

Are the physical arrangements for the meeting appropriate? A person must ensure that the meeting can be conducted without interruptions from people coming in and out of the room, the telephone ringing, or even having noise in the adjoining room. Disturbances do not permit the discussions to progress logically.

Will the meeting be conducted by a skilled person? It is common for the management to delegate the responsibility of conducting the meeting to an appropriate person who possesses the necessary skills. The person conducting the meeting could lead it to success or failure. Much would depend upon his or her skills to deal with people and also delicate issues.

An often-asked question is: what kind of skills should a person conducting a meeting must possess? By its nature every meeting is unique. As human beings every person conducting a meeting or participating in it is unique and special. The level of knowledge, understanding and experience would of course vary from one person to another. Each person would be a unique combination of skills. It has been observed that people with the following skills do well at conducting meetings:

Leadership skills. Every meeting requires one person to lead and the others to respond with positive suggestions.

Teamwork skills. A person who possesses teamwork skills carries everyone along without anyone taking offence.

Speaks convincingly. A person good at verbal communication knows how to frame sentences

and speak convincingly to quietly assert to move along in a particular direction.
Patient listener
present, one cannot be sure what the general consensus is. Listening patiently is a very valuable skill all leaders must possess.
Impartiality. It does not take long for people to realise that a leader is partial towards certain

A person must take a balanced look at all individuals and the issues under consideration.
Flexibility
attitude. This conveys the message that the person is not open to new ideas or activities and

Time management skills
A person conducting a meeting must budget time for each issue and move on to attain the purpose of the meeting.

How does a skilled person conduct an effective meeting? Possessing appropriate skills is necessary. What is more important is how these skills are used. Every corporate house follows a customary pattern

practices. Here are a few observations about ensuring that the meeting attains its purpose:

Arrive in time. Time is a crucial factor for a successful meeting. Most people are very

conveys, "I mean business!"

Begin on time. When the person conducting the meeting fails to start a meeting on time, the immediate message is that he or she is not serious about it. When the person decides to wait because one or more persons have not arrived, yet another negative message is conveyed that the opinion of those who are late is more important than those who respect time. The next time they will also not arrive on time.

Begin with apt opening remarks. The person presiding the meeting must attract the attention

They should convey, "No negative inputs, please!"

. Most organisers look at meetings as a routine

a true meaning when all the participants leave better informed, a little more evolved and enthusiastic about the subject of discussion.

Keep the meeting in control. The meeting must be businesslike, one person speaking at a time. Each person must address the chair, and not individuals. Nobody should be allowed to monopolize the time. Everyone must be given a chance to speak. If someone does not raise his or her hand to speak, it would be appropriate to ask him or her to say something on the subject.

Encourage the positive, discourage the negative. The ultimate success in any discussion

and appreciate what could be possible threats. Counter them with positive solutions and carry forward the discussion.

Do not let the discussion drag. This leads to boredom and negative results. Reinforce a dragging discussion with positive inputs, and lead to a positive conclusion.

Speaking at Meetings

End the meeting on time. The ideal time to close a meeting is when the purpose of the meeting has been attained even though it might be well before the closing time. Letting the

effectiveness. They will look forward to the next meeting. If the purpose of the meeting is not attained and it is already closing time, leaving the discussion incomplete, close on a positive note that the participants would give the subject still greater thought and propose positive ways to resolve the issue. This way everyone leaves the meeting with a happy frame of mind ignoring the time spent on an infructuous meeting.

Thank the participants. Irrespective of the outcome of a meeting it is simple courtesy for the person conducting the meeting to thank all the participants for their time and the valuable inputs during discussions. They would then look forward to the next meeting on the subject.

The role of the participants is limited to the exact role assigned to them, or to put forward their views to the person conducting the meeting to bring it to a logical end. The role of the person conducting

also be aggressive and rude. This makes the role of the person conducting the meeting like that of an oarsman steering a boat in a river that is both calm and rough at places. Just like an oarsman steers a boat to an appropriate point on the bank of the river, the person conducting the meeting must steer through it to attain the ultimate purpose.

How should a person do it practically? Let us take the example of the president of a housing society

conducting the meeting arrives before others, receives and greets them on arrival and leads them to where they are expected to be seated.

The moment it is time to begin the meeting, the president takes his place and begins, "Ladies and Gentlemen, could I please have your attention." Looking at his watch, the president continues, "We have important things to discuss. Those who are on their way can join us on arrival. Are we all ready?"

The participants would want to get over with it and would respond with a resounding "yes". The president should at this point make his opening remarks. To draw the attention of the participants, and trying to build eye-contact with them, he could greet loudly, "Good evening!" If the participants are attentive, they will respond to the greeting with an equally enthusiastic, "Good evening!" The president continues:

"Ladies and Gentlemen, I am grateful that you have acceded to my request and found time to be here to discuss a very vital issue that has bothered all of us for some time. I refer to the imbalance of the supply and demand of water in our society. There is a shortage of about 10 percent. We need to

secretary of the society would record them. Let one person speak at a time. If you would like to speak,

In these few lines, the president has:

    Thanked all the participants for their presence.

    Invited suggestions to counter the problem.
    Assured that the suggestions are being recorded.
    Asked everyone to maintain discipline.

Invited discussion on the issue.

Do all participants respond to such courtesies and requests? No, they don't. If everyone would respond in the same spirit a large percentage of meetings would be fruitful. It is for the person conducting the meeting to understand that the participants could respond in several different ways and he or she should be ready to face the situation accordingly. The behaviour of the participants has been observed at meetings and one would do well to know how to cope with different situations.

How should one respond to a person who continues to speak beyond time? The president must intervene:

"Mr. Sharma, I am sorry for the interruption, but we have limited time. Please conclude your remarks."

What about the person who digresses from the subject? The president must intervene to remind him:

"Sorry, Mr. Mathur, it appears that you have not understood the subject of the discussion. It is different. Please keep to the point."

How does one handle a person who interrupts others and speaks repeatedly? The president must immediately step in:

"I am sorry, Mr. Singh. We are seeking suggestions. Please do not interrupt when a person is speaking. You have spoken already. Let him offer his suggestions. If time permits, I will give you a minute in the end."

Some people get agitated very easily. Rather than give suggestions they lose control and accuse everyone for the problems. How should the president respond? He should intervene:

"Yes, Mr. Mishra, we appreciate your problems. If it weren't for the concern for your problems, why would this meeting have been called? Please tell us how you feel your problem can be sorted out?"

Those who accuse others freely are invariably those who are misinformed of the issue. They look at it only from their own angle. To bring the minds of such people to rest provide them with all the information available on the subject. The moment the doubts are dispelled people take a new look on the subject.

How should the person conducting the meeting handle a negative person? Such people do not offer solutions to a problem but frighten others how worse times are awaiting them. Things are bound to worsen, not improve. On such occasions the president must step in to say:

Do you have any? If you don't, leave it to others."

In every meeting there are some people who sit quietly listening and observing others without a comment. Should the president be content that there are some participants who are accepting all that is being said? No. Such people could have good suggestions to offer. The president could point out:

feel about the problem?"

No discussion at a meeting comes to a conclusion automatically. It is for the person presiding the

participants as stepping stones to move towards the purpose that is to be attained through the meeting. In the present case the imbalance in the supply and demand could be sorted out by increasing the supply of water, or reducing the consumption of water. If the supply of water in to be increased it would mean additional expense. What would it be, and how can it be paid without an undue burden on the residents. The person conducting the meeting must work on these issues, as the discussion progresses. This means that while the president must listen to all the participants and conduct them through the meeting, he must also think fast how to conclude the meeting appropriately.

What about the person, who comes late, has innumerable reasons for the delay, wants everything

afford to accommodate latecomers and offend those who came in time. He will have to be polite and

"Mr. Lal, we appreciate the circumstances that have kept you away from this meeting. Our friends who could make it to the meeting in time have been able to sort out the problem for all of us. You can speak to me after everyone leaves. We must close the meeting now. Everyone would have other engagements."

Close the meeting as soon as the purpose of the meeting is achieved. It is not advisable to prolong it. The participants will appreciate it.

attained and the participants gave their suggestions as they deemed suitable. What about the thousands of meetings in clubs and organizations held in altogether different circumstances. The purpose of these meetings would be to inform, educate or entertain. The president would know what is expected of him, but what about the participants who would be present to be informed or entertained? What should be their role? How should they respond to different situations?

Some of the participants could be entrusted with simple though special responsibilities. How should they behave, or what would they need to speak on such occasions?

What should a person do if a person is asked to give a bouquet to the Chief Guest or speaker at the meeting? All eyes and probably the cameras would be pointed at him or her at that moment. The person should not take the responsibility for granted. One must know where are the bouquets placed, and who will hand it at that point. The person should be so seated that it should take the least time. The bouquet must be presented with a broad smile and a short welcome, "A very hearty welcome to you, Sir!"

The situations and circumstances will vary from one meeting to another, but when asked to present a bouquet the method adopted and words chosen would be similar.

Sometimes a person could be invited to formally introduce a guest speaker. One cannot do that unless the individual is well known to the person who is to introduce him or her. Even in such circumstances it is customary that the introduction should be formal. This is possible only when the speaker has given a written biodata well in advance. Many a biodata is very lengthy and to read it would

it only to include important highlights and achievements. If a person is anxious that he or she could forgetsomething, it would be all right to read out from a paper.

The introduction should take not more than three minutes. It could begin in a simple manner:

"Mr. President, Ladies and Gentlemen: It is my pleasure this evening to formally welcome and introduce Mr. Srinivasan, an eminent scientist and guest speaker. He is currently the Director of …"

One could go on to describe the highlights of his career gradually building him to inform the

simplicity, concludewith:

"Ladies and Gentlemen, with this brief introduction, I present to you, Mr. Srinivasan, who will speak to us on …"

The secret of a good introduction is: Be well prepared, be brief and to the point, speak clearly and

It is customary to thank the guest speaker and other guests and those who have contributed towards the success of the meeting. The president would ask somebody to do the needful. The purpose of this thanksgiving conclusion is to convey the organizer's gratitude to all concerned. Don't do it casually. Those who have contributed their time and effort can be sensitive about it. The sincerity of intention is very important. The concluding thanksgiving could be brief, but should be very sincere.

remarks:

"Mr. President, Ladies and Gentlemen, we are indeed privileged this evening to have the opportunity to listen to our most learned guest, Mr. Srinivasan. We are grateful to you, Sir, for your presence and sharing your experience with us. We will look forward to your coming again when possible."

Never comment about what the speaker has said. You could or could not agree with whatever he might have said. The important thing is that he spared his time to be with you. Thank the other people next. Since you should know who are to be thanked have their names ready preferably written down in the order they are to be announced. You could just say:

this evening, and Mr. S.P. Singh who accepted to be here this evening, and all the ladies and guests who have added grace to this meeting. Could I now request all of you to join us for tea?"

People new to such occasions must keep their words simple and easy to remember. The more experienced people choose a variety of other words like "being grateful" or "obliged by your presence" or something similar. Some would also put in a line expressing how motivated or impressed they feel. They would also congratulate and convey their best wishes for the person's mission in life. Once again, the secret of a good thanksgiving speech is to be brief, to the point and being "sincere".

In many meetings, particularly club meetings, it is customary to greet members, their spouses and children on birthdays, wedding anniversary or on some special landmark. The responsibility to convey greetings through a bouquet or a gift could be entrusted to a member or members. Be prepared for the responsibility. When you offer the bouquet or gift, do it with a broad smile saying, "Many happy returns of the day" or "A very happy birthday to you". On a wedding anniversary you could say, "Please accept our greetings on your anniversary". When you are presenting a bouquet on a special occasion you could say, "Heartiest congratulations!"

Whatever responsibility is entrusted to you take it seriously. Everyone is watching you. Be well

Chapter 31

Next to death, nothing frightens a person more than asking him or her to speak in public. The mind goes blank, the face turns livid and the throat gets choked. The person feels close to hell. This is not to be seen in rare instances. It is more of a rule than an exception. Irrespective whether the person is a doctor, an engineer, a lawyer or a businessman, to most people speaking in public is the most dreaded of experiences.

The ability to speak in public can add a new dimension to one's life. It is a skill that is neither inherited, nor a gift of God. Like any other skill it can be learnt and perfected with training, practice and experience. People who come from homes where the father or mother can communicate well and possess good speaking skills learn the art of public speaking sooner.

The fear of speaking in public is so intense that people prefer to do without the skill even at the cost of pursuing mediocrity in businesses and professions. We see much of it everywhere every day. Very few people are aware that this skill can enable them to senior positions in all spheres in life. Good public speaking is an important step to a role as a leader at the workplace.

of speech. The parliamentary system has led to developing great political orators. Good public speaking can move millions of people into both positive and negative directions. Those involved in a business or profession use the skills at the workplace to develop the society, and in

magazines, books, radio, television and the Internet. All information is supposedly passed on as important. However, that is not the reality. One could not possibly use all the information. It is just a source of great confusion. At such times it is those who participate in public debates or speak to large audiences that one is able to discern what is right or wrong.

Circumstances have made it necessary for people in business and professions to address large meetings, symposiums, seminars, academic conferences and sometimes even large conventions.

professional growth and also popularity.

textbook on the subject based upon the experience of Greek orators was published. The Latin speaking

curriculum. It is not taught in the schools the same way now, but the importance of the subject has not diminished. We need it as much today, as we needed it then. Since formal avenues of learning this skill are limited, one would have to learn it through personal learning and practice. Two things are very clear:

1. **Speaking skills are acquired skills**. Nobody is born a speaker. Like any other skill, public speaking must be learnt. It can be acquired through training and practice. Experience helps attain perfection.
2. **Speaking skills lead to leadership roles**. A good leader is able to communicate very effectively. Since the art of public speaking is really the art of good communication, a good speaker is easily accepted as a leader.

When speaking skills are very important in business and professional life, why is it that greater emphasis is not given to train more people? Why is it that more people are not interested in acquiring these skills? The truth is that many institutions that teach languages and also personality development

fully acquire the skills. Individuals do not avail of the opportunity to practice it.

What is the difference between everyday normal speaking and speaking to public? Whereas everyday speaking is normal conversation, speaking to public is special for several reasons. The speaker:

Speaks to a larger audience. A normal conversation is between 2 to 4 people where each interacts with the rest offering personal opinions and suggestions. In public speaking a person

. A good speaker must attain these objectives to attain success. This is not an easy thing to do when the audience is large.

Understands audience psyche. When he knows the mind of the audience he can then touch

Has an arsenal of effective words. The only tool with the speaker is words that he can juggle

Knows his subject well
arguments and questions from the audience.

Understands human nature. People love to hear about other people and situations. Anecdotes and little stories given them an opportunity to visualize the situation and understand the subject better.

Knows when to close

For an effective public presentation there are four distinct components. They are:
1. **The speaker**   -
    ence.
2. **An appropriate message**
    audience, there is no need to speak to them.
3. **A receptive audience**. The audience will be receptive to a message only when it touches their lives. If the message is not to their interest it cannot make a mark.
4. **The audience reaction**. It is the audience reaction that conveys the utility of the message to the speaker. Only when the reaction is positive that it can be said that the presentation has been useful.

Every Speaker is Different

Are all knowledgeable speakers similar? Would they talk about a subject in the same way? The answer effective. Each person is unique. So is each speaker different from the other. Both possess different speaking skills. It is possible that both might be knowledgeable, but each would have different levels of sincerity, an understanding of the audience and presentation skills. Each would present the subject differently interpreting the subject in many ways. Some speakers are creative, innovative and present a variety of thoughts to make the presentation attractive and novel for the audience to enjoy it.

All speakers use different techniques to drive home their point of view to the audience. Some draw from personal life experiences, others illustrate by using stories, anecdotes and quotations. Some use poetry, while others are dramatic in making a presentation. Some will ask strange questions the audience has no answers to, and would then suggest a variety of answers. Some entertain through humour and subtle remarks. A few also use ancient tales and fables. The ultimate aim of every public speaker is to persuade the audience to his or her point of view. To speak well in public, every speaker must develop a personal style of speaking, and not try to copy others.

speaker after one great presentation. One builds up gradually. Little successes add on to become bigger successes. There is gradual growth of knowledge, better use of techniques and appreciation of audience

forget that climbing each little step would ultimately lead the person to the top.

Chapter 32

We have observed that every person is unique. It is, therefore, natural that everyone is different. The behaviour of each person is dependent upon personal strengths and weaknesses that affect the personality and attitudes. One could look at the same thing from different angles and also adopt different ways to arrive at a common destination. However, there are certain similarities and essentials that are common to all people who desire to learn public speaking skills. These must be well understood.

Let us begin from a common goal that all these people have adopted: to become good public speakers; to possess the necessary skills to speak before a group of people. Let us consider step-by-step how an average person develops public speaking skills

The fear of speaking in public comes next only to the fear of death. This fear has held back millions of people around the world from attaining their full potential. People accept mediocrity rather than make the little effort to overcome the fear and move on. The obvious question that arises from this situation is: how can a person overcome this fear? The simple answer is: face the fear head-on. The next question would be: how does a person do that? The answer is: understand how your body reacts to a request that you address a group of people. What next? Follow up by taking control over yourself and the situation. Let us try to understand the situation point by point:

What happens when a person is asked to speak in public? The fear of speaking in public triggers numerous reactions in the body causing apprehension, worry and eventually anxiety.

What is the condition called? It is known by many names: stage fright, speech anxiety, speech phobia and shyness. Technically it is known as glossophobia, meaning the fear of speaking in public.

Are only public speakers affected by this problem? No. Besides public speakers the problem also affects stage performers and singers

What is the immediate danger to the person? The fear arises from the mind that brings forth certain doubts about the person.

What are the immediate doubts? In brief, they are:

a. I don't know what to speak.
b. I will forget what I have to speak.
c. People will ridicule me when I cannot speak.
D. I will make a laughing stock of myself.

How does the person feel? The visible reactions include the skin turning pale, accompanied by sweating, nausea, chill and trembling. The mouth feels dry, the blood pressure rises, and the

Self-development as a Speaker

pulse beats faster. The digestion gets affected. One desires to visit the toilet. There is shortness of breath. The immediate desire is to run away from the situation.

Couldn't these reactions be pathological? No. These are physical reactions caused by the mind's response to a certain danger. When the mind foresees a danger the body believes and reacts to it.

Can't these reactions or symptoms be controlled through medical intervention? Yes, but only temporarily. Since the situation is not health-threatening, it is common for doctors to prescribe anti-anxiety drugs for temporary relief.

Is the use of these drugs harmful? Yes. Many people are known to get addicted to taking them regularly as mood-lifters. This is harmful in the long term.

How can the problem be controlled? The problem is best tackled by keeping the mind under control. This, in turn, means controlling the thoughts.

Should the person ignore the situation because it is imaginary? No. When you ignore a situation it means that you have accepted it and are trying to avoid it. This would be wrong.

What should the person do? The correct thing is to face the situation. It is a fear. It might be imaginary, but to the concerned person it is real. One must face the fear to overcome it. How does a person face the fear of darkness? You overcome it simply by going into darkness and convincing yourself that there is no danger lurking around.

How should a person get over the fear of speaking in public? A person has to develop the

and the fear would vanish.

follow these steps:
a. Believe in your ability to deliver, to speak well.
b. Visualise that you speak well, that you will succeed. There is great magic in visualisation.

    persistently.
d. Prepare yourself for success. There is a lot of preparation behind every great presentation however small it might be.

    possibly can.
f. Practice. Put in as much practice as you can. The more you do it, the deeper it will penetrate the subconscious mind. You will remember better.
g. Do not let performance anxiety overtake you. Stay calm. Do not use drugs or alcohol. They can hinder your success. To ensure that your stomach does not bother you eat little

    Laugh. Laughter helps keep nervousness under control.
h. Arrive early at the venue of your presentation. Look around. Get acquainted with the surroundings. Get a feel of the lectern. Note how the audience would be seated.
i. When seated, seek the blessings of God. See the blessings coming in the form of patience. Breathe deep to feel the patience. Visualize success.

of deep breaths, look around, and try to build eye contact with the audience. Remind yourself that you are special. You have been invited because you have a very special message to deliver. Give of your best.

k. The audience is always constituted of people with different mindsets. Nobody can please

of the people in the audience.

Step 2: Make Success Your Companion

make success your companion. Think success. It comes from your thoughts. When you think success, you visualize a dream to be capable, to do great things in life. The dream makes you desire to turn it into reality. Dreams motivate a person to act.

Visualise yourself as possessing good speaking skills. Visualise yourself being appreciated and applauded. Resolve to be a good speaker; make plans to turn this dream a reality. Seek the company of friends who appreciate and encourage you. Be grateful to them for this support. Avoid people who discourage you. Do not let small setbacks upset you. Do not panic. Small defeats are a part of life. Each one prepares a person for success. Obstacles are a part of life. Problems come and go to make each one of us a little bit better, taking us towards greater successes.

even though it is for something small like conveying gratitude to a guest. Each little effort is practice in

dressed. Let it be felt that you carry success wherever you go.

Step 3: Mind Your Body Language

We have earlier observed how each of us is constantly communicating through our body language. Many of the body gestures are involuntary and convey a message to the audience. The audience perceives a speaker from the involuntary messages he or she conveys. These might not always be in the favour of the speaker.

If the body language is based upon involuntary gestures the aspiring speakers question what they can possibly do to project a positive image. Just as children and adults "act" to convey a message in particular situations to others, a speaker too needs to convey a message to the audience when he or she

being responsible, from being well prepared for the occasion. The speaker too must "act" responsible by arriving on time, by having prepared the presentation thoroughly. Like an anchor or the Master of

Gradually it will become a part of the body language.

Self-development as a Speaker

Step 4: Mind Your Language
A speaker conveys the message through words, irrespective of the language one uses. Therefore, it is essential that the speaker must convey his message through words that are well understood both by the speaker and the audience. It is a two-way interaction. A good academician who knows English well

the knowledge of the language of the audience.

The spoken language is the common language people use to communicate with each other. It varies from place to place. The English language is no different. It also varies in use in different parts of the

When preparing the presentation the speaker must use words that are easy to understand, and weave sentences that touch the feelings and emotions of the audience. For those who learn English as a mother tongue it would be easier to write an appropriate presentation, as compared to those who have learnt English as a second language to interact comfortably around the world. It would require a little extra effort. In public speaking no effort is wasted because it ultimately leads a person to great success.

stop learning the language. It is so vast that a person continues to improve one's performance every day. An aspiring speaker needs to work still harder because words are the artillery of a speaker. The best advice to an aspiring speaker is:

    Improve your vocabulary
    Pronounce words correctly
    Draft grammatically correct sentences
    Do not use slang or hackneyed phrases.

Step 5: Prepare the Presentation
Some of the best speakers appear to speak effortlessly, but the truth is that great effort has gone into

re-read and practiced. It has been observed that good speeches have been prepared to a set pattern. The speaker would do well to:

    Write the speech just as one would speak.

    Convey the message logically.
    Try to hold the interest of the audience.
    Do not exceed the allotted time.
    Stop speaking when the message has been conveyed.

Step 6: Practice
The old English adage: Practice makes perfect is very relevant to public speaking. Read the speech loudly. How does it sound? Are you pronouncing the words correctly? Are you emphasizing the correct words? Does the speech sound convincing? Are you able to deliver it within the allotted time? The answers to these questions will give you a fair idea of what to expect. If you feel that certain parts are

repetitive or lengthy, cut them out. A good speech should be like a straight line – the shortest distance from the beginning to the end. The more a speech is practiced the deeper it goes into the mind and less likely that you forget what is important. This is an important step in being fully prepared for making the presentation.

Step 7: Make Notes
A written speech could be read out but that would not create the impact a good speaker desires from

accurately conveyed, as it is in most academic seminars, it would be appropriate to read the speech.

written, but delivered as though it is spoken spontaneously.

A speaker makes an impact on the audience when he is able to establish eye contact with the audience. This is not possible when a speech is read. To maintain eye contact the speaker must speak spontaneously. This would mean that he would not have his written speech. He would practice it several times at home, and rather than read from a paper he would have each point noted down on cards, 3 inches by 5 inches. The speaker can glance at the cards to maintain continuity of points and yet speak spontaneously and convincingly. The cards are easy to carry, can be easily placed on the lectern, and used without anyone knowing about them.

Step 8: Making the Presentation
Do not overlook that the audience keeps watching the prospective speaker from the time he comes on the head-table or stage. The way he is dressed, his body language and his movements are constantly under scrutiny. Invariably half the battle is won or lost even before the presentation is made.

Every speaker is different. The style of presentation differentiates one speaker from another. This style is not developed overnight. It develops gradually with the speaker experimenting with words on different occasions. Words do not only convey a message. Together they convey a rhythmic effect,

Most aspiring speakers try to copy those who are known to speak well. This is not the right thing to do. Remember, when you imitate the style of another, you are only a copy and not original. To make a mark be original, "be yourself".

For a message to get through to the audience a speaker must speak loud and clear. The words must be correctly pronounced or else they will be misinterpreted. Speak just as you would do so in everyday life. Only then it would appear natural. This requires a lot of effort and practice. No aspiring speaker skips on that. Every step takes a person towards the ultimate goal.

When you have said what you wanted to just stop and return to your seat after thanking the audience for their patient hearing. Repetitions and lingering on easily irritate the audience and speaker should not let that happen.

Chapter 33

The purpose of good public speaking is to convey an effective message. Irrespective whether a person is

or speaking to 50 people at the meeting of the housing society where he or she lives, to be recognised

This means that every speaker must have a purpose to speak. If there is none, just forget about speaking. It is only the politicians who can speak everything about "nothing". Those in business and professions should not try to cross their path,

The speaker must understand the exact purpose of the presentation. Is it to inform the audience on a vital issue, or is it to guide and show them direction? Or is it to inspire and motivate them to give of their effort or time to get something done? When the speaker is clear about the purpose of the presentation then he or she can think how to convey the message effectively to the audience. The thought processes of the speaker lead from one idea to another to persuade and convince the audience.

Another important factor in preparing a presentation to convey a message to the audience is the time allotted for the presentation. At any meeting or a function time is a limiting factor. Organizers usually inform the speaker in advance how long he can speak. The sanctity of this request must be honoured by the speaker. A speaker must understand it clearly that the organizers do not expect a speaker to give a thirty

his ability. When there is no time to add on frills just leave them out. Get down to the basics rightaway.

Many learned speakers feel that when they are expected to give a brief presentation they owe it to the audience to explain their stand and spend a couple of minutes doing so. This is wasted time. The audience looks at it as "making excuses", and immediately concludes that the person is not

often likened to a bikini – it is brief and yet covers the essentials!

When writing the presentation just forget about how many minutes you need to speak. Write a presentation to convey all the points that you would like to convey. It could become lengthy. You could

1. **An attractive beginning**
   begun is always half done towards success. It must immediately draw the attention of the audience to you and the subject. It must arouse interest. The audience must get to know the purpose

Business English

2. **The body of the speech**. This would include the main points that the speaker would like to emphasize, particularly how they affect the audience. At this stage it is also necessary that the speaker should continue to hold the interest of the audience. The effectiveness of the presentation would depend upon it.
3. **An apt closing**. The closing of the presentation is as important as the opening. While the opening aims at drawing immediate attention, the closing should leave behind a lasting impression, a strong message. Leave the audience with a feeling, "We would have loved hearing a little more."

An Attractive Beginning

Although the audience begins to judge a speaker the moment his name is announced, but the real test is when he walks over to the lectern and makes his opening remarks. These few sentences could make or mar the whole presentation.

It is customary for the speaker address the dignitaries on the stage and in the audience before

productive for the rest of the audience. Besides, it takes time, draws the attention of the audience from you to the person you name, and you are always at the risk of missing out an important name or even not pronouncing it correctly. Therefore, an ideal solution to this issue is to address the person presiding and the chief guest, if any, along with the audience. An ideal way to address would be:

"Mr. President, Hon'ble Chief Guest, ladies and gentlemen;"

"Hon'ble Chief Guest" could be substituted with "Hon'ble Chairman" or "Hon'ble Director". It is also common to substitute "Ladies and Gentlemen" with "My colleagues" or even as "Dear friends".

After addressing the audience the next step is to begin the presentation with an opening sentence that would immediately draw the attention of the audience. This would largely depend upon the subject of the presentation and the type of audience.

A very learned speaker addressing school children opened his presentation with:

"Little friends, how many of you love to hear a good story?"

Of course all the hands went up and the speaker had their attention, and in the next 15 minutes he spoke to them telling stories on ethical values in life.

On another occasion a very learned professor addressing a group of teachers opened his presentation with:

"I am indeed privileged to be amongst great people who quietly help shape the lives of the coming generation."

By praising the work done by the audience professionally the speaker drew their attention immediately.

to a person who was loved by one and all."

Addressing the sales force the company Sales Manager said:

"I am here this morning to tell you of a great new product that will overnight change the image of our company and also provide each one of you the greatest opportunity to reach for the sky."

The President of a building society began his address:

Conveying an Effective Message

"I am pleased to announce that the Executive Committee has asked me to tell you of a plan that would ensure comfort and security to every resident of this society."

At a meeting of a club where a mixed audience had gathered the speaker said, "I am going to talk to you about a community where every person continues to maintain good health even beyond 80 and 90 years of age."

Have you observed how each of these opening sentences attracts the attention of the audience them, and all within the a few minutes.

When you are required to prepare a presentation and are looking for an appropriate opening sentence, place yourself with the audience. What would interest them? Read speeches by reputed orators and statesmen. Watch people speak on the television. Analyse both the good and the bad. Adapt what you like to your presentation.

Some speakers begin a presentation with a touch of humour. When a speaker was lavishly praised

you said about me."

On another occasion when the person introducing the speaker said that he was grateful that the speaker found time to be with them whenever they invited him, the speaker said:

"Gentlemen, thank you for inviting me. You're right. Think of the devil and there he is."

At one function where two speakers were scheduled to speak and contrary to what were written on

and began:

(pointing at the other speaker) stole my speech from my coat pocket."

(pointing at the other speaker) stole my speech from my coat pocket."

It is common to begin a presentation with jokes and short anecdotes, but many of them do not create the impact they are intended to. The reason is simple. Either it was inappropriate for the occasion or the speaker did not narrate it correctly, forgetting keywords and the punch-line.

In using humour a person must be very cautious about the sensitivities of people. Nothing should

use humour that touches their own lives or of those who are well known and close to them. Many speakers are known to maintain a collection of funny and interesting stories to make the presentation interesting.

The Body of the Presentation

After an attractive opening sentence that draws the attention of the audience towards the speaker, the

system. It could be as follows:

. The audience must know why the presentation is important to them. In many situations where the opening sentence discloses the purpose the speaker should proceed further.

Inform the audience how and why the subject is important to them
the presentation interests the audience, why would they pay any attention to what the speaker has to say?

How would the problems arising out of the situation impact the audience? If the people in the audience are not affected by the problems, why would they want to hear about them?

Suggest possible solutions to the problems. Once the likely solutions are placed before the audience it becomes easy for them to choose solutions that suit them best.

Seek the cooperation and support of the audience. If the presentation touches the feelings and emotions of the audience there will be a positive response. This would also mean that the presentation was a success.

Public speaking aims at persuading the audience to accept a new idea and act upon it. It is an exercise in persuasion. This is not easy. The principal reason for this is that it is human nature to resist change. Everyone is happy in their own comfort zone. Any change that requires an extra effort from them is resisted. Therefore, to succeed, the speaker must understand the way the audience thinks and reacts. This requires special abilities like those of leaders. For this reason leadership and public speaking go hand-in-hand.

An aspiring speaker must remember the following steps when writing the speech:

Note down all the ideas and points that come to your mind. Do not restrict your thoughts. Let them go wild. Just keep noting down what comes to the mind.

Select 3 or 4 of the most important points that you have noted down. Do not try to cover too many aspects of the problem. Avoid vague and misleading issues.

Never mention the number of points you are going to talk about. The attention of the audience is diverted to counting the number of points instead of listening to the speaker.

For each major point write sub-topics, emphatic words, phrases and sentences. Do you know an anecdote or story to illustrate a point? Note it down.

Prioritize each of the points you have selected. The most important one should come on the

in the presentation. If called to speak for a lesser time the items with lower priority can be eliminated.

Making a speech point-wise helps the speaker remember it. It also makes it easier for the audience to understand it.

Every speech would be different from the other even if they are on the same subject. At an academic seminar several professionals speak on the same subject, but each has something different to say. They leave it to the audience how they would like to look upon the subject.

When you write the speech do not worry about what the audience will say about it. You should put in your best. That is what is important for you. After the main body of the speech has been written with everything in place, with the priorities set right, it is time to close the presentation with an appeal to act.

An Apt Closing

Many speakers have a problem closing the speech appropriately. They open well, explain the subject

they repeat whatever they said earlier. On hearing the repetitive remarks the audience immediately decides that the speaker has exhausted his arsenal of arguments, lose interest and all the good work done by the speaker is lost. What could be more unfortunate for the speaker? He loses a battle that he had already won.

What should the speaker have done? After he had said what he had wanted to he should have concluded with appropriate remarks and left the rest to the audience. Even if he did not have concluding remarks to make he should have stopped speaking.

the audience and return to your seat.

An experienced speaker does not close a presentation abruptly. While arguing the subject the speaker gradually builds up to a point where he has the complete attention of the audience. Then he throws the ball at them seeking their **support**, **cooperation** and **action**. It is now for the audience to think and act.

While speaking on the harmful effect of watching too much television by children the speaker concluded:

"Dear Parents: Drawing upon the experiences of parents all over the world I have said what I think all of you needed to know. It is now for you to decide whether you prefer to indulge your children, or would like them to attain their true potential in life? Thank you!"

Addressing the Parliament of Religions in Chicago, Swami Vivekananda concluded his address on

"If the Parliament of Religions has shown anything to the world it is this; it has proved to the world that holiness, purity and charity are not the exclusive possessions of any one church in the world, and that every system has produced men and women of the most exalted character. In the face of this evidence, if anybody dreams of the exclusive survival of his own religion and the destruction of others, I pity him from the bottom of my heart, and point out to him that upon the banner of every religion will soon be written, in spite of resistance: "Help and not Fight". "Assimilation and not Destruction." "Harmony and Peace and not Dissension."

When concluding a speech, a speaker would do well to remember the following:

    The closing remarks should be in harmony with the presentation.
    The remarks should endorse the purpose of the presentation.
    Always end a presentation on an optimistic note.
    When necessary, end the presentation with a request, a promise or a warning.
    Some prefer to end the presentation with a challenge. It makes people act.
    Always lead the audience to think and act.

Chapter 34

If a well-written speech or presentation alone could persuade the audience, we would probably have innumerable teachers and professors all over the English speaking world serving as top public speakers. But this is not so. Writing a good speech is only a part of the work of a good speaker. The real test of the speaker is to know how to deliver a great presentation that would touch the hearts of the audience.

Have you ever observed religious speakers speaking in a *temple, mosque, church or a gurudwara?* Almost all of what they are speaking has not been written by them. They are speaking from religious texts many of them written several hundreds of years ago. Their secret lies in choosing the correct texts and speaking as though from their heart. The key to a successful presentation, small or big, is in the way it is delivered to the audience. Success comes from an appropriate delivery.

For practical purposes the delivery of a presentation begins from the moment the speaker's name is announced. He or she is being watched for every movement or action. The audience sits gauging every little action. Their interest grows when he is formally introduced, the way he walks over to the lectern, adjusts the mike and tests it. The way he stands, looks around at the audience to seek their attention and builds eye contact immediately decides the rapport he or she has been able to build with the audience.

A presentation can be likened to a car. The speaker ushers the companions into the car, and sets it gear with great enthusiasm to present the most important points, shifts to the third and fourth gears to catch on speed and say whatever he has pre-planned. How smooth or rough the drive is depends upon how well the speaker delivers the message. He gradually drives the car to its destination bringing it to a smooth halt. The impression he leaves behind on the audience depends upon how smooth, rough or erratic the drive has been. After an enjoyable drive all passengers look forward to more of such experiences. The reverse is equally true.

What does the audience expect from the speaker's delivery of the message? The reality is that a good speaker takes away the mind of the audience from himself and the delivery and makes them listen sincerity and enthusiasm for the subject speak as much as his voice that carries the audience through the journey.

This sounds simple, but it is not so. One reaches this stage of performance through much practice. and then practises it repeatedly. *Perfection comes from training of the voice.* Just as singers practice the same song repeatedly, a good speaker does the same with his presentation. How and when does the speaker get to know that he is ready to deliver before the audience? He is ready to deliver when he can

Delivering an Effective Speech

Training the Voice

A good speaking voice is one that can be clearly and easily heard and understood. It should be free of accents, blurriness and unpleasantness that would detract a person. Some voices have a high pitch others are medium or low pitched. Voices that are high or medium pitched carry better when speaking to a group of people.

The best way to train the voice is to read loudly. Read from a book or a magazine. Some practise by reading the newspaper aloud. This will immediately give you an idea of how your voice sounds to the ears. Books and magazines are not intended for this purpose. Therefore, it would be better to shift to a book of speeches by eminent personalities. When reading a speech you should learn to appreciate the use of words. Try to experience the feelings that they convey. The more you think and understand them the greater the feeling you will develop for them. This feeling is important because when your voice conveys it the audience gets to experience it also. The conveying of these feelings makes a presentation effective.

or something similar. These should not discourage an aspiring speaker. In modern times it is possible to get over many speech defects through medical intervention. Speech therapists can help immensely.

for aspiring speakers to practise also. Breathing is involuntary, but when you deliberately practise deep breathing, drawing as much air into the lungs as possible, holding it for a short while and exhaling slowly, the capacity of the lungs increases gradually and the intake of oxygen increases. This helps clear thinking when speaking. As a part of voice training learn to breathe naturally and deeply.

Learn to use your vocal cords correctly. Reading loudly to an object that is at some distance from you helps develop the use of the vocal cords. When you speak at a distant object you tend to make a greater effort that is in contrast to the use of the vocal cords in a normal conversation. This is essential because public speaking is different from a normal conversation in that you need to make an extra speaking effort. Yet it is necessary that the speaker must appear to speak naturally. To add feeling to the words you use in the presentation it would be necessary to learn to modulate the voice to create an impact on the audience.

In delivering a speech it is not the spelling of the words that matter, but it is the phonetics, the way you pronounce the words that makes a presentation effective. Every dictionary gives the correct pronunciation of a word. However, the best way to learn this art is to spend time listening to English news channels on the television. Observe that those in other countries would have a different accent. The English spoken on Indian channels is the Queen's English.

When listening to others speaking English the greatest danger is that of adopting someone else's speaking style. This is not right. No two people are alike. When they think differently why should they speak in the same style? Let your style be exclusively yours. A speaking style develops gradually over a long time. You don't need to work on it. It would develop when you begin to appreciate what moves the audience and what doesn't.

the mood right for the presentation. Breathe deeply before you begin, draw enthusiasm from your own

to your voice that will immediately draw the attention of the audience.

How does one get to know whether a presentation has been effective or not? It is common for some people in the audience to compliment the speaker after the presentation. Their comments can be useful. However, you are your best critic. Many aspiring speakers record their presentation and then analyse it for its strengths and weaknesses. You can judge yourself best. Hear your presentation. Think about it. What could make it more effective? Better selection of words? Better control of the voice? Or may be a more receptive audience? The answers to these questions lead to more effective presentations.

Let us now move on to consider other important aspects of public speaking like reading a speech, things to avoid and understanding the audience the speaker is trying to reach through the presentation.

It is common for professionals like doctors, academicians, lawyers and engineers to read out academic papers at seminars, workshops and conferences. Many politicians and senior executives also read out speeches. Some of these are written by the speakers who present them, but many read out speeches prepared for them to read out.

Speeches that are read out are never very convincing. Without an eye contact and rapport between the speaker and the audience the speech lacks "feeling". It is rare when a read-out speechwould be accepted as a special presentation. Many of the speeches that are read are presented more for the content, the facts that give them some importance.

The audience lacks interest in speeches that are read out. Their interest would be limited to what is useful in everyday life. Speeches written by specialists and experts are often too technical for an average person to understand. The audience is usually apathetic towards a

without having much to speak.

When the speech that is to be read out is self-written, the speaker can read it out effectively provided he or she has rehearsed it several times. The emphasis must be on the correct words and sentences. If

it effectively unless the speaker and the writer think alike. Reading a speech is an art that must be learnt and practised to perfection

If the speech is written by someone else the speaker must adapt it to suit one's language and personality. This helps make a more realistic delivery. The audience is never interested in the knowledge or the intellect of the person who has written the speech. They want to know what is in it for them.

When a speech is well-rehearsed a speaker can read it and yet stay connected with the audience. The speaker reads the speech and yet keeps glancing at the audience to keep in touch. A few strategic pauses help special points register in the minds of the audience.

A read out speech might not be as well received as a spontaneous presentation, but when required a good speaker would still score well above an average person who is content reading it as though from a book. *Innovate, plan, rehearse and arouse the interest of the audience when you are compelled to read a speech.*

Chapter 36

There are several reasons why some of the most effective speakers fail to impress the audience. Many of these relate to organizational and physical failures that are invariably out of the speaker's control. However, there are several failures that are related to the speaker. The most effective speech can fail if the speaker fails to keep the sensitivities of the audience in mind when writing or delivering it. The audience looks up to the speaker as a knowledgeable and learned person. They expect him or her to live up to that reputation.

What are the things that can easily put off the audience? It has been observed that there are some things that can easily "turn off" the audience. The important ones are:

Making excuses. It is common for some speakers to begin the presentation with an apology like the subject being too vast and the time for presentation too short, about arriving late or

time allotted to you, why did you accept to speak?" Would the audience pay attention under such circumstances?

Expressing self-importance.
some who suffer from a feeling of great self-importance. These speakers feel they know too much. They begin by telling the audience of their great past and the high pedestal they occupy amongst those who know them. The audience response to their self-praise is, "If you are great, so what? Can you share this greatness with us? Of course, you can't. Why should I bother?"

Talking down. Some speakers do not express self-importance directly. They do it by talking down to people. They look at the shortcomings of others, and not at their strengths. They have a lop-sided observation. Talking down at people does add a little spice just as happens with gossip, but the self-respecting people would not like it from a person who is supposedly knowledgeable and wise. Such talking always puts them off.

Dirty jokes. It is common for people to exchange dirty jokes amongst small private groups. Just because people laugh at them does not mean that they should be narrated by a speaker in public. The average audience consists of serious responsible citizens who prefer that such jokes be kept within wraps. A public narration makes them hang the head in shame avoiding looking at others.

Sarcastic remarks. Just like a dirty joke a speaker could make snide remarks to show disrespect or mock a person or a group. This is a common thing amongst politicians. Each is looking for an opportunity to tear down the other with words. This might be all right amongst people with low intelligence, but no educated audience appreciates sarcasm coming from a learned speaker. On such occasions they just switch off their mind from what is being said.

audience cannot immediately verify or remember, they tend to "turn off" to what the speaker is

person in the audience to read and verify later, but these are not acceptable during a normal presentation.

Lack of preparation. It does not take long for the audience to understand that the speaker has

attention of the audience is "turned off" from the presentation and the speaker loses control.

Wrong use of visual aids. When speakers use visual aids like charts, projectors, etc. more because it is fashionable to use them than because they are required, the attention of the audience is divided between the speaker and the visual aids where neither makes an impact

Smoking and drinking. Irrespective of how knowledgeable or learned a speaker might

now, but one can still see it in closed business meetings when high-pressured executives use smoking as a crutch to speak to the staff. The use of alcohol, particularly during banquets, is not appreciated if there are pre-dinner or post-dinner speeches. The audience response is that of ridicule.

Taking excessive time. Nothing irritates an audience more than a speaker who crosses the time-line. It is only an exceptional speaker who can continue to attract the interest of the audience for a long time. This too would have some limits. Therefore, always ensure that one stays within the time limits given by the organizers.

The real purpose of each speech or presentation is to convey a message to the audience. The aspiring speaker must understand that all audiences are not the same. They are constituted of different kinds of people. It has been observed that even in the same organization audiences react differently to speakers and on occasions. This makes it apparent that the prevalent environment at the time of the presentation also has a great effect upon audience reaction.

Many speakers are able to draw the attention of the audience with apt opening remarks, but unless the presentation has something of interest and usefulness to them, the best of presentations could be irrelevant to the audience.

Another major problem is that while a speaker delivers 125 to 150 words per minute, the people in the audience are capable of listening to 500 to 700 minutes per minute. This simply means that a person has a four times greater capacity to listen than to speak. With this wide a variation the minds of the audience begin to drift from the presentation to other thoughts and if the presentation is not powerful enough to hold interest of the audience, no purpose is served.

To be convincing every speaker desires to have a steady eye contact with the audience. This is possible only when the seating arrangement is such that the speaker and the audience are face to face.

Since the ultimate success of the best of speakers is what the audience thinks of the presentation, or how they react to it, every speaker must look ahead and plan the presentation to suit the audience and the occasion. Therefore, the speaker must be completely aware of who would constitute the audience and what the occasion of their getting together is. The presentation must be prepared keeping these facts

Would it be a mixed audience, or a specialised one? A mixed audience would have people from different businesses and professions. A specialized audience would have people from a

How big would be the audience? An audience of a hundred or more people would react differently as compared to an audience of twenty people. Group dynamics change the audience reactions. A speaker would speak more informallyto a smaller group than to a larger audience.

What will be the age range of the audience? Even in an educational institution the children from lower classes would need a different treatment than those from higher classes, or from college. The teachers too would need different kinds of presentation. Elderly people think differently. In an audience that has children, young adults, the middle-aged and senior citizens, the speaker would obviously need to adjust the presentation to appeal to all age groups.

Understanding the Audience

Is the audience male, female or mixed? Men and women have been observed to have different mindsets when in a group. They react differently in a mixed group. A speaker would need to keep these considerations in mind when using stories, anecdotes and humour in the

What is the level of education of the audience? Audiences in academic institutions and

a high level of presentation that is in harmony with their needs. On the other hand a mixed audience of children, housewives and businessmen would be interested in a presentation that would be appropriate for a common man.

What is the level of audience understanding of the subject? Most people take life for granted and live within a limited understanding of things and people around them. Their general awareness of life's problems is limited. However, there are many who are well informed and can contribute to a discussion on a subject.

Is the audience sensitive to certain issues? Many people have rigid views on politics, religion, casteism and gender differentiation. These sensitivities could be easily aroused through inadvertent remarks by a speaker. This could sometimes be disastrous for the speaker and the organizers. It is important that when preparing the speech the speaker must steer clear from such sensitivities.

Is the speaker known to the audience?
the audience. They know what to expect from him or her. At such times, even the speaker is aware of the audience he is going to speak to. This makes it easier for both the speaker and the audience. However, speakers are often invited to speak to new audiences and they should be prepared for the experience.

Handling the Audience

Every experienced speaker makes an effort to collect as much information about the audience as is possible and then tries to prepare and make a presentation that is in harmony with their expectations. This works out well most of the time, but not always. The speaker might need special skills to handle the audience sometimes.

A common problem is an apathetic audience. They might have been in the meeting for a long time, heard too many speakers, are bored and look forward to an early closing of the meeting. The audience can be likened to a child who is fed up being tugged around by the mother who is busy shopping. The child is restless and desires to get back home. Only a powerful speaker can handle the situation with an attractive opening, holding the audience interest through humour and short anecdotes, racing to quick closing remarks.

Sometimes a speaker is confronted with a hostile audience. Individually the people in the audience

to what the audience thinks. This requires very special handling. An experienced speaker would begin

they let their guards go down. That is when the speaker explains that there could be other ways of looking at the same subject. Finally, he asks the audience to listen to their conscience and make an appropriate decision.

Another situation between the speaker and the audience that needs tactful handling is when the speaker offers to answer questions by the audience. At this point there could be some who would ask irrelevant questions. Some could even be intimidating. Some might even try to point out that they know more or are better-informed than the speaker. A mature speaker takes such remarks tactfully with a

When some of the audience is insistent, the speaker could close the discussion by saying, "I appreciate your viewpoint. Everyone has the freedom to think as they like."

Audience Seating Arrangement

Although the seating arrangement would be the prerogative of the organizers of the meeting but a speaker appreciates that the effectiveness of a presentation depends to a great extent upon how the audience is seated, and how well the speaker can maintain an eye contact with them. Where possible the speaker should insist upon a seating arrangement that would suit him best.

A very popular form common for company meetings is sitting around a round or a rectangular table. The atmosphere is more informal, the speaker speaks sitting with his notes in front of him on the table. This would be all right for a small group.

A larger audience of 10 to 25 persons should preferably be seated with the tables and chairs arranged

could have a white board or the screen behind him so as to be visible to everyone. This arrangement allows the speaker to maintain eye contact and rapport with everyone, facilitating informal discussion. The participants can respond directly with the speaker and also take notes.

halls of corporate houses and government agencies. There is a long table with the audience seated on three sides, and the speaker sits on one side. This way the speaker can address the audience as a whole, and also have one-to-one discussion. He could have the projection screen behind him where everyone can see it.

A popular form of setup is known as the classroom setup. Just as in a class, everyone sits in rows facing the teacher's table occupied by the speaker. There is a passage between two blocks of rows. The speaker could write on a whiteboard or could have a projection screen behind him.

Another option of the classroom setup is known as the herringbone setup. In this setup the rows are not straight as in a classroom, but for a better interaction with the speaker they are inclined with a passage between two blocks. If tables are not required, the chairs can be arranged in a herringbone setup.

When the audience becomes larger, tables in front of the participants are removed, and we have rows of chairs arranged in two blocks with a passage in the centre. The speaker and the organizers would sit on a head-table, which could be on a stage for better visibility. The lectern too could be placed on the stage where everyone can see the speaker. This arrangement is known as the theatre setup and is very popular where the audience is big.

Another popular arrangement is when the speaker and the organizers sit on the head table and the

area and the speaker cannot maintain an eye control with the audience. Another serious problem is that when drinks, snacks and meals are served the audience is unable to concentrate on what is being said. Such presentations are formal and rarely useful to conduct serious business.

him to seek a setup of his choice.

Chapter 38

Considering the importance of effective speaking in business and professions it is common for speakers to take advantage of different kinds of aids to help communicate the message better. The immediate

even in a small group. However, when the group becomes bigger and with lack of eye contact holding

the message more effective.

Most people feel that all that a speaker needs is good knowledge of his subject, a well-prepared presentation and the ability to speak effectively and the job is done. This is not true. There are many factors involved in conveying a message effectively. Therefore, it would be appropriate to use whatever aid would help attain the purpose of the presentation. Common aids that help making a presentation effective are as follows:

A good public address system. When the audience becomes big it is not possible for a person to speak loud enough to be heard by everyone. If even a few fail to hear the speaker the purpose is easily lost.

A white board. It is common to see black or green boards in classrooms. These facilitate the teaching process in the classrooms. In the same way a while board makes it possible to explain facts to a medium-sized group. On a white board one can write with markers in different colours.

Flip Charts.

sheet to show the next one.

Slide projectors. These use 35 mm colour photograph slides and were once very popular to add colour and excitement to a presentation. These are now restricted to use in school laboratories.

Overhead projectors. These are still used in some schools because they enable the use of ready slides, and also to write on blank slides, but the changing technology is fast replacing them with laptops and LCD projectors.

LCD projectors. These have replaced most of the earlier display aids because the presentation is made on the computer and can be viewed on a large screen by a fairly big audience. The more powerful projectors are suitable for large auditoriums. In most seminars the organizers have these projectors ready connected to a laptop and the speaker needs to carry his presentation on a CD.

Pointers. Long wooden pointers were earlier used to point at written charts or displays, but today it is more convenient for the speaker to carry a laser pointer, which is like a pen and projects a dot that can highlight whatever is to be shown.

Other aids. Amongst other aids that speakers use is a **dais**, which is a low platform for placing the lectern. In colleges, the lecturer's table and chair are placed on the dais. A **lectern** is a tall

a guide, or can even read from them. A **podium** is a small platform on which a person stands when conducting an orchestra or giving a speech. Many people misuse the word: podium to mean the lectern. The podium helps the speaker stand a little higher and be visible over the lectern. The word: **rostrum** also means podium.

With good software available for visual presentations using the laptop and the LCD projector most speakers feel that their presentation problems are a thing of the past. They feel that visual presentations are appreciated more than those that do not use visuals. This is not true. They feel this way because they are not aware of the facts.

An eye-opening fact is that 9 out of every 10 visual presentations fail to make a mark on the audience. A principal reason for this is that most speakers do not possess the skills to prepare effective visuals. Another very important reason might be that visuals were not necessary. They were included more for novelty than for a need. Another common reason for the failure of visuals is that these are

possible for the speaker to have an eye contact with the audience.

When a speaker feels that visuals would help communicate the message more effectively to the audience, particularly for training programmes in colleges and at the corporate level, the speaker must give special attention to certain elements of the presentation. The speaker must ensure the following:

Use appropriate images. Just as the written matter is planned so must the images be appropriate. They must be such that the written matter stands out against the background image.

Use as few words as possible. Most speakers write too much making it necessary to use

Restrict one point to each slide. It should stand out against the background. Do not use too many sub-points that would confuse the audience.

Do not use headlines.
the presentation.

The wordings should be brief remarks rather than a complete message. The complete message must be conveyed by the speaker.

Display limited facts only.
audience. They give them no importance because they cannot remember them anyway.

Avoid fancy fonts.
simple fonts that are readable from a distance. Restrict the use of fonts to only two, or a maximum of three.

Do not use slides as prompts. Many speakers are guilty of using the slides as prompts to elaborate upon the presentation. This can easily lead to confusion.

Never use printed copies of slides as handout material. If a handout is to be given to the audience, prepare it separately for the purpose. Do not confuse it with the presentation.

Never expect miraculous results. It is the person making the presentation that can really prepared.

Just as one needs to rehearse a speech before delivering it to an audience, it is equally important that a presentation using visual aids is rehearsed repeatedly until perfected. It would also be necessary to inform the organisers in advance that you would need a LCD projector and screen along with a laptop, or you might prefer to carry your own. It is also necessary that the organizers are aware that you would need a dark environment for the presentation. Many a presentation has failed miserably because of the lack of it.

Despite all kinds of aids that are available to the speaker, it is the knowledge, preparation and the effort made that lead to a successful presentation.

Chapter 39

The development of technology has made it possible for several businessmen and professionals to confer with each other over the telephone and also be able to watch each other over long distances to promote mutual interests.

A teleconference or tele-seminar is a live exchange of information between three or more persons in remote places connected through a telephone or mobile network. A videoconference uses advanced technology that enables two or more locations to communicate simultaneously through video and audio transmissions. It differs from a videophone in that it is designed to serve a conference of multiple locations rather than a person speaking to another.

The technology makes it possible calling or conferencing on a one-to-one, one-to-many, or many-to-many to talk face to face for personal, educational, business or professional purposes.

medicine and mass communication. It has enabled people in remote corners of the world to talk to each

or to share documents and display information in a remote conference hall. Earlier, the technology was too expensive to use, but the developments in the recent past has made it enter the workplaces of businessmen and the professionals. Even home users are now using the cheaper technology for one-to-one video-conferencing.

The new technology has made it possible for a judge in a court to talk to and hear and try a prisoner in jail without taking the risk of moving him from jail to court. It has enabled professors to talk to their students, or for students to talk to each other and also view places of importance in other countries without having to move out. It has also made it possible to have cross-cultural exchanges around the

The medical profession has used the technology to consult each other on serious issues involving patients. Without moving the patients from the hospital doctors have been able to carry out consultations, diagnosis and suggest treatment for use by local doctors and support staff. This has helped save lives by avoiding the risks of transferring patients from one hospital to another. With technology becoming cheaper and available at more locations the medical profession is likely to take full advantage of the potential of video-conferencing in the near future. This would have far reaching impact on the health of people around the world.

Business operations require a lot of conferencing particularly when the operations are at remote places or at the international level. It involves great expense in manpower and travelling. The use of new technology is progressively being employed by these corporate houses not only through their conference rooms, but also through handheld sets that can be carried easily and persons reached swiftly.

The communication media are front-runners in using the new technology because it enables them to communicate directly where facilities are available.

The deaf, hard-of-hearing and speech-impaired persons see new hope in communicating through video-conferencing because they can use it to communicate through sign language, which was not possible with the conventional phone or mobile.

How will the new technology impact business and professional activities over the long term? How of the questions often asked by people. The new technology works on equipment that is expensive, but progressively coming within the means of more people. When corporate houses cannot have personal conference halls equipped with the best equipment, they could hire one on rent. Like the mobile phone the technology is likely to take big strides in the near future.

The users of the new technology complain that it does not permit the eye contact that is possible only in a face-to-face conference. It is also devoid of the observation of body language that gives many cues when negotiating a deal. Some also complain that the presence of cameras at a conference make the participants self-conscious stealing spontaneity from their reactions. These are issues that a person will have to address personally just as one does when speaking at a meeting or in public. Every situation offers its own challenges, and those of the new technology are no different. While the new generation will accept it in its normal stride, the older generations will have to adapt themselves in the new ever-changing working environment.

Section 3

Business English is important not only as a spoken language, but equally so as a written language. It is the written records that have enabled the communication of knowledge and wisdom from one generation to another. If it were not for the written language we might never have learnt what some of the greatest philosophers of the world said thousands of years earlier. Many of these truths are as

No business or profession can develop or survive without the thousands of books and journals published each year. All important transactions in business and professional life are recorded in writing.

problems that are hard to resolve.

written Business English has evolved its own usage of words, terms and phrases out of academic English young people learn in schools and colleges. A study of written Business English enables a

Business English is literally more businesslike than academic English. The emphasis is not on the perfection of grammar or choice of correct words, but to attain the goal of business and professional effectiveness. This can be achieved by perfecting a business style, writing effective letters and memos, preparing excellent reports and giving due importance to the legal aspects of all business and professional activities.

Technology is forever changing the way people think, work or run business and professional activities. A common man could for some time ignore these changes. This is not possible for those in business or a profession. Failure to adapt to changes could restrain their success, or even lead them to failure. It is important to keep up with the changing scenario at the workplace.

Attaining perfection in written Business English depends upon the simple skills of learning the

are innumerable uses of communicating effectively through written documents. All businessmen and professionals need to write and also understand documents written by others. Different situations would

workplace. A large variety of situations are covered in the pages that follow.

While the spoken English is the original language and is used in the conduct of businesses and professions,

of society. With world growing into a global village, and English being the international link-language, one cannot carry on the development of mankind, of businesses and professions without the use of English. We have seen how the spoken version makes it possible to carry on activities in every possible

written version of Business English:

To describe yourself.
vitae, which is a written record of academic and professional achievements. Can anyone do without it?

Writing letters. Everybody needs to write letters to each other, to employers, customers and clients, to the agencies that provide civic services, to banks and in many other situations. Good letters lead to effective communication.

In-house journals and newsletters. These promote better relationships within the organization and also help build good public relations. These are an essential need of the corporate world.

All kinds of meetings. Millions of meetings are conducted all over the world each day. These cannot be possible without a written agenda, background material and recording of minutes. These are not only important to the corporate world, but equally so to the common man.

Accounting procedures. Effective accounting is the backbone of all business and professional life. Much of it is done in English.

Writing reports. In every business and profession project reports, annual reports, auditor's reports and a whole lot of other reports are written each year.

Filing returns.
reports. Most of them are in English.

Company memorandum of incorporation. All companies, societies, trusts and organizations have deeds written in English.

Company documents. All companies and corporate houses maintain a record of the administrative policy, HR policy, leave rules, directions about use of company residences, vehicles, telephones and other facilities in English.

Legal work in courts. Although some legal work is done in the regional language of the State or in Hindi, all High Courts and the Supreme Court of India conducts work in English. Legal briefs and rulings are in English.

International trade. The correspondence and documentation of all international trade is done in English. It is not possible to be involved in export and import activities without knowledge of English.

Dealing with banks. Much of the work done by the banks including the issue of passbooks, receipts, cheque books and other documentation is in English.

Press notes. Most of the press notes issued by the government and corporate houses are released to the media in English, some in Hindi and a few in regional languages.

Systems within corporate houses. Every corporate house develops systems like employment policy, marketing policy, market research, accounting, public image building, receiving feedback and several other similar activities. These are all done in English. Much of this is done in harmony with international standards using English as the main language.

Writing email. Millions of email messages in English are exchanged at every level in English every day.

SMS messages are exchanged each day at almost no cost.

Trade magazines. All business houses and professionals subscribe to trade magazines to promote their own work. Most of these are in English.

Refresher courses and seminars. Teachers, businessmen and professionals are regularly participating in refresher courses and technical seminars, most of them in English, to upgrade their knowledge and skills.

With such widespread use of English in business and professional life, is it possible to do without practical aspects that are a part of business and professional life taught. These will need our special attention.

People involved in business and professional life view the English language from their own perspective.

profession would certainly disapprove of people taking liberties with the language. The business and professional community do not intend to damage the language. Their interest lies in using the language

use the spoken and the written language to attain this end.

The facial expression, gestures or the body language can also affect the level of effectiveness of the communication. In a written message the possible variations in the meaning are restricted within certain limits. To convey a written message precisely it becomes necessary for both the person conveying the message and the person receiving it to have a good working knowledge of the language.

The written language is at an advantage over the spoken language in that a person is at lesser pressure for the choice of words. One can think and frame sentences. If a sentence or paragraph is not convincing, the person can always re-draft it in another way. A person is at liberty to experiment with

the human mind. In the spoken language there is no time to think. Words, once spoken, can never be retrieved. They will always be accepted in whatever way they have been communicated.

Businessmen and professionals need to promote their vocations by communicating through letters, memos, bulletins, messages and several other written documents. It is essential that these must be effective

effective communication everyone must remember the 5 Cs. To be useful the communication must be:

1. **Clear**. It must clearly convey what is to be done. In the English language there are innumerable words that have more than one meaning. This makes it essential for a person to choose the right word and also use it correctly when writing a sentence. Business English has given new meanings to several words.
2. **Concise**. In the quest for being effective most people have a tendency to use many words to convey a message. The real meaning of the message could be lost in words when the communication is lengthy. With more words there is also the likelihood of misinterpretation of the message.
3. **Courteous**. Business is all about building relationships with people. This is possible only when

dends. It has been observed that people respond sooner to requests than to an order.

4. **Convincing**. It is human nature to be suspicious of the other person's intentions. If these suspicions are not addressed they can become doubts. The message must be written in a manner that the reader is convinced that the request must be understood and acted upon.

5. **Complete**. It is common for people writing a message to take a narrow personal view of a situation not realizing that the readers could look at the situation in different ways. Whenever there is an element of doubt in a communication, it would be incomplete and ineffective.

Another school of thought suggests that to make written communication effective, we must follow the **ABC** of writing.

A is for **attention**
the person is attentive to the message, no action can be expected.

B is for **brevity**. The message must be as brief as possible. A person can easily get lost in words when the message is lengthy.

C is for **convincing**
message would be ineffective.

Another straightforward way to promote effectiveness in a message is to clearly specify the following:

What is to be done?	How it is to be done?
Why it is to be done?	By whom it is to be done?
Where it is to done?	When it is to be done?

An effective communication must answer all these questions. Good written communications help businessmen and professionals to attain their purpose.

Chapter 42

It is estimated that English has more than 500,000 words. These did not emerge at one time. Initially, the language might have started with a few hundred words. Through use new words emerged; each word began to have several meanings. People borrowed words from other languages using them as a part of the language. The process is still progressing with more words added to usage each year.

To appreciate the exact situation, pick up the dictionary and choose a word. Read out the meaning. On randomly opening a page in the Concise Oxford Dictionary, at the end of the page there is a three-letter word: see. It is a word that every English knowing person, even a child, would know. Everyone would overlook it as a common word. Let us take a look at how it is described or explained in the dictionary:

See *v (**sees, seeing, saw**; past part **seen**) **1**. Become aware of with the eyes. **2**. Experience or witness. **3**. Work out after thinking or from information: *I saw that he was right.* **4**. Think of in a particular way. **5**. Meet (someone one knows) socially or by chance. **6**. Meet regularly as a boyfriend or girlfriend. **7**. Consult (a specialist or professional). **8**. Give an interview or consultation to. **9**. Guide or lead to a place: *don't bother seeing me out.*

it is not a special case, let us take a look at another word. On opening another page, there is another three-letter word: lie. Again this is a word that every person would know and understand. Let us take a look at how it is described or explained in the dictionary:

Lie *v (**lies, lying, lay**; past part **lain**) **1**. Be in or take up a horizontal position on a supporting surface. **2**. Be in a particular state. *The abbey lies in ruins.* **3**. Be found. *The solution lies in a return to traditional values.* **4**. Be *n. the way, direction, or position in which something lies.

There is another description for the word:

Lie *n**1**. A deliberately false statement. **2**. A situation involving deception *v (**lies, lying, lied**) **1**. Tell a lie or lies. **2**. (of a thing) present a false impression.

dictionary has thousands of words with several shades of meanings. It is not possible for a businessman or a professional to go deep down into a language searching for the exact meaning of words, but this

misused, one must be sure that the clarity of the message has not been overlooked. With a large number of words in the language there is likelihood of making mistakes. These can be avoided with a little understanding and care.

Another common problem when writing in English is that of similar sounding words. The language has lots of words that sound similar, but have altogether different meanings. Since a person writes just as he or she speaks with the inputs coming from the same mind there is the likelihood of writing the

Clarity in Writing

wrong word changing the meaning of the message. It would be worthwhile to understand and appreciate the differences in these words. For your convenience here is a representative sampling of these words:

1.	Accede	Agree to a request or demand
	Exceed	Be greater in number or size than
	Concede	Admit that something is true
2.	Accent	A way of pronouncing a language
	Ascent	Rise in status
	Assent	Approval or agreement
3.	Accept	To receive
	Except	Not including
4.	Access	Enter a place; way to a place
	Excess	More than necessary
5.	Accessory	A person who helps someone to commit a crime
	Accessories	Items that increase the glamour and utility of something
6.	Adapt	To make suitable
	Adopt	Choose to take up; take a course of action
7.	Advice	Counsel
	Advise	To give advice
8.	Affect	
	Effect	Accomplish; result; consequence
9.	All ready	Quite ready
	Already	Previously
10.	All together	In a group
	Altogether	Wholly
11.	Allusion	An indirect implicit reference
	Illusion	A deceptive appearance or impression
12.	Alternative	Available as another possibility
	Alternate	Occur or do in turn
13.	Amiable	Friendly and pleasant in manner
	Amicable	Behaviour characterised by a friendly temperament
14.	Ante	Before
	Anti	Against
15.	Anyone	Any person or people
	Any one	Any single person
16.	Anyway	In any case; at any rate; nevertheless
	Any way	In any manner; by any means

17.	**Apathy**	Lack of interest or enthusiasm
	Antipathy	A deep-seated feeling of aversion
18.	**Apposite**	Appropriate
	Opposite	Situated on the other or further side; facing
19.	**Appraise**	Assess the value, quality or performance
	Apprise	Inform or tell someone of something
20.		Causing a good result; advantageous
		Charitable; generous
21.	**Beside**	Close to
	Besides	In addition
22.	**Canvas**	A kind of cloth
	Canvass	To solicit
23.	**Capable**	Having the ability to do something; competent
	Capacious	Having a lot of space inside; roomy
24.	**Capital**	Wealth; a city; uppercase letter
	Capitol	
25.	**Cease**	Come to or bring to an end; stop
	Seize	Take hold of suddenly and forcibly; take an opportunity eagerly
26.	**Ceremonial**	Relating to or used for ceremonies
	Ceremonious	Relating or appropriate to grand formal occasions
27.	**Childish**	Immature; silly; foolish
	Childlike	Having qualities associated with a child
28.	**Cite**	Quote a book or author as evidence; mention as an example
	Site	An area of land where something is located or occurred
	Sight	The power to see; vision
29.	**Clothes**	Things worn to cover the body
	Close	To shut; to be near
30.	**Coarse**	Rough in texture; inferior
	Course	A direction taken, onward movement; a series of lessons
31.	**Command**	Give an authoritative order; the ability to control something
	Commend	
32.	**Complacent**	
	Complaisant	Willing to please others or accept their behaviour
33.	**Compliment**	A polite expression or praise and admiration
	Complement	That which contributes extra features to improve it
34.	**Comprehensive**	Including or dealing with nearly all aspects of something
	Comprehensible	Able to be understood; intelligible

Clarity in Writing

35.		Feeling of certainty about something
36.	**Conscience** **Conscious**	A person's moral sense of right and wrong Aware of responding to surroundings; to be aware
37.	**Considerable** **Considerate**	Notably large; having merit or distinction Careful not to harm or cause inconvenience to others
38.	**Consistently** **Constantly**	Acting or done in the same way over time Occurring continuously; remaining the same
39.	**Contemptible** **Contemptuous**	Deserving or worthy of contempt; despicable; mean Showing or feeling contempt; scornful
40.	**Contiguous** **Contagious**	Sharing a common border Spread by direct or indirect contact with people or organisms
41.	**Continual** **Continuous**	Constantly or frequently occurring with intervals in between Without interruption; forming a series without exceptions
42.	**Counsel** **Council**	Advice; to advise; a legal adviser A body elected to manage the affairs of a city
43.	**Credible** **Creditable**	Able to be believed; something convincing Deserving public acknowledgement and praise
44.	**Decent** **Descent**	Moral or right A slope going down
45.	**Dependent** **Dependant**	Relying on someone for support; relying on
46.	**Desert** **Dessert**	A dry barren waste land; callously abandon; leave a place A sweet dish eaten at the end of a meal
47.	**Device** **Devise**	A thing made or adapted for a particular purpose Plan or invent a procedure or mechanism
48.	**Diary** **Dairy**	A personal journal An animal farm
49.	**Discreet** **Discrete**	Careful and prudent to not offend others or seek attention Individually separate and distinct
50.	**Discuss** **Discus**	To talk about something A heavy disc thrown at athletic events
51.	**Economic** **Economical**	 Good value for the resources used or money spent
52.	**Effective**	Producing a desired result Capable of producing an intended result over a long time

53.	Elicit	Evoke or draw out
	Illicit	Forbidden by law, rule or custom
54.	Elusive	
	Illusive	Deceptive; based on false idea or belief
55.	Emigrate	Leave one's country to settle in another country
	Immigrate	Come to live in a foreign country
56.	Eminent	Respectful and distinguished within a particular sphere
	Imminent	Likely to happen very soon
57.	Empathy	The ability to understand and share the feelings of others
	Sympathy	Feeling of pity and sorrow for someone's sorrow
58.	Especial	
	Special	Set apart for a particular purpose
59.	Excite	Cause to feel eager and enthusiastic
	Incite	Encourage a violent or lawless behaviour
60.	Exhausting	Tiring up completely
	Exhaustive	Fully comprehensive
61.	Finally	At last; in conclusion
	Finely	Delicate or intricate workmanship
62.	Flair	Natural ability or talent; stylishness and originality
	Flare	
63.	Forceful	Powerful; assertive; vigorous
	Forcible	Done by using force
64.	Forego	Precede in place and time
	Forgo	Go without something desirable
65.	Formally	In accordance with rules; in a proper, polite manner
	Formerly	In the past; previously; in earlier times
66.	Fourth	That is number four in a sequence
	Forth	Onwards in time
67.	Graceful	Having or showing of elegance of movement; courteous
	Gracious	Courteous, kind and pleasant
68.	Hair	Thread-like strands growing on the skin in animals
	Heir	A person who has the legal right to inherit property
69.	Hear	Perceive sound with the ear
	Here	In, at, or to this place or position
70.	Heard	To have listened something
	Herd	A large group of animals

71.	Hoard	
	Horde	A large group of people
72.	Human	Relating to or characteristic of humankind
	Humane	Compassionate or benevolent; act in a civilized manner
73.	Imperative	Of vital importance; an important or urgent thing
	Imperious	Arrogant and domineering
74.	Incredible	
	Incredulous	
75.	Industrial	Of, used in, or characterized by industry
	Industrious	Diligent and hardworking
76.	Ingenious	Clever, original and inventive
	Ingenuous	Innocent and unsuspecting
77.	Instance	An example
	Instants	Moments
78.	Insure	Arrange for compensation for damage to life or property
	Ensure	To make certain
79.	Jealous	Envious of someone's possessions or achievements
	Zealous	Having or showing great enthusiasm for a cause
80.	Judicial	Relating to administration of justice
	Judicious	
81.	Later	Afterwards; at a time in the future
	Latter	The second of the two mentioned people or things
82.	Lay	Out something down gently; set in position for use
	Lie	Be in a resting position on a supporting surface
83.	Lesson	An exercise
	Lessen	To diminish
84.	Loose	
	Lose	
85.	Meat	Flesh of an animal
	Meet	Come face to face; come together formally for discussion
	Mete	Dispense or allot justice or punishment
86.	Moral	Concerned with the principles of right or wrong behaviour
	Morale	
87.	Negligent	Failure to take proper care about something
	Negligible	
88.	Ordinance	An authoritative order
	Ordnance	Mounted guns; cannon

89.	Passed	
	Past	Gone by in time and no longer existing
90.	Peace	Freedom from disturbance; tranquility
	Piece	A portion of an object; an instance or example
91.	Persecute	Subject to prolonged hostility and ill-treatment
	Prosecute	Institute or conduct legal proceedings against
92.	Personal	Affecting or belonging to a particular person
	Personnel	People employed in an organization
93.	Precede	To come or go before in time, order or position
	Proceed	To begin a course of action; carry on or continue
94.	Preposition	A word governing and usually preceding a noun or pronoun
	Proposition	Statement expressing a judgment or opinion
95.	Presents	Gifts
	Presence	Being present
96.	Prevaricate	Speak or act evasively
	Procrastinate	Put off doing something; postpone action
97.	Principal	First in order of importance; main
	Principle	Fundamental truth serving as foundation for belief and action
98.	Quite	Fairly; moderately; to a partial extent
	Quiet	Making no noise; undisturbed; moderate or restrained
	Quit	Resign from a job; leave permanently
99.	Raise	Lift or move to a higher level or position; increase salary
	Raze	Tear down and destroy
100.	Respectable	Regarded by society as being proper, correct and good
	Respective	Relating to each of two or more people or things
101.	Respectfully	Giving respect to a person or group
	Respectively	In order as described
102.	Right	
	Rite	A religious or other solemn ceremony or act
	Write	Mark letters, words or symbols on a surface with pen
103.	Seem	Give the impression of being; be unable to do despite trying
	Seam	A line where two pieces of fabric are sewn together
104.	Servitude	State of being completely subject to someone more powerful
	Servility	Excessive willingness to serve or please others
105.	Sewn	To have stitched with a needle or machine
	Sown	To have planted seed in the soil

106.	Share	A part of a larger amount contributed by people
	Shear	Cut off with scissors
107.	Spacious	Having plenty of space
	Specious	
108.	Stationary	Not moving; not changing in quantity or condition
	Stationery	Paper and other material used for writing
109.	Tamper	Interfere with something so as to cause damage
	Temper	A sudden outburst of anger; to become angry easily
110.	Than	Conjunction used in comparison
	Then	At that time
111.	There	In that place
	Their	Belonging to people
	They're	
112.	Threw	To have thrown something
	Through	By way of
	Thorough	Exact
113.	To	In the direction of
	Too	In addition
	Two	The number following one
114.	Transient	Lasting only for a short time
	Transitory	Not permanent; short-lived
115.	Variation	A change or difference in condition, amount or level
	Variance	The fact or quality of being different or inconsistent
116.	Virtual	Almost or nearly the thing described, but not completely
	Virtuous	Having high moral standards
117.	Wary	Suspicious
	Weary	Tired
	Vary	Differ in size, degree or nature
118.	We	People in general
	Wee	Little
119.	Weak	Not strong
	Week	Seven days
120.	Weather	State of atmosphere in terms of temperature, wind and rain
	Whether	Expressing a doubt or choice between alternatives
121.	Where	In or what place or position? In what direction or respect?
	Wear	Cover one's body with clothing, decoration or protection

122.	**Willful**	Intentional, deliberate, stubborn or determined
	Willing	Ready, eager or prepared to do something
123.	**Wreck**	The destruction of a ship at sea, building, vehicle, etc
	Wreak	Cause a large amount of damage or harm

Have you observed how simple words in the English language could have several meanings? You would also have realised how similar sounding words could be misused when writing a letter, a memo or a report. The list that you have just gone through is only a representative list of some common words used every day. With a little effort the list could become overwhelming.

Businessmen and professionals would not have the time to perfect their language skills by delving

essential that a communication must have the clarity so as not to be misinterpreted by the people receiving it. The list given above covers the common everyday words that are used in daily interaction, both spoken and written. These can greatly improve the clarity of messages conveyed each day. It would be useful for a conscientious businessman or professional to be aware of the likely misuse of words.

Over a long period of use businessmen and professionals have adapted words for use at the workplace. Many of these words have several meanings. Some of the adaptations are strange and the sound of the words could be misleading. To avoid the misuse of these words and also to acquaint the conscientious businessmen and professionals of these words a glossary of business terms is given in the reference section of this book. One would do well to go through this list to acquaint oneself with these terms for greater clarity in writing.

With the world becoming a global village and businessmen and professionals working as freely at international level as they do in their own hometowns, it has become necessary to understand that different currencies are in use all over the world. It is also important to understand that the way people weigh or measure or check things around the world it is necessary to appreciate the correct conversions

measures around the world are also included in the reference section of this book.

"Have I clearly written what I intend to convey?" When a person is conscious of the need for clarity he or she will check repeatedly before moving the document to the receiver. Clarity will come with some effort and experience.

Chapter

The word: concise simply means giving a lot of information clearly in few words. When a person adopts the second principle of effective writing by making it concise, it really means that while clarity of meaning should not be compromised, the least number of words should be used to convey the message.

A popular advice given to people is to speak less so as not to be misunderstood. If everyone would understand this simple truth there would be greater harmony and peace in this world. This sounds easy,

Just as speaking less is virtue writing concisely is an equally valuable virtue that promotes effectiveness in writing. Here is a sample of some sentences that have been revised to make them concise:

1. We <u>are of the opinion</u> that the goods are of poor quality.
   We <u>believe</u> that the goods are of poor quality.
2. You have <u>at all times</u> delayed making payments.
   You have <u>always</u> delayed making payments.
3. Please respond <u>at an early date.</u>
   Please respond <u>soon</u>.
4. We have suffered a loss <u>as a consequence</u> of your delaying the consignment.
   We have suffered a loss <u>because</u> of your delaying the consignment.
5. Please send the goods <u>at your earliest convenience</u>.
   Please send the goods <u>soon</u>.
6. I am writing <u>in regard to</u> the order you had personally booked for me.
   I am writing <u>about</u> the order you booked for me.
7. Enclosed <u>herewith</u>   <u>form.</u>

8. During <u>the course of</u> discussions it was agreed that you would give us credit facilities.
   During the discussions it was agreed that you would give us credit facilities.
9. At <u>the time of</u> writing your company owes us more than Rs 25,000.
   At <u>present</u> your company owes us more than Rs 25,000.
10. Please pay for the goods <u>at the earliest possible moment.</u>
    Please pay for the goods <u>immediately.</u>

Business English

Have you observed how these simple sentences found in everyday business mail have been made concise by substituting phrases with simpler words? These changes help make the sentences crisp. When revising sentences, you should look for unnecessary words. Can you delete them? Can you

Simplicity helps make the message readable.

Avoid Repetition
Another common fault made is to repeat the same thing by using different but similar words in the sentences. For example: *The team members entered the hall one by one in succession.* Wouldn't it have been better to say: *The team members entered the hall one by one?* The sentence would be concise yet it would convey the meaning correctly.

To lay greater emphasis on something it is common for some people to add an additional word to the main word. For example, people say, *"absolute guarantee"*, *"absolutely certain"*, *"absolutely essential"* or *"absolutely necessary"*. Wouldn't it be effective if we were to do away with *"absolutely"* and just use the single word that conveys the message clearly, and would make the matter concise?

Another common example of repetition is when people say, *"completely destroyed"*, *"completely full"*, *"completely empty"* or *"completely random"*. Again, wouldn't it be better if *"completely"* was deleted and we used the words: *destroyed, full, empty* or *random*?

There are dozens of words that people use unconsciously to give greater emphasis to a fact in the message. The writer needs to be conscious of this common fault particularly when revising the text. The repetitive words can be easily eliminated making the message concise and readable.

Using Pedantic Language
A common problem with some learned people is when they decide to express their superior knowledge of the language by using words and phrases that might appear fancy but fail to impress people at the workplace. Many academicians and bureaucrats are guilty of using such language. It might be

and the professionals do well without it. Such language robs the message of both clarity and conciseness and must be avoided always.

Mackenzie warns, "Pedantry, in the common acceptation of the word, means an absurd ostentation of learning, and stiffness of phraseology, proceeding from a misguided knowledge of books, and a total ignorance of men." S. Smith adds, "As pedantry is an ostentatious obtrusion of knowledge, in which those who hear us cannot sympathize, it is a fault of which soldiers, sailors, sportsmen, gamesters, cultivators, and all men engaged in a particular occupation, are quite as guilty as scholars; but they have the good fortune to have the vice only of pedantry, while scholars have both the vice and the name for it too." Businessmen and professionals would do well to keep all the written communication plain and simple.

Using Jargon

understand. Have you observed that when you are in the midst of a group of doctors they will exchange conversation that might not be understood by you? Similarly, when you are in the midst of a group of lawyers they would also use certain words and phrases that you cannot understand. Bureaucrats have their favourite words and phrases just as teachers and professors would have their own.

Every business and profession uses words and phrases that are typical to them. These words and phrases popularly called "jargon" would be a part of the language understood by the group, but not by everyone. The glossary of business terms in the reference section is a compilation of such words and phrases. The important thing is that when a communication is intended to be used within a group where everyone is acquainted with the terminology used, it would be perfectly all right. However, when the

people to understand the message clearly. This must be avoided.

Using Clichés

some of the clichés attractive and interesting, but they do not realize that they have been overused to make them stale and uninteresting to most people. They are not accepted happily. Here is a list of some of the common clichés that are to be seen in everyday use:

above the call of duty	accident waiting to happen	acid test
add insult to injury	after all is said and done	a gift from god
all's well that ends well	a pillar of society	as luck would have it
a sight for sore eyes	a step in the right direction	at a loss of words
back in the saddle	backseat driver	back on track
beat a dead horse	be an open book	ball is in your court
both sides of the coin	bury the hatchet	by and large
call the buff	cold as ice	centre of attention
count your blessings	come full circle	counting on you
dead wrong	dog-eat-dog	down and out
done to death	down in the dumps	
easy come, easy go	easier said than done	easy target
face the music	fair and square	fall from grace
far reaching consequences	few and far between	
	free as a bird	from time immemorial
game plan	get down to brass tacks	get to the bottom of it
give a damn	give rise	go for the kill
go it alone	go the extra mile	go to places
goes without saying	good for nothing	green with envy
head over heels	have had their day	hammer out details
hedge the bet	hit the nail on the head	hit the ceiling
icing on the cake	in hot water	I couldn't care less
increasingly apparent	in a nutshell	in seventh heaven
	kill the idea	kiss the dust

let the cat out of the bag	learning curve	leave no stone unturned
little does he know	live it up	lock, stock and barrel
make the blood boil	make ends meet	
method in madness	mince words	moment of truth
naked truth		nip in the bud
needle in the haystack	needs no introduction	no strings attached
on cloud nine	on top of the world	off the cuff
out of the woods	on a trip	over-riding importance
pass the buck	powers that be	proud as a peacock
pulling the leg	put words in one's mouth	put on hold
rags to riches	ripe old age	rule the roost
sell like hot cakes	shot in the arm	sitting duck
skeleton in the closet	smooth sailing	spill the beans
steal the limelight	stick to your guns	stick your neck out
take one's word for	take the liberty of	the die is cast
the order of the day	tighten your belt	through thick and thin
throw caution to the wind	to each his own	to avoid the plague
unfairly courteous	upset the applecart	vicious circle
where angels fear to tread	wild goose chase	welcome with open arms
wishful thinking	with bated breath	without further delay

    Has the use of these clichés been totally stopped? No. Despite the best efforts of the academicians who consider these phrases stale and outdated, newcomers will continue to use them despite the

particular situation. When preparing a written message a person should understand the concepts of effective written messages, but should never restrict oneself to limited use of words. English has some

ability.

Chapter

Just as people are attracted to a person who speaks courteously, they are equally impressed when a written message conveys courtesy and good manners. Courtesy is related to human behaviour. It is being polite and considerate towards each other. It is immediately noticed in a conversation between two or more people. It is equally well noticed when people interact at the workplace.

When business really means building good relationships to help each other earn a livelihood, we cannot really overlook the need for courtesy in all written messages. One does not communicate only with colleagues and subordinates. The senior management represents the employers and is worthy of extra courtesy and respect as that extended to one's colleagues. Just as we use "Sir" to address them in everyday conversation, we need to address them appropriately in the written messages and documents.

Montaigne said, "Courtesy is the science of the highest importance. It is like grace and beauty of the

"Small kindnesses, small courtesies, small considerations, habitually practised in our social intercourse, give a greater charm to the character than the display of great talents and accomplishments."

Written communications in business and professional activities are not restricted only to everyday routine billing, documentation, accounting and other similar activities. On many occasions these communications relate to misunderstood or misinterpreted contracts and agreements, non-payment of bills and debts or about other disagreements. When such situations arise the common reaction is

Experience has repeatedly proved that the most complicated misunderstandings can be resolved through patience, tact and above all by maintaining a courteous behaviour with each other. More

courts of law. Being courteous is an attitude towards life. Those who are polite and considerate will always be so at all times and in all situations. Goethe has rightly remarked, "There is no outward sign of true courtesy that does not rest on a deep moral foundation."

It is immaterial what kind of a message is being communicated through a written document. Even in the most provocative situations a person should not lose one's cool. A retaliatory attitude will only

leading to better professional relationships.

Chapter 45

The purpose of every written communication is to inform, seek information or cooperation and to act in certain situations. In every case the sender would desire that the message should attain the purpose it intended to have, but eventually it is for the recipient of the message to decide how he desires to act on it. This is what makes it necessary for a written message to be convincing.

To be convinced by a message the person should either share the same beliefs with those of the sender, or should accept them as better than his own. This happens in several situations such as when the message is from:

The employer The boss A respected person	A judicial court A person in an important position

If the sender of the message is in one of the aforesaid positions he or she is at an advantage in that the recipient would not ignore the message and would comply with whatever is desired. However, the majority of the messages does not come under such situations, and are one-to-one requests for something to be achieved. This makes it necessary for the sender to make a little extra effort to ensure that the message is convincing to the recipient.

What restricts a recipient of a message from accepting it as correct? Every person has his or her own beliefs, and when these are not in harmony with those of the sender of the message, the person would not be immediately convinced. In such circumstances it would be necessary for the sender to use persuasive skills in writing the message to change the existing beliefs of the recipient.

For example, when the sender is drafting a message to promote the sale of a new detergent FAST,

recipient to change his belief easily. To convince him the sender would need to reinforce his request for change with persuasive facts that claim that FAST is the result of the latest technology, it cleans faster, is equally effective with cold water, washes double the number of clothes, requires lesser rinsing water and also conditions the fabric just as it cleans the garments better. It is these facts that set the recipient thinking and gradually changing his belief in favour of trying the new product.

yet they would aim at selling an idea to the recipient. Good written messages would need motivational and persuasive skills. These are not as easy to learn as they appear to be. Human beings are complex and one can learn these through an understanding of human behaviour and good writing skills. Some of the popular methods used by people are as follows:

>**Appeal to reason.** Most people are reasonable and respond positively when something is suggested within reason. To reason, one must use logic.

Facts convince people through results. People do not results.

Appeal to basic instincts. People respond immediately when basic human instincts are touched upon. Everybody is sensitive about the need for food, clothing, shelter, health and family.

Appeal to feelings and emotions. People have their sensitivities. If you can touch them, their response would be swift.

Appeal in the name of faith and religion. All religious leaders use this human weakness to persuade millions of people effectively. However, they do it more through the spoken language than through the written language.

Appeal in the name of tradition and cultural needs. Many people respect traditions and cultural values and would be persuaded.

Some people use unethical methods such as making false claims or making unrealistic promises, or even deception and coercion to persuade others to do things. These would be against law and must never be tried.

People are known to use both ethical and unethical methods to persuade people. One would do well to remember that only the ethical people succeed and are recognised in society. The ultimate success comes from using one's imagination to change the way people think. All successful businessmen and professionals have continued to so over the centuries gone by.

Chapter 46

A message cannot be complete until it conveys all the information related to it. It is a common mistake made by millions of people every day.

this evening."

One of them immediately responded, "Where?" Another followed, "At what time?" Would it not have been better if the Sales Manager had written, "Please join me for a meeting today at 4.00 p.m. at

making the meeting fruitful. Such lapses made hurriedly and unconsciously in a busy routine are costing businessmen and professionals a lot of wasted effort and money.

Even in everyday life we receive incomplete invitations to meetings, weddings, social gatherings and workplace activities, making the effort unfruitful and also losing the opportunity to have more people join in and attaining greater success.

Any message that is incomplete is a waste of time and effort. In business it could be a very costly mistake. Meeting notices are sent out without details of the agenda for the meeting. When the agenda is handed over at the last minute the participants are not prepared to put forward their views. They seek time until the next meeting. This happens repeatedly at every workplace just because of a little carelessness.

Just as it is important to write a complete message, it is equally important to ensure that the enclosures with a message are attached and placed in the envelope. It is also essential that the envelope is appropriately stamped if the message is sent by post.

To ensure that a message is complete, check the draft for its contents. Is the purpose of the message clear? How is the message related to the recipient? Are there any action points for the recipient? Are these points clear? Is the message time-related? If so, are the dates and timings clearly mentioned? Is a feedback desired? How soon do you expect it? Is the message readable? Is it being sent through a reliable service? When you have checked on all these points you can be sure that your message is complete and will get the expected response. One learns to make the message complete through a little extra effort and work experience.

Chapter 42

Some suggest that to write effectively a person should follow the principles of ABC of writing. In

    A *for attention,*
    B *for brevity, and*
    C *for convincing*

This simply means that the written document should draw immediate attention, must be brief and easy to read, and should be convincing for the recipient to act upon it.

For a document to draw immediate attention it must be well presented, be readable and must clearly express the purpose of the message. If the message is related to the recipient, it must be clear how it

upon it?

B should not only be for brevity, but also for belief. Brevity in a message makes for easy reading and also ensures that there are no misinterpretations. The message goes straight, as it should be. Fenelon advises, "Genuine good taste consists in saying much in few words, in choosing among our thoughts, in having order and arrangement in what we say, and in speaking with composure."

Belief in the message is a step towards making it convincing. Bulwer explains, "In belief lies the secret of all valuable exertion." Ovid adds, "We are slow to believe that which if believed would hurt our

We have already discussed how to write convincingly. It is of utmost importance that the recipient

sender of the message to use words that motivate and persuade a person to act. This is not easy, but not

adopts and follows success comes from making a persistent effort in the right direction.

Chapter 48

Punctuation marks are symbols used to identify the beginning and end of a sentence, breakup of sentences, to express a pause within the sentence, an exclamation or a question. These symbols help understand the written text better.

Most people do not give the attention punctuation marks deserve in a written document. This is because they do not know how to use them correctly. When appropriately used, the punctuation marks add vigour and clarity to a written document. They help to separate words and ideas, group and keep together related ideas, and set aside words that need special emphasis. Contrary to what some people think, it is not their purpose to give a broken look to a document, but to enhance clarity and effectiveness of the document.

There are as many as 30 marks, but only a few are in common use. Here is a quick revision on the important punctuation marks, and also how they can be used effectively:

Full stop (.) Uses:	Examples:
at the end of a sentence	I will be joining work tomorrow.
after some abbreviations*	Mr., Mrs., Dr., etc.
as a decimal point in numbers	23.75
to separate parts of email address	sriram.sahram@yahoo.in
to separate parts of website address	vspublishers.com
after a number or letter in an outline	1. Stationery items
	a. Note nooks
	b. Pencils
in groups of three when words are eliminated	"…is sturdy, easy to use and long-lasting"
*Not used when abbreviation is for:	
certain organizations	
currency	$, €, £ ¥
short names	Sam (for Samuel)
for some words	Memo, exam, math

Using Punctuation Marks

Question mark (?)
    after a direct question.
    to express doubt or uncertainty
	What is your name?
	 We expect to complete the work by January 1(?) if all goes well.

Exclamation mark (!)
    at the end of a sentence to express surprise, shock, doubt or irony
    to indicate a loud sound
    to emphasize what has been said
	I can't believe that in two years you have grown so tall!
	 Boom! Aah!
	 I am warning you for the last time!

Comma (,)
    between items in a list.
    to show a pause in a long sentence.
    when you add extra information.
    in direct speech.
    in a list of adjectives before a noun.
    before question tags.
    in large numbers, to separate them
    in writing the date
    after a complimentary close
	I have asked for a copy, pencil and rubber.
	 We would run, rest a little, and then run again.
	 My friend, who is bald, loves to tell jokes about bald people.
	 He said, "Just wait a little".
	 She was a tall, pretty woman.
	 You are in a hurry, aren't you?
	 3,75,842 or 1,452,567
	 June 1, 2013
	 Yours sincerely,

Apostrophe (')
    for possessives, to show something belongs to someone.
    for missing words
	This is Sharda's book.
	 He couldn't care less.

Semicolon (;)
    to separate two parts of a sentence
    to separate items on a list where there are many items and commas have already been used
	turned up till late at night.
	 The options are Physics, Chemistry and Math; Physics, Chemistry and Biology.

Colon (:)
    to introduce a list
    to introduce what follows
    the opening of a letter
    when quoting someone
	You will need: 2 exercise books, 1 pen.
	 The following observations were made:
	 Dear Sir:, Dear Mr. Sharma:
	 Your salesman promised: "We will have the consignment ready today."

Hyphen (-)		
	for some compound words	Well-established business
	for compound numbers	Twenty-seven
	to join words together	The hungry-thirsty children could bear it no longer.
	to divide a word at the end of a line	The situation requires that the manage-ment must intervene immediately.
		Pre-industrial
		President-elect, president-nominee
Dash (--)		
	to separate parts of a sentence	Please check the inventory—place the returned items together.
	near the end of a sentence to repeat an important thing	She bought grocery, fruits, vegetables, milk—almost everything.
	to express an interruption in speech	The bomb sounded like hell—I closed my ears.
	to express an omission	Mr. – was present that day.
Quotation Marks ("or")		
	to show that the words are spoken	She said, "Please get back in time."
	to show someone's thoughts	"I must apologise", he thought.
	to show that someone else said or wrote the words	The councilor explained "they had done what was possible."
	to show a word that is new or unusual	Follow the simple "mantra".
	to change the meaning of a word	I thought you were "honest"?
Ditto Marks (")		
	imply repetition	20 pieces of toilet soap.
		10 " " toothpaste
		10 " " toothbrush
Parentheses ( )		
	to add extra information but keep it separate from the rest of the sentence	You will need an extra change (at least one) in the event it rains.
	to enclose numbers, references, directions and question marks	(1), (Smith & Jones[2]), (see Chapter 2), (was it true?)

Using Punctuation Marks

To most people all that you need to write is a paper and pencil or a pen. In earlier days the businessmen

was to be written and let him or her type it out on a typewriter. Much of the writing was done at that

To be effective in the modern times one needs to be well-versed with many things. It is essential that a person must know the language well. At the same time a person must know how he can access

to replace the typewriter with a computer and a printer. There is need for other tools. To write well a person must have:

A good dictionary. Businessmen and professionals feel that a dictionary is something for a school or college-going young person. That is not true. Young people are taught the use of a dictionary because it is an essential tool for good writing. The word dictionary has been derived from Latin meaning "a manual of words". A dictionary lists words from the language you are using. We have earlier observed that a larger vocabulary enables effective writing.

A good thesaurus. A thesaurus is a book that gives lists of words that have the same or similar meanings. This makes it possible for a person to choose the right word for a particular occasion. While it gives a person a wide choice of words to choose from, it also helps increase

A book of synonyms and antonyms. Synonyms are words with similar meaning and antonyms are words that have a meaning opposite to a word. These too are an asset for effective writing in that they give a wide choice of words to choose from.

A business dictionary. Every business or profession today has dictionaries that list words and phrases of great importance in everyday work. Rather than grope in the dark in a particular situation it would be appropriate for every person in a business or profession to have a work-

A good word processor. All businessmen and professionals are using computers at the workplace. However, a computer is only as good as the software we use on it. Word processing

Using A Good Word Processor

A person can easily get away by speaking broken sentences, inaccurate words and phrases and still express what one desires to say to someone. When it comes to writing, one is always on test. The words must be spelt correctly, the sentences must be right grammatically, the capitals and the punctuation must be right. Every little mistake negates the effectiveness of the written message. All errors are brought to your notice and also corrected when you use good word processing software on your computer. One of the most popular word processing software used is MS Word.

Good word processing software warns the writer about capitalization, misused words, negation, possessives and plurals, relative clauses, subject-verb agreement and verb phrases. It suggests reframing of sentences and correct punctuation, the use of clichés, colloquialisms and jargon, fragments, gender-

The word processing software guides a writer throughout the document warning about sentence structure or length, unclear phrasing or about wordiness. Besides, it helps you have the type of spacing you desire on the left and right, or top and bottom. It enables the use of a variety of fonts, italics or words in bold letters. It also makes it possible to include graphs, illustrations and photographs within the document, with the written matter wrapped around them. It also enables the use of colour printing on an appropriate printer attached to the computer.

Using the Tools

A tool is only as good as the use it is put to. Good craftsmen use their tools very effectively. It is just the same with writing. Those who use the tools regularly begin to appreciate their potential use very quickly. Word processing software that includes a dictionary and a thesaurus and many other facilities has made writing documents very easy. *Practice is the key word to attain perfection.*

Chapter 50

People who write regularly develop a personal writing style over a period. If you observe closely every author has a distinct style of writing. Like individuals, even newspapers, magazines and technical journals have their own writing styles that distinguish one from the other. The style is a selling point.

A writing style could be formal or informal. As the word suggests, a formal writing style requires that all the rules about writing must be followed. Informal writing is similar to making a conversation where the sentences are short, abbreviations are freely used and the writer expresses empathy towards the reader. One style is not better than the other. Both have a purpose. At the workplace both the styles are used; the informal style within the workforce and the formal style when communicating with the outside world.

Some classify the writing style as a technical style or a conversational style. In the technical style, principally used to write reports, clarity and conciseness are very important. Wordiness and long sentences are avoided. The technical details must be clear and understandable to the reader. Business writing comes within the technical style with the minor difference that longer sentences can be used. The conversational style is like the informal style.

A personal writing style depends to a large extent upon the audience to whom a person is writing. A capable writer has a good understanding of his audience and adapts his writing to a particular need and the audience. Business and professional writing is not like writing a short story or a novel. It needs

are always busy and have little time to devote to reading correspondence and documents. One has to

this truth always.

In business and professional writing, a writer must keep the following in mind irrespective of the subject one is writing on:

The audience. In business writing the audience is the very purpose of writing. The audience

audience. The writer must adjust the style to the ability of the audience to understand the document.

The subject
professional activities also, but only to a limited degree. Generally, one needs to write on a variety of things, as varied as writing a letter to a client and writing an explanation to the

a variety of situations that need to be dealt with effectively and the writer must appreciate this requirement.

Be yourself. It is common to see people talk comfortably, but the moment it comes to writing they become self-conscious and adopt a stiff posture. This affects what they write. To write

perfect. You have something to begin with. Revise it to be in harmony with your personality. Every written document must project a positive image of the person who has written it.

Keep it simple

it simple. The audience for written documents at the workplace is very limited. Nobody

purpose, and this is best served when the document is simple and easy to understand.

Always be explicit. Write what you want to say. This is not to suggest that one should be too open, unmindful of courtesies. One should be straight and honest. Ethics and integrity are very important in business and professional activities. At the same time, keeping in view the competitive environment, one must express oneself unhesitatingly. In the long term it is appreciated by everyone.

Keep it brief. Some people are fond of reading. They read for leisure. But when it comes to reading a business letter or a report, they feel it is time-consuming. The majority of people do not enjoy reading, least of all business documents. This makes it necessary that all written business and professional messages must be short and to the point. Good writers are known for providing a lot of information using very few words.

Give of your best. A good writer never compromises on effort, accuracy or quality of presentation. Every written document should project the image of the person who has written it. A document must be well written and equally well presented to the reader. It will always leave behind a lasting image.

Following these simple rules, people in different businesses and professions have been able to develop a writing style that distinguishes them from others. You can do it too!

Chapter 51

If you were to send an article to a newspaper or magazine for publication it would go to an editor for assessment and polishing before being printed. In the same way a proposed book too would go to an editor even if it is worthy of being published. In each case the purpose is to make the article or the book more salable or attractive for the reader to pay for it and read it. Editors have knowledge of many subjects and are trained to look at written scripts not only for spelling and grammar errors, but to polish them to make them readable and useful.

All written work at the workplace is also intended to be attractive and readable. This intention is

even by the best of writers is not always attractive or readable. A good writer is aware of this fact

making corrections to make the reading crisp, attractive and readable. A good writer is really never fully

Corporate houses and professionals employ people who can write well. However, their work does not require a professional editor. Therefore, the responsibility of editing and polishing a document has to be taken on by the person writing the document. This is an important additional responsibility.

documents:

Follow the rules of writing. *Businessmen and professionals need a variety of written documents.* Each kind has its own writing rules besides the general rules of writing discussed earlier. Do not take these for granted. They have been compiled on the basis of wide work experience. A wise person learns from the experience of others.

Know the corporate style. Have you observed that every newspaper and magazine has a style

over a period? In the same way corporate houses, professionals and also individuals develop a style in writing letters, presenting reports or other written documents. Follow this style in your writing.

Wait before you edit a document. Do not get down to editing a document immediately after you have completed the draft. You could do this to improve the preliminary draft, but not to

look at the document afresh ready to polish it to make it attractive.

Look at the document objectively. Do not look at the document as your work. Look at it how

correctly and accurately? Will it create the desired impact? Can it be misinterpreted to mean something else? How can it be improved further?

Check for spellings and grammar. Modern word processors installed on our computers

the error.
Check for conciseness. Can you eliminate unnecessary words? Can you replace a phrase with a word? Can you cut short a sentence? Or break one sentence into two for easy reading? Don't hesitate. Do it right away. Your document will become attractive and readable.
Check for accuracy. Only zero inaccuracy can be tolerated in a business or professional

a document useless.
Share your document. Many writers share the document with a colleague to be sure that

upon the document. If some changes are suggested you are not bound to accept them. But do consider them. If they would be useful, you could incorporate them. If not, forget about them.
Seek excellence

Do not slacken your efforts. After a period of acceptance most people tend to become slack. Do not let this happen to you. Ensure that every noting, memo, letter or document that goes

The truth is that every document can be improved to make it readable. Ask any author. He will tell you that he would write a better book if he could do it again. At the workplace time is an important

written. Polish the document as well as you can and let it move on. With experience you would be producing excellent written documents.

Chapter 52

have well-written curriculum vitae about you, as that is your introduction to the world of business and professional world.

achievements. Some prefer to call it a résumé. Whereas the words: curriculum vitae have been derived

convenience, the words curriculum vitae are abbreviated to CV, and used as such in the business and professional world. It is essential to send a copy of the CV along with a job application.

A CV is really a tool that helps you sell your services to a prospective employer. It is practically not possible for a person to go from one prospective employer to another in search of an appropriate

purpose simultaneously.

employee has the necessary abilities required for the job, he invites him for a personal interview that gives both an opportunity to speak to each other, match each other's expectations and then create a

experience has shown that most CVs are badly written and shoddy, not attaining the purpose it was intended to do so.

written document. Just as a person continues to change, acquiring new skills and experiences, it is

Understand Your Needs

Before a person can get down to writing one's CV it is essential that one must understand oneself and also what one desires to attain. A person's career begins long before one seeks employment. It

aspirant must remember that there are no shortcuts to success. A person must begin at the lowest rung experience and develops new skills, the CV can be updated for future use. Begin from where you are today.

Whereas for a prospective employee a job provides a source of livelihood and an opportunity for or more employees to do the work that lead him towards the set goals. The prospective employee must answer the following questions:

Do I understand the job requirements?
What appeals to me the most about the job?

responsibilities?
Would I need to change my current mindset and routine for the job?
Would the level of job stress be normal or above normal?

The answers to these questions will help you understand yourself better in relation to the job you have in mind. Choose a job where you get an opportunity to do things that you like. If it makes you enthusiastic, that's the job you should be looking for.

Begin Early for A Job Hunt

Most aspirants begin the job hunt long before they are ready for the job. They apply for positions when still in college. Others look for possible employers and maintain a list to apply shortly before they are ready. Always remember the following:

Job hunt is a full-time job. Always keep on the lookout for prospective employers in the area.

Make an organised approach
copies of applications you make and the responses that you get.

. There are no tailor-made jobs. Some adjustments are always necessary. Be prepared for them.

Stay motivated. Every application would not get a positive response. Let that not disturb you.

Have realistic expectations. Employers are shrewd people. They seek people with appropriate abilities and experience.

Stay connected with the trade. Even after a person gets a job it is best to stay connected with the developments in the trade. It keeps one aware of the prospects for further growth.

Writing the CV

brief and yet must convince the person reading it. This simply means that it must be of interest to the prospective employer. While he knows what he is on the lookout for, it is for the prospective employee

There are three kinds of CVs. These are:

1. **Chronological CV.** This kind of CV provides a detailed account of academic and career history in a chronological order. It is written in reverse order, that is, the most recent information

career history with no gaps to explain. It highlights both the career goals and achievements.
2. **Functional CV.** This kind of CV provides a detailed account of a person's strengths and skills is on matching the available skills with those required for the job. People use this kind of CV career gaps that are looked upon suspiciously. They also use it when they have done a variety of jobs for different employers.
3. **Chrono-functional CV.** This is a combination of the two types of CVs where the best features of both the kinds are put together. While the career and educational history is given in chronological order, a detailed account of transferable core skills is also included. This way this kind of CV provides the details that would have been provided in both of the chronological and functional CVs, but it is done in lesser detail. This kind of CV highlights the best in a career. It highlights clear career goals, the positions held in companies you have worked for with no time

Which of these CVs is the best? It has been observed that the most popular formats used by people are either the chronological CV, or the chrono-functional CV. Employers look at the functional circumstances like careers in healthcare or project management. It is suggested that people entering a career or those with short-term experience should have a short one-page CV written as a chronological or a chrono-functional CV.

A typical CV could have some or all of the sections, as follows:

Heading. This section would have your name, personal details, address, telephone and mobile numbers, email ID, etc. that identify you.

Career objective. This would include your goals or whatever you desire to achieve through your career.

. This section would include details like your background, skills, achievements and experience.

Key skills. This section would give details of your knowledge, core skills, abilities and strengths that would be useful in pursuing the career.

Academic background. This section would include details of your school and college education, professional training and development as a basis for a career.

. This section would include details that are relevant to people who have already been working for some time.

Work history. This section is important to both, the person changing a job, and the prospective employer who would like to analyse facts to consider if the person would deliver in the changed circumstances.

Voluntary work done. This section would be of interest to people who are active in the society. This can be a great asset in some careers.

Membership in professional associations
up-to-date with professional developments.

Research and development. This section could give details of research papers written,

guidance provided or books published on the subject.
Computer skills

professional life.

Language skills. With business houses and professionals working all over the world language skills are a great asset in many situations.

Additional information. This section could give details about a person's holding a valid passport, driving license, or similar information.

References. Some employers desire that the applicants give the names and addresses of people known to them so as to check the facts provided by them.

A review of the list of items that are generally included in a CV would set a newcomer thinking

understand that inclusion of all the sections is not necessary. They have been mentioned because senior personnel would have many skills and experiences to talk about. If so, different items could be included in relevant sections. Since a CV is an introduction of a person, it must be short, crisp and attractive. This is possible only in a CV that is brief and to the point. The real test, therefore, in writing the CV is to keep it short, attractive and factual. Let us see how it can be done.

Heading

Heading generally refers to the title at the top of a page or section of a book. As a part of a CV it refers to the name, address and contact details about a person. Writing the heading appears to be simple work, but it deserves special attention because it must convey the details at one glance.

Also include your title such as Mr., Mrs. or Ms., as it eliminates the need to write the gender. Since the focus should be on the name it is best to write it in larger font size or in bold letters.

Do not use abbreviations when writing the address. Write the complete address for the mail to reach you conveniently through post or courier. Do not forget to mention the PIN code and the name of the country if you are writing to a person in another country.

If you are already employed and are not averse to your present employer getting to know that you

In some situations a person could have a current address and a permanent residential address. It might be best to mention both.

Since it is convenient to contact people on the phone, mobile or through email it would be necessary that these details are included below the address. If you have a landline number and a mobile number do mention both of them to make it easy for a person to contact you. Write the email ID only if you use it regularly, opening the mailbox at least once a day.

How should the heading of the CV typed? This is a matter of personal choice. Here are two common methods used:

Suresh Chand Sharma
14, Mahipal Towers, Swami Ram Road, Mumbai – 400 050
Tel: 022 1234 5678, Mob: 94170 12345
Email: sureshchand@abcd.in

or

14, Mahipal Towers,
Swami Ram Road,
Mumbai – 400 050

Suresh Chand Sharma

Tel: 022 1234 5678
Mob: 94170 12345
Email: sureshchand@abcd.in

Should there be a photograph alongside the heading? Opinions vary on this issue. Whereas the trend is not to include a photograph because it does not say anything about your skills and abilities, but still many employers ask that a photograph be sent. Some employers ask for a photograph after the person is asked to join work. This is for their personal records about the employees.

Career Objective

career statement. This is not a mandatory part of a CV. Writing a career objective is a personal choice. It

like to impress the potential employer with it. It would not be necessary when a person is pursuing and

A career objective could be included if a person has set clear career goals and the job applied for

included, it must be brief, truthful and realistic. It should not be more than two sentences. It would be necessary that the rest of the CV should focus on supporting the career objective and the potential employer must be convinced that you possess the necessary skills to attain it. Here are two samples of a career objective:

1. *To pursue a career in law to rise gradually through honest hard work to the position of a judge.*
2. *To seek employment in organizations that encourage research and development that promotes ideal healthcare and longevity.*

must speak well of a person in the least number of words that truly describe a person's abilities and

their own work excessively and unrealistically.

When writing about you, ask yourself: Who am I? What are my characteristic qualities? What skills make my work special? What do I specialize in? Are my achievements in harmony with my skills? Do I enjoy what I am doing? The answers to these questions will lead you to a factual and

be written in as few words as possible.

how they would be useful to a prospective employer. Explain how you are enthusiastic about the work and motivated to give of the best of yourself. Those who have already been working should highlight

expertise that you have acquired over a period. The prospective employer would also like to know what drives you towards your goals.

1. An ambitious and enthusiastic young man having accountancy skills would like to be part of a team in a progressive business organization. Possesses analytical and problem solving capabilities along with good communication skills. Would be happy to work in a challenging situation.

   ence in project management with two leading organizations seeks growth in a fast-growing infrastructure organization that has challenging projects, A hard-working team-member with

   ations.

right words that describe personal attributes and skills. Some words are more descriptive than others and arouse immediate interest. Here are two lists of words that describe common attributes and skills. You could select words from the two lists to suit your personal circumstances.

Common Attributes:

Accurate	*Adaptable*	*Ambitious*	*Articulate*	*Assertive*
Boisterous	*Broadminded*	*Brilliant*	*Calm*	*Candid*
Capable	*Committed*	*Competent*		*Conscientious*
Consistent	*Contented*	*Cool-headed*	*Cooperative*	*Courageous*
Daring	*Decisive*	*Dedicated*	*Dependable*	*Detached*
Determined	*Devoted*	*Diligent*	*Disciplined*	*Dynamic*
Effective		*Energetic*	*Enthusiastic*	*Faithful*
Far-sighted	*Firm*	*Flexible*	*Focused*	*Friendly*
Generous	*Goal-driven*	*Hands-on*	*Hardworking*	*Helpful*
Honest	*Humble*	*Humorous*	*Imaginative*	*Independent*
Industrious	*Innovative*	*Intelligent*	*Inventive*	*Knowledgeable*
Lively	*Loyal*	*Loving*	*Mature*	*Methodical*
Meticulous	*Motivated*	*Novel*	*Objective*	*Observant*

Open-minded	Organized	Original	Outgoing	Patient
Perceptive	Persevering	Persistent	Persuasive	Positive
Principled	Proactive	Productive	Professional	
	Quick-thinking	Rational	Reasonable	Reliable
Resourceful	Responsible		Scrupulous	
Self-motivated	Self-reliant	Sensitive	Sincere	Smart
Spirited	Steady l	Straightforward	Successful	Supportive
Tactful	Talented	Thoughtful	Thorough	Tolerant
Trustworthy	Thoughtful	Unassuming	Understanding	Upright
Versatile	Virtuous	Well-behaved	Worldly	Zealous

Desirable Skills:

Administrative skills	Analytical skills	Communication skills
Crisis-handling skills	Decision-taking skills	Delegating skills
Inter-personal skills	Leadership skills	Management skills
Motivating skills	Multi-tasking skills	Negotiation skills
Numerical skills	Organizational skills	Planning skills
Presentation skills	Problem-solving skills	Public speaking skills
Relationship building	Strategizing skills	Team-building skills
Technical skills	Trouble-shooting skills	Writing skills

your services to the prospective employer.

Key Skills

A skill is the ability to do something well. The ability comes from knowledge, practice and experience. Some people are blessed that they develop the ability better than others. Since prospective employers are always on the lookout for skilled personnel who could help them attain their purpose, they are

Turn back to the last page and once again go through the list of desirable skills. Nobody could possess all the skills. However, most people are very good at some skills and possess some knowledge of a few others. Tick those that you are good at. These are your strengths. Each one opens up several opportunities in your vocation. These must be included in the CV so that the prospective employer can know about them. You might like to match some of the skills that are required by the prospective employer.

The situation would be different for those who are setting out on a career and those who have been in it for long. While the former would have to rely upon the skills they gained during studies at school and college, during internship or through voluntary work or part-time employment, the latter could fall back upon the experience and achievements in their earlier part of the career. When in doubt list all of the skills that you possess. Do not overlook that with a little effort you could add on new skills to your list.

these in this section. When you possess several skills it would be advisable to mention a few in the earlier section, and the important ones in this section. It would be useful if you can match your key skills with those required for the position you are applying for. Here are two examples that you could modify to your requirement:

Target Position – **Accounts**	Target Position – **Project Management**
Numerical ability	Leadership ability
Analytical ability	Management skills
Team player	Team-building skills
Good time manager	Problem-solving ability

Academic Background

development. Begin with the highest level of achievement and proceed backwards to school level. Do mention special achievements, if any. Some prefer to include their marks or division attained against

obvious for teaching positions, it would be useful to list the educational achievements on a separate sheet of paper attached to the CV as an appendix.

When listing your educational achievements it would be useful to mention the names of the educational institutions you have studied in, the degree or diploma obtained, subjects of specialization, if any, and the year you completed the course of study. The names of the degrees and courses could be abbreviated. Those who are graduates or post-graduates could avoid giving details of schooling unless they are relevant to the position applied for. Although most employers desire to know the grades

Some people could also be faced with the situation where they do not have much to write about because they dropped out after school. In such cases a person could include details of school education. In such situation the person would of course apply only for a position that does not require higher levels of education.

Here is an example of academic information on the CV for an accounting job:

2013	Diploma in computer. accounts	School of Computer Accounting, New Delhi.	
2012	M.Com	ABC College of Commerce, New Delhi	1st Division
2010	B.Com	ABC College of Commerce, New Delhi	1st Division
2007	Class 10+2	Sri Ram Public School – CBSE Board	1st Division
2005	Class 10	Sri Ram Public School – CBSE Board	1st Division

some special success attained through exemplary effort, outstanding skill or courage. Those who are already working could look back at the successes they might have achieved much more than those who

like being a school captain or house captain, or that one was the president of the college students union. One could mention special achievements like being declared "the outstanding student of the year" at college. Here are a few common examples of special achievements:

> *Member of the Delhi University Students Union Executive Committee in 2002.*
> *Received the Rotary Vocational Award for Outstanding service in 2011.*
> *Received the Best Salesman Award from my company in 2010.*

Work History

work history particularly when you have worked for reputed companies and gained useful experience.

This section could be titled: Work History, Work Experience or Employment History. You could list internships and voluntary work separately. Begin with the current position and employment and go backwards. Give details like company name and address, position held and the period worked. You could list responsibilities and special achievements in each position, but this could make the CV long. Avoid writing unnecessary details. You could make a note of these achievements and if asked at the interview stage you could talk about them.

When discussing achievements the prospective employers are interested to know whether you employer and not with you until you have proved your credentials.

If you have not worked for long periods and the time-gaps are glaring the prospective employer could be suspicious about the reasons for it. You must have valid reasons to explain what you were doing during that period.

Here are a few samples of how work history could be included in the CV:

May and June 2010	Internship	XYZ Bio-chemicals Ltd, Worked in the HR Department
May and June 2011	Short-term employment	ABC Chemicals Ltd. Worked as Supervisor in Packaging Department.

or

July 2009 to Sept 2010	Accounts assistant	XYZ Bio-chemicals Ltd. Managed data entry and all account documents.

| Oct 2010 to date | Accountant | ABC Chemicals Ltd.

Managing accounts with two assistants. |

or

March 2010 to date	Sales Manager	Beauty Soaps Ltd., Mumbai.
Aug 2007 to Feb 2010	Sales Supervisor	
June 2003 to July 2007	Salesman	A-one Soaps & Detergents (Pr) Ltd., Thane.
April 2001 to May 2003	Shop assistant	Everyday Needs General Store, Thane.

Voluntary Work Done

Most people would think that voluntary work is not work because a person is not paid to do it. Therefore, they would avoid including it in the CV. Have you realised how voluntary work does not only help the community but also hones personal skills? Teaching street children to read and write in the evening would certainly change the outlook of the children, but it would also prepare you for training jobs at the workplace. In the same way managing events in the society could pave way for managing company meetings and conferences.

quarterly company newsletter. All positive activities help hone personal skills. It would be worthwhile to mention them in the CV. Leave it to the prospective employer to decide if he would like to utilize a particular skill. You could include a brief note about voluntary work. Here are a few samples:

>*I was the editor for the English section of our college newsletter for two years.*
>*I managed the company "Diwali Bash" with the help of two assistants last year.*
>*I motivated all the residents of our housing society to repair the roads within the society and provide security at the entrance.*
>*I am the President of the Parents & Teachers Association of my son's school.*

Membership In Professional Associations

professional organizations. However, it is generally felt that it is an asset to be a member of such an

event of a situation that is not very clear a person could always revert to the professional association for

it would be to one's advantage to mention such details in the CV. For example:

>*I am a member of the Computer Users Association.*
>*I am a member of the State Bar Association.*

Research and Development

technology, medicine, different sciences and even law where people make in-depth studies of situations

people could always include such information in the CV. Attendance and participation at technical seminars also helps hone personal skills and these too could be included in the CV when appropriate.

Computer Skills
Computers have been in existence for long, but their popularity because of easy availability at a reasonable price is barely two decades old. Many of the elder generation are still not versed with

being developed each successive year making life easier. Since many technical professions require knowledge of certain software it is necessary that the prospective employer must know about your

make all the difference in getting a job.

Language Skills
Since the whole world is now a global village and businessmen and professionals move from one country to another it is an advantage if a person knows several languages. When a job requires a person to work in several localities around the world it would be necessary to clearly indicate the languages a person can speak or write. In appreciation of this requirement most business schools are encouraging

Additional Information
What other information would be of interest to a prospective employer? In most of the developed countries it is customary to just write one's name and address on the top of the CV. In India and some other countries it is necessary to mention father's name, age or date of birth, marital status, children, if any.

Many employers also want to know if the applicant has a personal vehicle like a scooter, motorcycle or car. In that case they would want to know if one has a valid driving license. Jobs that require a person to travel abroad it would be necessary to have a valid passport and sometimes a valid international driving license. Since some jobs could be hazardous appropriate insurance cover would also be necessary. Even in normal situations all employers desire that a person must have personal health insurance when travelling to other countries. Since situations would vary from one person to another a person could include information, as desirable under the circumstances.

References
The majority of people are not in favour of including references of important people in the CV. These are usually not called for in the developed countries. Some employers ask for them for jobs at lower levels where they would like to be sure that the applicant is an honest, hardworking person, and would not leave without giving prior notice.

situations the parents' friends can be useful. The family doctor is another person who would know a person reasonably well. Old teachers and professors could also be helpful if you have a good relationship with them.

When references are required write the name, position, address and the telephone or mobile number of two persons. Do inform them that the prospective employer could call them to ask about you.

Preparing the CV

a good impression. The reader must be tempted to read through it. It must be brief but must cover the essentials. Just as a sales brochure tempts a person to buy a product, the CV should gently persuade the prospective employer to call the applicant for an interview. This is possible when the CV is clear, concise, convincing and well presented.

When a salesman sells a product he presents the best features that would attract the customer. In the same way, when a person is selling his services, the best in the person must be highlighted. When it is newcomers seeking a job it is their academic background, professional training and experience gained through extra-curricular activities and voluntary service that is important. For those who are already working and changing jobs the work history is important. Here is a suggested sequence of sections for CVs for those who are setting out on a career, or those already serving for long:

CV in early stages of career:	CV after having worked for some time:
Name	*Name*
Contact Information	*Contact Information*
Career Objective	*Career Objective*
Key Strengths	*Key Skills*
Education and Training	*Important Achievements*
Achievements	*Work History*
Leadership	*Voluntary Work*
Scholarships and Awards	*Professional Associations*
Work Experience	*Publications*
Voluntary Work	*Computer Skills*
Professional Associations	*Languages*
Publications	*Education and Training*
Computer Skills	*Additional Information*
Languages	
Additional Information	

Just as clothes make a person stand out, the way a CV is typed and presented is the most important part of writing a CV. It is more essential than the contents of the CV. To ensure that it meets these requirements, here are a few suggestions:

> To type the CV on the computer use Arial or Times New Roman fonts. The size of the font could be 11 or 12 for Arial and 12 for Times New Roman. Write consistently without changing the size of the font.

Writing about Yourself

The name should be in font of size 16 or 18. Never use fancy font. To highlight headings use capitals or bold font.

Restrict the size of the CV to 2 A4 size pages. If you have little to write cut it down to one page. A technical CV with details could be a maximum of three pages. Have a minimum of 2.5 cms margins on the left and right and 2.0 cms on the top of the page.

the CV. A paragraph should not be more than four lines.

Check spellings and grammar. Wrong spellings and poorly written sentences convey a wrong representation of a person. Write short sentences with a maximum of 15 words.

and if they are wrong or exaggerated they could get the person into serious trouble.

Print the CV on good quality white paper. Avoid fancy paper, fancy fonts, logos or printing in colour. Print in black only.

Always keep spare copies at hand.

If the CV is to be sent through email take as much care in preparing it as you would to send a

Sending the CV

The CV must be sent along with a cover letter addressed to the prospective employer. Since letter writing is in itself special to attain the purpose it is intended for, it will be taken up along with other forms of letters used in business and professional life. Send the letter and the CV in an appropriately addressed enveloped that should appear inviting, and not over-stuffed for its size.

Writing a letter is one of the most popular forms of communication in business and professional life. Those who can do it well are more effective than those who are average. Letter writing is taught in school as a part of learning languages, but few students take it seriously because they lack the vision that someday effective letter writing would form an important part of their career.

Letters are written to cope with a variety of situations. It could be as simple as informing a friend that you would call on him this weekend when you visit the town, or as complex as one being written by a businessman threatening a person that he would take him to court for not paying the amount overdue from him. While some letters are simple to write there are many that require special effort to make them convincing. In general there are three principal kinds of letters:

1. **Letters that provide some information.** These include the informal letters people write to each other to keep in touch, convey greetings and good news, provide information about incoming events or products being launched, and usually end with the request to the recipient to respond in some way.
2. **Letters that aim to persuade someone.** These letters could be like the ones students write from college to the parents seeking an additional allowance to meet a special expense, or from the company sales manager seeking to sell something to a prospective customer.
3. **Letters which are unpleasant to write.** These letters include refusing an employee to go on leave, breaking bad news like an accident or death, and sometimes having to tell an employee that his services would no longer be required at the workplace.

Irrespective whether a letter is informal or formal, it is constituted of several parts put together depending upon need. Each of these parts can be adapted as required in a particular situation. It is important that the person writing the letter must understand the function and necessity of each part of the letter. Let us look at each part of the letter.

1. **Heading.** The heading of the letter aims at telling who has written the letter and what are his or her contact details like address, telephone number or email ID. This is usually written on the top right side of the paper. Many government agencies provide this information on the top left side of the paper. If you are using a printed letterhead that has this information already printed on it, it would not be necessary to rewrite it. In an informal letter it is optional whether the sender desires to give this detail. Here are a few samples:

50, Subhash Road,

or

From:
Chief Labour Commissioner,
ShramBhawan,
Mall Road,
Shimla, H.P.

or

Industrial Products Ltd.

Tel: 0134 123456, 123789 Fax: 0134 123 790

2. **Date.** Just below the heading or the letterhead the date of writing the letter is mentioned. This provides useful information to the recipient because he might like to connect it with the matter

These sounds are all right to hear, but not to write. Write the year complete.

Wrong:	Right:
June 20th, 2013	June 20, 2013
March 2nd, 2013	March 2, 2013
03-08-2013	August 3, 2013

3. **Address of the recipient.** This includes the name, position, name of the company and the complete address. This is placed on the left side of the page at a lower level of the date. In an informal personal letter this part is usually omitted. This could be written as follows;

M/s Satish Book Store,

Mall Road,

Shimla – 171 001.

There are a few simple rules that must be followed when writing the name and address of the recipient of the letter. These are:

    This address should be the same as would appear on the envelope in which the letter would be sent.

    The title or position should follow the name.

    If the letter is to an individual in a company show his name (and title) followed by the company's name. For example; Mr. Satish Sharma, Proprietor.

    If the address is long and must be carried over to the second line, indent the second line three spaces.

    registered name uses an abbreviation like Co., (Pr), (Pvt), or&. The names of countries,

    street is also numbered, separate out the two numbers with a dash or write clearly: House no: 7, Street no: 4. Do not write 4th street.

Don't use "Care of" in abbreviated form. Don't use "Care of" before a hotel's name if a person is a guest in the hotel. Also do not use "Care of" before a company's name if a person is an employee in the company. It could be used in a special case if a person is temporarily receiving mail at the company address.

4. **Salutation.** This is a greeting at the beginning of a letter. This is written in different forms in various situations. This constitutes of two portions, the honorary title that precedes the name -

bered include the following:

who have not remarried.

or abbreviated as "Sh."

"Sarvshri".

Just as "Reverend" is used in English to address a priest, the Indian adaptation for it is "Swami".

The title or position should appear only in the address, and not in the salutation. It should not be abbreviated.

Please note the right and wrong ways of using the salutation and titles.

Wrong:	Right:
Mr. SomNath, Sr. Ed.	Mr. SomNath, Senior Editor,
Ms. SudhaSwamy, Prin.	Ms. SudhaSwamy, Principal,
Rev. John Burke	The Rev. John Burke
Reverend John Burke	The Reverend John Burke
Dr. I.S. Rana, Ph.D.	I.S. Rana, Ph.D.
Mr. S.B. Singh, Colonel,	Col. S.B. Singh
Mrs. Sadhana Singh, MD (Gynae)	Dr. Sadhana Singh (Gynae)
Sw. Nityananda	Swami Nityananda
Mr. Samuel Smith, Ambassador,	Hon'ble Mr. Samuel Smith,

5. **Subject line.** This is generally introduced by Sub: or Re: followed by the matter, which must be brief and preferably be at the centre to draw immediate attention. Many prefer to underline it or write in bold type.

Sub: Refund of advance for car

or

Re: Refund of advance for car

6. **Body of the letter.** This is the most important part of the letter. This part communicates the message that you are trying to convey. The message would obviously vary in different situations and circumstances. Each time one would need to think how to make it effective. We will look into this matter a little later. There are certain things that every person must remember when writing the body of the letter. These are:

> **Why are you writing the letter?**
> Your letter would be effective if this purpose is achieved.
>
> **Who are you writing to?** The person must accept the message you are conveying in the same spirit as you are writing it.
>
> **What relevant facts support your message?** You must have all the facts in order of their importance, the most important one on the top.
>
> **How would you present the message?** Every person develops a style of writing over a

Once you have the answers to the questions it is time to organize your thoughts and write the

the following in mind:

> **Make the message simple.** The most complex messages can be conveyed in a simple manner so that they can be easily understood.
>
> **Use simple language.** It must be easily understood by the person receiving the message.
>
> **Use short sentences.** Shorter sentences are easily understood. A sentence should not have more than 15 to 20 words.
>
> **Write short paragraphs.** Restrict one item to one paragraph. If there are too many restrict yourself to the important ones. Don't have more than 10 lines to a paragraph.

the draft would need to be checked and edited to make it effective. In making corrections, ask yourself:

> Does the message convey the meaning that I desire to convey?
> Is the message clear, or can it be misinterpreted?
> Can I reduce the number of words and yet have an effective message?
> Are the spellings, grammar, capitalization and punctuation right?
> Will the letter look good when typed on paper?

7. **Closing.** This would be the farewell word or phrase and would vary depending upon whether the letter is personal, formal or informal. In a formal letter that begins with "Dear Sir:" the complimentary close could be "Yours truly" or "Very truly yours". Some prefer "Yours faithfully," "Sincerely" or "Yours sincerely," is written when you know the person well enough to

address him or her by name. It should be used only with individuals and not when the letter is addressed to a company. When writing to a person of authority, the complimentary close would be "Yours respectfully." When writing to someone close you could end with "Affectionately," or "Yours affectionately." Never use trite phrases like "Your obedient servant," or "Seeking your sympathy,"

8. **Signature line.** This would have the sender's name and position typed, and he would sign his

the name typed at end, and the person would sign above it. However, if the letter is a business letter or written on behalf of an organization it would be appropriate to have the name of the company, the person writing it and his position. Here are two examples:

Example 1: Example 2:

Yours sincerely,   Very truly yours,
                                                 For Industrial Equipment Ltd.

Mahesh Sharma

                                                 Mahesh Sharma
                                                 Sales Manager

9. **Reference initials.** These initials indicate who dictated the letter and who typed it. The initials are written below the signature line. For example, if Mahesh Sharma dictated the letter to his

10. **Enclosure notation.** If there are any enclosures with the letter these are mentioned here. If there are no enclosures this part is avoided. Enclosures are mentioned as: Enclosures, Encl: 2

11. **Copy notation.** This part states the names of persons to whom copies of the letter have been endorsed. This part can be eliminated if no copies have been sent. Copies sent can be written

12. **Postscript.** Written as P.S., additional information is written below the copy notation. This part should never be included in a business letter. It is an indication of lack of organization and would create a bad impression in a business letter. A postscript should form a part only of an informal letter.

Chapter 54

Every letter would have some impact upon the person receiving it. The letter-head, the way it is typed and presented, the language and the way the sender has signed it would create an impression when it comes into the hand of the person receiving it. Every sender would desire that his or her letter should be well received otherwise it would not create the correct impression and the attention it deserves.

Have you observed how particular people are about packing gifts with the best of paper, decorating it further with ribbons or name cards? These serve no practical purpose, but add to the value of the gift by expression of extra love and care. These are valued much by the person receiving the gift.

An envelope in which a letter is enclosed when sent by post or through courier serves a purpose similar to the packaging of a gift. It is not suggested that one should use fancy envelopes to send letters. Far from it! It is best to use white business envelopes to mail letters, but the way the address or the name of the sender is written, and also the way the stamp is pasted speak much about the image the

year after year.

Follow these simple rules to ensure that the envelope creates a good impression on the person receiving the letter:

The sender's address should be written either on the top left side or the bottom left side of the envelope. Write the complete address along with the PIN code.

The receiver's address should be written midway between the top and bottom on the right side of the envelope. Ensure that the title, name and address are correctly spelt. Write the PIN code after the name of the city. If the letter is sent through courier or Speed Post, include the telephone or mobile number of the person receiving the letter.

Paste the postage stamp/s on the top right hand corner of the envelope. Paste them straight

sent Air Mail. They might be put aside or returned to the sender.

When using gum to seal an envelope ensure that you do not use excess of it to spill over inside

it whole, creating a bad impression even of the best written letters.

Do not write anything on the back side of the envelope.

Here is a sample envelope correctly addressed and stamped:

	POSTAGE STAMP
78, MadanLal Road, Delhi – 110 006.	47/1, Ring Road, Shimla – 171 001.

Chapter 55

Writing a personal letter is perhaps the easiest form of writing a letter because it is written to relatives, friends and close associates, who have accepted you as you are. Yet all businessmen and professionals would like to give the letter a personal touch of their identity and make it as perfect as possible.

Personal letters are letters that provide information of a person's welfare, family activities, extending invitations, seeking guidance and other similar situations. Over the past few decades the use of the personal letter has reduced considerably because of the use of mobile phone where a person can very conveniently provide this information directly from one person to another. The mobile has also provided the facility of SMS, which is discussed later.

A personal letter does not follow rules; it is written from the heart. It is an expression of a person's feelings and emotions. It could be type-written, hand-written or even be scribbled. It is an expression of feelings between two persons. Here is a sample letter from one friend to another. Much is communicated

> *Dear Rohit:*
> *It is a long time since we met. My company has assigned me some work in Pune. I thought before I return to Delhi, I could take two days leave and spend it with you at Mumbai. We could perhaps relive those days when we were together in college, visiting our favourite eating places, walking at the beach, and updating ourselves of everything that has happened since our last meeting two years ago.*
> *I would be reaching Mumbai by the Air-conditioned Express on Sept 13 evening and proceed to Delhi by Rajdhani Express that leaves on Sept 15. I do hope that it will not bother you much, or unduly disturb your work schedule.*
> *More when we meet, with best wishes,*
> *Sincerely,*   *Sudhanshu*

Despite the extensive use of the mobile phone it is still necessary to write personal letters inviting relatives and friends to weddings or other special functions in the family. It is common practice to write an advance letter informing of a function that is due at a later time, and formal invitations would be sent only shortly before the occasion. In the meantime the advance letter gives the invitees an opportunity to adjust work and make appropriate reservations for to and fro travel. It also gives the hosts an opportunity to make suitable arrangements for the guests. Here is a sample letter:

> *My dear VK:*
>
> *We would be grateful if you and the family can join us on all the occasions. A formal invitation would be sent two weeks before the wedding. I am informing you in advance to enable you to make appropriate travel reservations, and also to inform me so that we can receive you and make arrangements for your comfortable stay during your visit.*
> *With regards and best wishes,*
> *Sincerely,*   *Satish*

There are innumerable occasions when personal letters are written by businessmen and professionals to their suppliers, customers and clients. Organizations celebrate the anniversary of the founding day. Schools and college invite the alumni. Many invite the visiting faculty. Businessmen make special offers through personal letters. Many send greetings through personal letters to customers on their birthdays and wedding anniversaries. These letters are not strictly personal because they are written with the purpose of business or professional goodwill. When writing such letters ensure the following:

The name of the person is correctly spelt.
The letter is short, simple and conveys the message correctly.
The letter bears the sender's signature.
The letter is sent to the correct address and reaches at the right time.

Chapter 56

A cover letter is an explanatory letter sent with an enclosure. In business and professional work there could be a variety of enclosures that need to be sent every day at the workplace. A popular use of a cover letter is in forwarding one's CV to a prospective employer. Since this can make all the difference between being called for a job interview, or be ignored, we would especially look at this aspect of a cover letter. The other uses are similar and one could easily adapt a cover letter in such situations.

A cover letter is very much like the beautiful packaging we see every day for products sold in the market. The packaging enhances product visibility and sale though in itself it might appear to have no use. We could also liken a cover letter to the beautiful wrapper we put on a gift for the excitement and thrill it provides to the recipient. It adds to the attractiveness of the gift and makes it special. In the same way a cover letter serves as the packaging of the services you are offering to a prospective employer. Do not overlook that the person receiving your job application is a busy person. He or she would be led to

Just as the packaging enhances the value and sells a product, the cover letter and the CV would help sell your services.

Understanding the Potential Employer

work to his satisfaction and also make a living out of the services they offer. We must understand that it is

When a potential employer advertises to seek personnel, or sends out a team to scout for talent in some of the leading colleges, he is very clear about the kind of work he needs done. He knows what skills and abilities he is looking for and makes a great effort to match the same with the prospective employees

role at the workplace. If the potential employee can understand the basic skills and abilities desired by the employer, and can offer them, then a good cover letter can quickly bridge the gap between the employer and the potential employee.

Why A Cover Letter?
The alternative to a cover letter is a little note saying: "
advertised," followed by your name and signature. How does it sound to the ears? Does it encourage a

you for an interview? In the normal circumstances the chances of being called are slim despite the skills and abilities that you might possess.

It is interesting to observe that 4 out of every 10 prospective employers desire that there should be a proper cover letter with the CV, 3 confess that they are too busy to read another letter, and the other 3 have mixed feelings about it. Half of these suggest that the letter should be a half page letter, 2 feel that

a CV is a cold, matter of fact document. The letter enhances the value of the CV by highlighting how you look at your skills and abilities, and how you connect them with the skills desired by the employer. The letter simply adds life to a usually dull document and encourages the employer to invite you for an interview.

Writing the Cover Letter

Before you can get down to writing the cover letter you must be clear on certain issues. You must have answers to important questions:

      Who do you address the letter to?
      How should you address the person you are writing to?
      What skills and abilities is the prospective employer looking for?
      How do your skills and abilities match with those required by the employer?
      What would be the appropriate length for the letter?

whom is the application to be sent. It has been observed that more than half the applications are sent to the wrong persons. One out of every four address the letter: To whom it may concern. It should best be sent to the advertiser, or if only the name of the organization is given, it could be addressed to the Director, Human Resources. In many advertisements the name of the person issuing the advertisement is given. If an advertising code is mentioned then it must be mentioned on the cover letter and also on the envelope in which the letter and the CV is sent.

The next question is: How should you address the person you are writing to? When the name of the person issuing the advertisement is known, the letter could be addressed: Dear Mr. Sharma: or Dear Ms. Joshi: When the names are not known it is best to write: Dear Sir or Madam: Some prefer to address: Dear Hiring Manager: It is best to avoid writing: To whom it may concern, as it is too impersonal and would not get the desired attention sought by the applicant.

The next step in writing the letter is to mention the job you are applying for, and also the source of information that the company has need for a person in a particular position. This should be restricted to just one or two lines. It could be written as follows:

I am making an application for the position of Personal Secretary, as advertised by you in The Times, dated July 7, 2013.

The next step in writing the letter would be to write the main body of the letter. To do this you

and the abilities the employer desires and also how your skills match with those desired by him. This information would vary with every position and the kind of work being done by the hiring organization. In the immediate case the employer is seeking a Personal Secretary, possibly for a Manager, and would

maintaining the dignity of the position through good etiquette and manners. The person must be able to

When writing the main body of the letter, you will do well to remember the writing rules suggested by George Orwell:

> Never use a long word where a short one will do.
>
> If it is possible to cut a word out, always cut it out.
>
> Never use the passive voice (e.g. "Bones are liked by dogs.") where you can use the active voice ("Dogs like bones.")
>
> Never use jargon if you can think of an everyday equivalent.

One must also remember that in the main body of the letter the information must come in the following order:

> Why you are interested in the position?
>
> What attracts you to the organization you are applying to?
>
> What are your strengths?
>
> How these are related to what the job requires?
>
> When you could be available for a personal interview?

The main body of the letter could be written as follows:

working as the Personal Secretary to the proprietor of a company that distributes paints at the state level. I would now like to serve a larger organization where I can develop and use my full

the country.

I would be available for a personal interview at your convenience. My mobile number is: 12345 67890. If found suitable for the position I could join in 15 days from the day I receive the appointment letter.

The cover letter must be closed with a respectful closing statement and the complimentary close. When the letter is addressed to a person by name, the complimentary close should be: Sincerely, or Yours sincerely. If the letter begins with Dear Sir or Madam, it could be ended with: Yours faithfully, or Very truly yours,. Here is a sample close for the letter:

Looking forward to a favourable response,

Very truly yours,

Yogesh Sharma

When writing a cover letter with a CV you must remember certain rules that have enhanced the effectiveness of the letter. These simple rules are:

spelling and grammar. Revise it to make it effective.

Make the letter as personal as it can be. This is an effort of your extending a friendly hand towards the prospective employer.

Write the letter on plain white paper of A4 size. Do not use fancy paper. Do not use a fancy personal letterhead. The letter paper must match the paper on which the CV is printed.

a master copy. Paste the dispatch receipt on the letter.

bold letters. Include the sender's name and address on the envelope. Stamp appropriately or send through courier.

An Email Cover Letter

It is possible that a prospective employer might seek the application for a job through email. In that event it would require that the cover letter is written like any other email letter and the CV sent as an attachment to the mail. When forwarding an application through email it would be useful to remember the following observations:

Reading an email is not like reading a normal letter. It is also likely to be sent to the Junk Box in some software applications, and could be missed altogether.

An email cover letter could be written like a normal letter, but care should be taken to write simple sentences in short paragraphs, each paragraph covering one point. Have one-line spacing between paragraphs.

a person.

It would be advisable to follow the email cover letter and CV with a hard copy sent through post or courier.

Some Popular Opening Lines

you could adapt to your own situation and circumstances:

I enclose my CV for the position of ... in your company.

I am making an application for the job advertised by you in The Times.

2013.

I will be qualifying for a B.Tech degree in Mechanical Engineering soon, and would appreciate

I am writing to enquire if you have any vacancy for an accountant.

I am looking for an entry-level position in your Sales Department.

This is in response to your advertisement seeking salesmen in every district in the state.

the CV and also of the cover letter. Follow the general rules of addressing the employer and writing the

A Word of Caution
Every person writing a cover letter with a CV to a prospective employer would like to attain success

would have several options open to him and he would select one that is most suitable from his point of

letter or the CV is ineffective. Review them by all means, but do not let the lack of response from the prospective employer discourage you. Perhaps still greater opportunities await you.

Cover Letters in Other Situations
Writing a cover letter to be sent with a CV is just one situation. Special emphasis has been given to this particular situation because getting a call for an interview depends upon it. There will be innumerable situations when cover letters will have to be sent with trade promotions and enquiries, forwarding invoices and accounts, inviting tenders and quotations from suppliers, sending details of meetings or forwarding a project report or a typescript to a publisher. In each case the body of the letter would be different, but the writing style would be similar.

Rules for Writing Effective Cover Letters
Here are a few common rules that you must remember when writing a cover letter:

New Roman in size 12 pt.

As far as possible address letters to individuals or to positions. Write generally only when you are not aware of the details of the recipient.

view. Do not over-praise your work or achievements. Do not overdo the use of "I". Check

Always end the letter with a request for some kind of action.

Print the letter on good quality white paper. Mail it appropriately to the concerned person.

Do not forget to attach the principal document.

Chapter 52

Every business and profession would require a variety of letters to be written. Many letters are written each day in several organizations. In others there is an occasional need to write a letter. There is no getting away from writing them. Since every letter is a form of communication from one to the other, its effectiveness would depend upon how well it is drafted and presented. The matter of each letter would depend upon the situation. Let us look at some of the common situations.

Letter of Acknowledgement

Whenever someone writes to another, there is a suggested need for action. Since everyone is slow at taking decisions, it might not be possible to react to a letter immediately. Good businessmen respond immediately. However, if the letter or any other form of communication is not acted upon but acknowledged immediately, the sender appreciates that the communication has been received and would be attended to soon. This is a sure way to maintain good relationships and promote business.

Several occasions require that a letter of acknowledgement be sent. Here are a few common situations:

When you are invited to a function or a party.
When someone makes a special sales offer to you.
When you are appointed to take up a job.
When you are given a special honour.

A letter of acknowledgement would necessarily be short and to the point. Here are a few samples for different occasions:

Acknowledging an invitation to a function:

My wife and I are grateful for your kind invitation to join at the Annual Day Celebrations of your school at 4.00 p.m. on September 15, 2013. We will be pleased to be present on the occasion.

Wishing the function all success,

Acknowledging an offer from the General Manager of a hotel to become a premium customer by availing of certain facilities at special rates:

Thank you for your letter dated July 7, 2013, making a special offer of using certain facilities in the hotel.

I must compliment you for making a very attractive offer. I would certainly like to avail of the special offer, but before I do so I would like to share the information with my wife because some of the items pertain to the Ladies Parlour in your hotel. She is presently out of station for a week. I would revert back to you with my cheque on her return.

Thanking you in the meantime,

Acknowledging an offer for a job:

I had explained to you during the interview that I would need to give 15 days' notice to my present employer before I join your company. I will be pleased to join on October 15, 2013.

With best wishes,

Acknowledging a special honour:

invited me to receive an award on the occasion of Teacher's Day.

I will be pleased to be present at 5.00 p.m. on September 5, 2013, at the auditorium of the Nav Jyoti School.

With best wishes,

Thank you for your kind reminder. I am aware that the deadline to submit my article for the special issue of your magazine is July 10, 2013. The article is almost ready. I have only to polish it a little before I forward it to you well before the deadline.

With best wishes,

Letter of Acceptance

A letter of acceptance is another form of a letter of acknowledgement. Through a letter of acceptance a person acknowledges what is being offered. It could be a job, an assignment to do something, an invitation, or something similar. The sample letters of acknowledgement can also be described as letters of acceptance. When writing a letter of acceptance, remember the following simple rules:

Respond promptly. There is always an element of urgency in an offer. Writing immediately

Express appreciation. Any good offer is worthy of appreciation. A line of appreciation immediately draws the attention of the reader to what follows.

Repeat the offer. In a letter of acceptance one must repeat what you understand is being offered to you. This is a feedback to the person making the offer assuring him or her that you have understood the communication.

you might not have understood. Some words and phrases could be interpreted in more than one way.

Suggest amendments, if necessary. Some offers might not be acceptable in the form they are presented. A small amendment could make it acceptable.

Be brief and to the point. Let the message be as short and clear as would convey the meaning convincingly.

Writing A Letter Declining An Offer

On many occasions it is not possible to accept an offer, and therefore you need to decline the offer. Just because an offer does not interest you it should not mean that you ignore or avoid acknowledging

maintain good relationships. Do not overlook that the offer might not interest you today, but it might in the near future. In that circumstance it is good relationships that one generates through effective communication that help a person. You would need to write a letter declining an offer in the following situations:

An offer of a job. You might have applied for a job earlier and you were not invited to take it up for different reasons. The offer has come now when you have already taken up another job that you like. A letter declining the offer would help maintain a good relationship with the prospective employer.

An offer from a hotel offering premium facilities. You would not like to subscribe to them because you have to move to another place from where it would not suit you to use the facilities. A letter declining the offer would help maintain good relationships.

An offer for a product that you already have. You would not need the new brand even though it is offered with a special discount. It would be simple courtesy to decline the offer stating your reason for it.

Other situations. It is common to receive offers for things that you do not require, or membership into organisations that you are not inclined towards for various reasons. A simple letter would generate goodwill and good relationships.

When writing a letter, declining an offer the following simple rules must be observed:

Express appreciation. When someone is offering something of value it must be appreciated even if we do not need it.

State reasons for declining the offer. State correct facts. Every person is open to reasoning. He or she will understand your circumstances.

Write courteously. A person wonders when a good offer is refused. It could be misunderstood. When you write courteously the person making the offer would understand and accept the refusal with a positive attitude.

Do not apologise. You do not have to be apologetic because your circumstances do not permit you to accept an offer irrespective of how generous it might be. Every person has the right to live the way he or she desires to, and one should not apologize for it. All that is required is a gracious "thank you".

Here is a sample letter declining an offer for a job. It could be adapted for writing letters in similar circumstances.

I am very grateful to you for your offer of the position of Works Supervisor for which I had made an application several months ago.

It would have been a pleasure to work for your esteemed organization, but I regret that I cannot accept the offer because I took up another job since I did not hear from you. I have signed a contract for working with my current employers for working at least for two years.

I appreciate your kind offer and would revert back to you in the event I am available to serve in your organisation.

Thanking you, with best wishes,

Besides the business letters that we have considered there are several other kinds of letters that need special attention. These are discussed under appropriate headings in different sections of this book.

Chapter 58

A follow-up is an activity carried out to check or further develop earlier work. It is a method to build up on both the successes and failures experienced earlier. All businesses and professions aim at providing products and services to people. In a competitive environment people are continuously making persistent

letter is a positive step in developing and maintaining good relationships.

A salesperson visits a new town in the hope of appointing a local distributor to sell to local retailers and meets three prospective persons who are doing similar work already. He spends substantial time meeting and talking to them about his line of products, and also to understand how well each could

keeps the possibilities of growth open.

Another salesperson goes out to sell an X-ray machine to a hospital. He meets the Hospital Superintendent who is generous to give him time to talk and discuss the proposal, but expresses his inability to buy the machine because the management is in favour of buying the machine from another vendor. Does the salesperson return home dejected at having lost a sale? No! He might have lost the sale but he would not like to lose on the relationship he has built with the Hospital Superintendent. He knows that good relationships mean good business. There would be other needs and chances. He would strengthen the relationship with a follow-up letter.

Balakrishnan was invited to an interview by a company for the selection of "management trainees". The interview was conducted by the HR Director, who discussed a variety of issues with the candidates. The results of the selection were held back for a future date. Balakrishnan was impressed with the way he was treated. On return home he was not sure whether he would be selected, but he did feel that he must thank the Director for the courtesy extended to him. This would best be done with a follow-up letter soon after the interview.

Success comes from persistent effort. A follow-up letter is part of this exercise. It does not take long to write a follow-up letter. Yet it can make all the difference. It can convert what might have been a defeat into a success. An expression of one's feelings to another would touch every heart. In each case the situations would be different and would need appropriate action. The person writing the letter would have to choose appropriate words each time, but there are certain common factors that must be remembered when writing a follow-up letter. These are:

Expression of gratitude. Every follow-up letter must convey gratitude for the time and courtesy that another person has given as a part of his business or professional activity. Always remember that he had the option to refuse it, but he gave you the opportunity willingly.

Sincerity of expression. Every follow-up letter must convey a feeling of sincerity. The words must come from the heart. When they come from the heart they touch the heart of the person receiving the letter. It is sincerity that helps build and strengthen relationships.

Convey a positive reaction. It becomes easy to convey a positive reaction when a person looks at every situation with an open and positive mind. A positive attitude is infectious and the receiver of the letter immediately catches on to it.

Be brief and to the point. Busy people have little time and when going through their mail have the tendency to put aside long letters for later reading. The short letters are read immediately.

Write immediately. The follow-up letter must be written at the earliest. It would lose its importance if the person was to receive it after several days when he has already forgotten the occasion. If you write email, follow it with a hard copy through post.

Let us now consider how a person could tackle the situation under different circumstances. We will look at the three situations described above a little more closely.

Interviewing Prospective Distributors
When the salesperson visited the new town to seek an appropriate distributor he would have the consent

possibly best candidates and then meet them. There would only be one distributor, but he interviews three because he is not sure who the best is. In future it might be necessary to shift work from one to another. In all likelihood the Area Sales Manager would accept the salesperson's recommendations, but might like to check each party personally before issuing a letter of appointment, which would depend upon his workload and availability to visit the town. In the meantime a follow-up letter from

appointment is made. A sample letter, which could be the same for all of the three prospects, but written individually with their names could be as follows:

It was a pleasure to meet you when I was in your town in connection with the appointment of a distributor for our products. I am grateful for the information you shared with me.

On my return I have shared my impressions with our Area Sales Manager who would like to meet you soon. I will inform you before we visit you.

Looking forward to meet you again, with best wishes,

After A Failed Sale
When the Superintendent of the hospital expressed his inability to buy the X-ray machine offered by the salesperson, it was not the end of business. You might have the best product with the most competitive price tag, but there are several factors that go into making a sale. Some situations cannot be easily

in building good relationships to promote business in the future. A sample letter to the Superintendent could be as follows:

I am very grateful to you for having given your valuable time despite your very busy schedule. It was a pleasure meeting you.

I can understand your constraints when the hospital management has already decided to purchase a machine of their choice. We have a wide range of medical equipment that meets international standards. Please do not hesitate to get in touch with me for your future requirements. I can assure you the best quality at most competitive prices. I am always available

With best wishes,

After An Interview

Balakrishnan could easily have waited for the company to write to him if he was selected as a management-trainee, but he felt that the conversation he had with the HR Director of the company was a unique experience. The manner in which all the candidates were received and treated spoke highly of the practices of the company. He felt that he must share these feelings through a follow-up letter addressed to the Director.

A sample letter could be as follows:

I am grateful that I got the opportunity to converse with you during the interview for management-trainees for your company.

I appreciate that the purpose of the interview is to seek the best persons who can help take forward the business of the company. I answered your questions to the best of my ability, but my conversation with you was a learning experience for me on building ideal relations at the workplace. The people working for such an organization are truly blessed.

I must also convey my gratitude to your staff for receiving all the candidates courteously and offering assistance, which truly conveys the message of the best business practices adopted by your organization. I will consider myself fortunate to work in such a positive environment.

With regards,

Other Situations

You will appreciate from the three samples given above that throughout the purpose of the follow-up letters were to convey gratitude with sincerity. They also express a positive attitude of the person writing the letters. The message becomes clear to the person receiving the letter. When the person looks at situations with a positive outlook, he or she would be an asset to the organization and to the society.

In everyday business and professional life there would be many occasions when people are touched with special care and kindness. A short follow-up letter, or just a note, can do wonders in cementing relationships on these occasions. Many businessmen and professionals have a small card printed to their name and follow-up on their visits with a small hand-written message inside to convey a distinct message:

Dear Mr. Rohit:

It was a great pleasure to spend more than an hour with you during my visit to Delhi. I was impressed with the excellent work you are doing. Please keep up with it. It is our partnership with people like you that gives strength to our company.

With regards,

Sincerely,

Aditya

There is magic in writing follow-up letters. Write them and feel the difference. You will add to the effectiveness of your activities.

Chapter 59

In business and professional life a person needs to sell oneself through new ideas, products and services. Selling seems easy, but it is not. To sell, one needs to be persuasive. This has been discussed earlier. One persuades another through reasoning and argument. It is necessary to be persistent without being aggressive or offensive. One must speak and write convincingly.

When speaking a person uses the voice accompanied with appropriate body language to appeal to a person's feelings and emotions. This helps persuade the person to do something. Salesmen are also known to use deception as a tool to sell. One cannot use these methods when writing a letter. The options

strength to what they write. That is not possible for an average businessman or a professional. They must write persuasively using their own abilities.

When writing the principal method to persuade a person is to use logic and reasoning. It becomes

own beliefs and it is only through reason that one would step out of the comfort zone to experiment as desired by the persuasive tactics of the other person. A person would also need to have good writing skills to convey a message persuasively. Just as an effective salesman "uses the gift of the gab" to sell, a writer will need writing skills to persuade another.

How should a salesman selling a popular food supplement write a follow-up letter to the catering head in a school where 1000 children drink milk every morning using another brand of food supplement? The changeover of brand would mean good business to the salesman's company. **Here is a sample letter:**

Dear Mr. Khanna:
Thank you for your time and courtesy when I visited you yesterday.
I trust that you must have considered the advantages of using our brand X against the brand Y you are currently using as a food supplement served with milk each morning to the children in your hostel.

For your convenience I would like to repeat:

1. *That the formula of our brand X is superior to brand Y in that it not only strengthens the bone structure, but also has a marked effect upon the growth and memory of children, making the learning process effective.*
2. *That the bulk institutional pack specially created for institutions like yours makes the brand X*

3. *That our manufacturing schedules are such as to make the brand X available throughout the year.*

Writing Persuasive Letters

I look forward to a favourable response from you. Thank you,
Yours sincerely,
R.C. Sharma
Sales Supervisor

You will observe that the writer has in a short, readable letter repeated that the product is superior, cheaper and available throughout the year. These points are important to the prospective purchaser.

A common problem with many business houses and professionals is to recover past dues from customers and clients. They would not like to offend the debtors, or lose their business but they know that getting back what is due to them is important. How should such people be persuaded to pay? Here is a sample letter:

Subject: Outstanding balance in our accounts

I am pained to observe that despite persistent reminders by our accounts department there is a large amount payable by you for a long time. I am writing to draw your kind attention to it.

You will appreciate that as a business house we are very competitive. Our margins do not permit us such credit facilities. Please arrange to have the account settled within the next week.

We value your business and our past relationships. Please do not stretch matters to compel us to use legal options.

Seeking your cooperation and favourable response, with best wishes,

Yours sincerely,

In this letter the writer has courteously appreciated the business relationship with the other party but made it clear that extended payments are not acceptable. The letter has also courteously threatened

One learns through experience to write appropriate letters.

Chapter 60

Everyone has a right to receive value for money. When a person is denied this a complaint emerges. Millions of complaints emerge every day because of faulty products and services. If one were to overlook them it would lead to anger and frustration. At the workplace overlooked complaints could result in unnecessary expenses and losses.

The complaint could pertain to a faulty telephone line, equipment not serviced properly, items over-priced or under-supplied, a service not provided honestly or a whole lot of other things that we experience every day. It is normal to express such a situation verbally directly or over the phone. This rarely works unless the service provider is serious about his work. In that event a written complaint must be sent either through email where such facilities are available or as a letter of complaint sent through post.

Name of the complainant. The name and address of the complainant must be clearly

get back to you.

Telephone and mobile number. These help a person to locate the complainant and the point of complaint quickly to address the complaint.

Name of the service provider. A complainant must be sure that he or she is complaining to the correct person. Many complaints remain unattended because they are addressed to the wrong people.

Status of complaint. What is the nature of complaint? If some equipment has gone out of order, is it under a warranty? Do you have proof of purchase? When did you buy it? From whom? Is the warranty valid? Mentioning these facts helps the service provider to address the complaint quickly.

Problems with utilities. When services like electricity, water supply or telephone are involved it would be necessary to have a bill handy to identify the status of your right to complain.

Follow-up on the complaint. Some complaints are attended to immediately, but not addressed completely because of lack of spares or staff. These will require a follow-up until the complaint is satisfactorily addressed.

Closure report. Once the complaint is fully addressed, the service provider will seek a closure report in writing.

on record until such time that the complaint is not fully addressed. In many cases it would be necessary to submit a complaint in writing directly or through email where such facilities are available. A letter of complaint must be simple and short. Here is a sample letter written by a company on its letterhead to the Electricity Supply Co. about a damaged electricity meter:

Electricity Supply Co.
Raja Road,
Raipur.

Dear Sir:

Replacement of damaged meter

us that the meter has burnt out because of lightning, and would require to be replaced.
   No further action has been taken since then. Please arrange to have the meter replaced at the earliest. Please also note that in the event the meter is not replaced immediately, and we use unmetered supply, we will be liable to pay you on the basis of average daily consumption made by us during the last three months.
   We seek your cooperation and an early replacement of the meter. Thank you.

Yours faithfully,

Manager

department. Such complaints are common in the accounts department. Here is a sample letter drawing the attention of the department to an unpaid travel bill:

Subject: Reimbursement of Travel Expenses
I had submitted details of travel expenses incurred on company account in writing to you last

have not been reimbursed to me till date. Could I please request that the same be reimbursed to me soon?
   I will be grateful for your early action. Thank you.

the person you have complained against again. Seek that your complaint be corrected, and not that the person be unnecessarily punished. Even in a complaint be polite. Your problem will be sorted out faster.

Chapter 61

Since good and bad are a part of life and it is as applicable at the workplace as it is at home or in the society, it becomes necessary to learn how to convey unpleasant news.

What would constitute unpleasant news? Any message that is not likeable or feels unfriendly could of the common ones include:

>   Not being permitted to go on leave.
>   Not promoting an old employee to a higher position.
>   Not allowing a desired advance or loan.
>   Not giving an increment in salary.
>   Transferring an employee to a place where he would live without his family.
>   Reprimanding a person for a sexual harassment complaint.
>   Reporting an accident of an employee to the family.
>   Reporting the death of an employee to the family.
>   Terminating the services of an employee.

You will observe that to the concerned person none of these situations are likeable or pleasant. Conveying any one of them would appear to be an unfriendly act. When conveying such a message verbally, one can take the advantage of body language conveyed through a variety of facial and body gestures. The person can convey the news gently and could act reassuringly. This is not possible in a written message. It has to be written in plain, cold words. The situation cannot be altered. The immediate problem before the person writing the message is how to soften the blow when the hard reality reaches the person.

When writing a letter conveying an unpleasant message it would be worthwhile to take the following steps to take away a part of the sting from the feeling of hurt in the person receiving the message:

>   **Convey the message straight**. The person receiving the communication wants to know the reality. Do not try to bury the bad news with words. A straight message hits hard. If you look at it rationally any unpleasant news would hit hard. Let the person know it and gradually come into grips with it.
>
>   **Adopt a tone of sympathy**. You cannot change the situation. But you can always be sympathetic when conveying the message. The tone of the letter will convey your attitude in a particular situation. A sympathetic attitude lessens the intensity of the blow. The person appreciates that it is beyond your control.

Choose words carefully

. A person would like to know why he was denied leave or a promotion. There would obviously be valid reasons for such things. If these can be communicated to the person there will be lesser heartburn.

Convey one thing in one paragraph. Breaking up ideas into paragraphs enhances the clarity of the message. The reader can understand the facts better.

Suggest a solution, if possible. Many times a situation arises because of the person's own fault. When it can be corrected suggest how it can be done. Perhaps he could review his earlier

Close with a positive note. We cannot change the hard facts of life. Yet no calamity is so large that it will never be forgotten. Life has to go on. When you end the letter with a positive note, you would have started the healing process.

Writing the Letter

We have just observed that there could be a variety of causes for the unpleasantness that needs to be

adapted in different situations. There could be some similarities, but invariably each situation would be unique because it pertains to individuals. In drafting the letter think of words and terms that would make it easy for the reader to accept the reality of the situation. This isn't easy. However, it is a part of work and the task must be performed. Let us consider how some of the situations could be tackled when writing the letter.

Situation: Not being permitted to go on leave:

We regret that it would not be possible to grant you leave for the period you have desired in your application.

We appreciate this would be disappointing to you, but as you are aware a team from the

everyone.

If you can adjust your leave schedule to dates after the team completes its inspection, please write a new application with revised dates for favourable consideration.

With best wishes,

Read the letter once again and observe how an effort is made to soften the blow of refusing leave, explaining the reason for it and also suggesting a solution. Let us consider another situation where an

given to a younger newcomer.

We are sorry that despite your vast experience and service in our company your application for the position of Brand Manager could not be accepted, and the position given to a new person.

The Board was looking for a person with special skills because it is intended to extend the brand to a variety of new products. Knowledge pertaining to these products was essential for the position.

The Board appreciates your commitment and contribution to the progress of the company.

With best wishes,

situation where the work of a senior person had to be overlooked to accommodate a new person who had special skills to support him. Let us look at another situation where a person is transferred to a new place where he would have to live without his family.

You have been selected to lead a team of four persons to Raipur where the company is putting up

records, obtaining permissions and completing formalities on behalf of the company. This could take more than three months.

Unfortunately, the circumstances would not permit you to take your family with you. Arrangements are being made for your stay and that of your team at Raipur during this period. A company car will also be at your disposal. Each team member would also get an allowance for staying away from home. Two team members can visit their homes on weekends once every fortnight.

The relevant documents pertaining to this assignment are being assembled for your convenience.

With best wishes,

In this particular situation, the letter is a mixture of pleasant and unpleasant news. Whereas the

followed it with the unpleasant news of having to stay away from the family. This would cause hardship to him and the family. It is some relief that the assignment is most likely for three months, or a little more. It is also heartwarming that it would be possible to spend the weekend at home once a fortnight.

particularly the workplace. It could be a complaint of pilferage, misuse of company assets or something more serious like sexual harassment. These have to be stopped immediately. Here is a sample letter written to a person on a complaint for sexual harassment:

I am directed by the HR Director to draw your attention to a complaint of sexual harassment against you.

You will appreciate that this is a very serious matter. The company has very strict rules about such complaints and could lead to termination of your job and also a complaint to the police.

the concerned person. Since these instances lead to ugly publicity the company would like to close the matter at the earliest.

Please respond urgently,

You will observe that the language of the letter is simple and yet to the point mincing no words that legal action is imminent in such cases. However, taking a compassionate view he has suggested how the problem can be resolved.

In yet another situation when an accident takes place at the workplace and the injured employee is rushed to the hospital the circumstances can always be misunderstood by the family. No family likes to accept that the injured person could have been at fault. They will contend that the fault was with the machine or elsewhere, and certainly not with the injured family member. How does one communicate with the family in writing in such a situation? Here is a sample letter:

Dear Mrs. Sharma:

It is unfortunate that Mr. Kailash Sharma met with an accident in the factory. Although complete care is taken and all workers trained to maintain high safety standards in the factory, sometimes one is a victim of the act of God.

We appreciate that Mr. Sharma will have to be in hospital for some days. As per company policy all medical bills will be borne by the company. Even when Mr. Sharma recuperates at home he will be duly compensated because all our workers are covered by insurance until such time that he returns to work.

We are sorry for the inconvenience that would be caused to you. Please do not hesitate to get in touch with me if you need any help.

Wishing Mr. Sharma an early recovery,

Yours sincerely,

is to write about the death of an employee. In this situation the family is obviously shattered when the bread-earner dies at the workplace for whatever cause. Such a situation also shakes up the colleagues who have been working with the deceased person over a period. Like other situations this one also requires very special care and correct choice of words. Here is a sample letter:

Dear Mrs. Awasthi:

medical help could reach him. Your loss and that of the family is much greater. We offer our sympathies and condolence to you and the family. We pray that the departed soul may rest in peace, and may God grant strength to the family to bear this irreparable loss.

Instructions have been issued to the Finance Department that all amounts payable to Mr. Awasthi may be accounted for immediately, and a cheque for the amount issued in your name. This would require some documents to be signed by you. A representative from the company would visit you after

With our sympathies,

Yours in grief,
R.C. Sharma
Branch Manager

Observe how the Branch Manager has offered his sympathies and also offered help so that the bereaved family's suffering on the occasion can be reduced. Writing these letters requires the

workplace is to inform a worker that he/she would not be required and therefore the services are

interest of all workers law requires that a person should be given a month's notice before the services are terminated. In situations where an employer feels that the person could cause damage through his presence at the workplace, it is common to ask a person to leave and one month's salary given without asking the person to work during the notice period. Here is a sample of a letter of termination of service of an employee:

Dear Mr. Khanna:

I regret to inform you that the company would not require your services with effect from October 1, 2013.

The terms of employment require that one month's notice be given to you before termination of service. I have instructed the accounts department to give you one month's salary in lieu of the notice period, along with your salary for September. Please do not hesitate to let me know if any other outstanding amount is payable to you.

Wishing you success in your endeavours,

Yours sincerely,
R. P. Sharma
Branch Manager

In another situation the company could be closing down some of its operations and would require reducing the staff accordingly. In such a situation the letter would have to be worded differently. Here is a sample letter:

Dear Mr. Randhawa:

I regret to inform you that the company is closing down its operations in several regions where the sales have not picked up despite all efforts. This will require the company to reduce manpower looking after these operations. Unfortunately, you are one of the persons looking after these regions. The company appreciates the efforts you have made, but sometimes one is left with no choice.

Please take this as one month's notice that your services will no longer be required after November 30, 2013.

I have instructed the accounts department to check your account for any outstanding payments due to you so that your account can be settled to your satisfaction at the expiry of the notice period. Please do not hesitate to let me know if I can help you in any way.

With best wishes,

Yours sincerely,
R. P. Sharma
Branch Manager

A variety of situations will continue to emerge at the workplace making it necessary to convey unpleasant news. Handling these situations requires patience, tact and maturity. At the same time it is necessary to handle the situation sympathetically, using writing skills to ease the unpleasantness of the situation. A persistent effort enables a person to learn these skills.

All kinds of meetings play an important role in business and professional life. A vast majority of meetings are ineffective because of incompetent handling. To be effective, they must be appropriately circulated. The participants would also like to be informed of the action taken on the decisions taken at the meeting.

Every organization has its rules about calling meetings. Some meetings are mandatory such as a monthly sales meeting, or a quarterly Board meeting. Many meetings are called at the pleasure of the president or secretary of the organization. Some meetings are called on a notice by two or more members. The choice would depend upon the circumstances. It is important that the person calling a meeting must understand the rules and call a meeting only when he is entitled to do so, or through the authority vested upon him by someone who enjoys that authority. All organizations also have rules pertaining to the number of days between sending of the letter of invitation to the meeting and the actual date of meeting. An interval of 15 days is normal keeping in view delays in the post. Emergency meetings can be called at short notices.

A letter inviting the participants to a meeting would just extend an invitation informing everyone about the time, date and venue of the meeting followed by any additional information. It could read as follows:

To Members of the Board:
Dear Sir:

2013, at Nav Jyoti School premises. Please stay for tea and refreshments after the meeting.
    A copy of the agenda for the meeting is enclosed.
    With best wishes,

                                                                           Yours sincerely,
                                                                           Suresh Rawat
                                                                               Secretary

The Agenda for the Meeting

Agenda is a list of items to be discussed at a meeting. When an agenda is sent with the letter of invitation for the meeting, it gives the participants time to think about what is to be discussed. When in doubt they could seek additional information. When all the participants are prepared for a discussion the matter is easily sorted out and the purpose of the meeting is attained.

The agenda should include all the items that need inputs from all the participants. In the event an item crops up at the last moment the participants have a right to defer it for the next meeting. However, smaller issues that do not require much discussion could be included provided the president deems it

AGENDA

The following items will be discussed at the meeting:

    meeting.
2.   *Action taken on the minutes.*

5.   *Approval of the Auditors for the next year.*

Suresh Rawat
Secretary

Many people prefer to combine the letter of invitation and the agenda writing it on a single sheet. It would then be as follows:

Writing the Minutes of the Meeting

Minutes are a written summary of the points discussed at a meeting. It enables an organization to move steadily onwards referring to earlier decisions, if necessary. In the minutes it is not necessary to record the opinions of the participants individually. Only in the event a person desires to record something

at through consensus among the participants. The minutes of the meeting for which the agenda was circulated would be written as follows:

MINUTES OF THE MEETING OF THE BOARD OF DIRECTORS HELD AT 4.00 P.M. ON MARCH 12, 2013, AT NAV JYOTI SCHOOL

The following were present:
1.   *Mr. R.S. Pahwa*   *- President*
2.   *Mr. P.K. Sharma*   *- Vice-President*
3.   *Mr. Suresh Rawat*   *- Secretary*

5.   *Mr. Sushil Gupta*

Mr. P.R. Swami expressed his inability to be present.

2.   *The Secretary informed that as desired in the last meeting the Auditors were requested to complete the work as early as possible. They have assured that the audited accounts would reach us latest by April 30, 2013.*

    ments. A copy of the approved Budget is made a part of these minutes.

running short at times and would affect the daily routine. It was suggested that it should be increased. It was unanimously resolved to raise it to Rs 12,000/-

5. *It was unanimously agreed that our Auditors, M/s S.K. Jain & Co. continue as our auditors for the next year at the same remuneration as for the current year. They may be informed accordingly.*

additional person before the next meeting.

from the Auditors.

Secretary

Circulation of the Minutes

It is customary to circulate the minutes of the meeting to all the concerned persons whether they were present at the meeting or not. Sometimes it is possible that there might be some error due to some misinterpretation of facts by the person writing the minutes. In such a case the same can be corrected before the next meeting. A copy of the minutes should be pasted on the Minute Book and duly signed by the person writing the minutes. It is usually the secretary who does this work.

Follow-Up Action on the Minutes

You will observe that soon after the meeting and writing of the minutes of the meeting some responsibilities have been created. In the present case these are:

1. Circulation of the minutes of the meeting.
2. Informing the Auditors of their appointment and remuneration.

4. Circulation of audited accounts for the current year as soon as these are received.

It will be the responsibility of the secretary to follow-up on each of these items, and have a short report ready for the next meeting that each of these four items has been complied with.

Appropriate documentation of all meetings ensures that the meetings attain the purpose for which they are called.

Chapter 63

always the danger of important information shared and written by the personnel being leaked out or

Memos. A short document written by one person to another.

A noting. Short remarks written on a document.

A diary. Day to day notes taken each day for personal use or action.

Writing A Memo

A memo is a brief form of the word: memorandum, which is a note sent from one person to another. This note could provide some information; it could also make a suggestion or request for something. A memo can also be described as an informal letter or a report written in conversational style. However, a memo is not a letter or report in the strict sense. It is a short informally written document from one person to another within the organization. Some organizations have a template for writing a memo. This template has the organization logo, name and details.

A typical memo would include:

The date.

To: The name of the person it is sent to. This could be written formally or informally, depending upon the circumstances.

From: The name of the person writing the memo. In formal memos the full name should be given; in informal memos it could just be the popular name.

Subject: The purpose of the memo must be clearly described.

Message. It is written in conversational style. It could be divided under sub-headings, if necessary. The message should be written with short sentences.

Signature or initials: The sender could put his initials or sign the memo.

How would the Area Sales Manager write a memo to the sales supervisors working in his sales team to collect data? Here is a sample memo:

Date: *November 20, 2013*
To: *Sales Supervisors*
From: *ASM, Uttarakhand*
Subject: *Monthly sales data*
Message: *You are advised to collect data of monthly sales from each salesman by the 5th of the same to the Sales Manager by the 10th. I have to present the*
Signature / Initials: *SPG*

With computers and laptops on the tables of all personnel would it not be advisable to send this

to the other person the memo would have to be written on paper. Here is an example:

Date: *November 20, 2013.*
To: *Sales Supervisor, Garhwal.*
From: *ASM, Uttarakhand.*
Subject: *Proposal for appointment of new dealer.*
Message:
in district Uttarkashi. Please visit Purola, study the potential, meet the applicants, and let me have your recommendations within the next fortnight.
Signature / Initials: *SPG*

Manager informing him about something or for making a request. Here is an example:

Date: *November 20, 2013.*
To:
From: *Supervisor.*
Subject: *Food warmer for staff.*
Message: *In response to your instructions I have checked the availability and prices of food warmers available in the market. The prices are:*

Brand A – Rs 1,550/-
Brand B – Rs 1,715/-
Brand C – Rs 1,800/-

Signature / Initials: *Ram Kishore*

Must be complete
documents pertaining to a particular issue, understood the impact of each factor, and brought forth the crux of the matter, the note cannot be complete.
Must be reliable. All the information must be factual. There must be no assumptions. It is for

should not take on this responsibility.
Must follow the 5 Cs of writing. It must be clear, concise, courteous, convincing and

Must be readable. It should be so written as to make it useful reading for the person for whom it is intended. The reader must grasp the basics of the issue immediately. If he were to struggle

note is, one cannot highlight the correct facts or make suitable suggestions that would help the decision-maker.

Even within the organization different people would look at the note from their perspective.

The person writing the note should confer with the person for whom the note is written and understand what he or she desires.
What are the important considerations? It is on this basis that the facts will have to be studied in detail.

It is only a well-structured note that serves the purpose best.

notes must have the following components:

It must be clear as to what is the issue, topic or purpose of

The facts of the case. There could be several important considerations. The facts must be listed with the most important ones on the top, followed by those that have a lesser impact on the issue. These could be broken into sub-sections as follows:
The background. This would include a brief history of the issue. How a problem emerged? How it shaped up?
The current status. What is the current magnitude of the problem or issue? How is it affecting the organization?
Important facts. What are the facts? These must be reported authentically. There should be

Options available
issue.

The conclusion. What can be inferred on the basis of the facts? Would the writer like to make a suggestion or offer advice on the issue? It is optional to offer suggestions. If these are given they must be the best options available.

useful. To ensure that it is complete check for the following?

Are all the facts correctly stated and explained?

Making A Noting

A note is a brief written record, usually for a later date. It could also be described as a short written

on an issue. It could serve several purposes as follows:

Draw the attention to certain rules and regulations pertaining to the issue.

State questions that emerge from the issue and would need to be addressed.
Make suggestions to address questions that need to be addressed on the issue.

Propose a course of action on the issue.
Seek sanction from an appropriate authority to address an issue.
Close an issue using one's authority.

the following when writing a note:

It must be short and yet keep in mind the 5 Cs of writing.

use green or red in rare cases.

A note must be written point-wise, as necessary in a situation.
When notes have to be written by several persons expressing their views on the issue, when a person agrees with what has been written by a person earlier, rather than repeat the information, the person can write, "I agree with the view of…".
When a rule or regulation is to be mentioned in the note, do not write the complete text of the rule or regulation. Just mention it by name and section number.
When several notes are desired, they should be written on a separate sheet, writing only on one side of the paper.
When a note is desired on a particular aspect by another department, the opinion of different

must be written by the senior person in the department listing all the opinions in a single note.

written, but the earlier one should also remain as it existed initially. It should not be deleted or cancelled.

Repetitions of any nature must be avoided.

A person must sign and write his designation and date at the end of the note.

Writing A Diary

maintain a diary giving the details of cases they need to attend to each day. Doctors and professionals use a diary to record appointments mentioning time when the person would call. In the same way, businessmen use a diary to write appointments, people they need to visit, and also important details like cheques that need to be honoured on a particular date. Many retailers record details like goods they need to order or other similar details. The accounts departments keep a diary to trace outstanding payments.

A diary is a good tool to remind a person about insurance premium to be paid, taxes and bills to be paid, licenses to be renewed. Digital diaries and computers have taken on the work of writing a diary, but these function only when they remain switched on to remind a person. That would depend upon individuals and the systems that they have adopted. Even those who use a computer still maintain a diary placed on the work-desk to record any information that would be required at a later date. The details can be transferred to a digital diary or computer later. It is common to record phone numbers on a mobile for easy dialing, but it is advisable to maintain a hard copy in an address-book in the event a mobile gets damaged or lost.

Chapter 64

in forms, records and returns. Many of these are optional depending upon a person's activities, but some of them are statutory requirements for purposes of different laws of the country.

Every organization requires that the attendance of all employees must be recorded every day. It would also be necessary to maintain a record of an employee's casual leave, medical leave, leave without pay, annual vacation. To pay every employee it would be necessary to issue cheques, or transfer the salary to a designated bank account.

Employees need to travel locally, outstation or even abroad. This makes it essential to maintain appropriate records to seek reimbursement and settle the advance payment. Where many vehicles are maintained by an organisation it becomes necessary to maintain log books. The mileage and fuel consumption is recorded each day. Every organisation would have its own rules on checking these records periodically.

A very important record in every organization is the incoming and outgoing inventory every day.

details to the auditors at the end of the year. Incoming and outgoing mail too would require to be recorded in a register.

new cheque books.

require indent slips, sanctions and approvals. The renewal of licenses and passports would also require

Businessmen and professionals need to be aware of all such forms, records and returns.

and also Service Tax. When making payments it is essential to deduct taxes in many cases. These taxes must

a feedback from the customers on the services rendered. Airlines and railways seek feedbacks through

servicing equipment. The schools seek a feedback whether the child has shown his progress report to the parents.

Read the form carefully. Go through the whole form. What is the purpose of the form? Why

mentally it is time to begin writing.

in blue or black? Follow instructions on the form.
Relevant and irrelevant portions. Since forms are devised for a vast population certain portions might not be relevant to you. Are there any instructions to cope with such situations? If there aren't any, do not leave the space blank. Write: Not applicable or NA.
Personal information. Fill in personal information only when it is a statutory requirement.

anniversary disclose the day and month. You could avoid writing the year.
Fill records regularly

Fill returns on time

Ensure that the return is complete
instructions on it? Mention your name, address, and other details correctly. Mention your PAN

Seek a receipt

Chapter 65

Few businessmen or professionals think in terms of writing any kind of report. The majority feels

true. To be a good businessman or a professional it is essential that one should be able to write a good report. That also enables the person to understand, evaluate and use the information in business reports written by other individuals or groups. These reports are the foundation of development of business and professional activities.

Generally, a business report is a concise document that informs through summarization and

The report could be for one person, a group of people, or even a large audience depending upon the purpose of the report. The report could be the work of one person or a group of persons working collectively.

A business report could be a brief document in a few pages, or could be fairly exhaustive running into 50 to 250 pages. Reports on government affairs could be much longer. Since time is an important consideration to businessmen and professionals the emphasis is always on writing short and effective reports.

The nature of a business report would vary in different situations. A report could be formal or informal depending upon the purpose and the person/s it is addressed to. It could provide desired information, or analyse certain facts or situations or could just recommend methods to address different situations. It could just be a written report, or could include charts and illustrations to make comparisons. To enhance the visual impact it could also include a PowerPoint presentation.

The common types of reports in business include sales reports, sales forecasts, inspection reports, progress reports, annual reports, audit reports and also feasibility and project reports pertaining to

their experiences through written reports presented at seminars. All professionals grow with time and

recommendations pertaining to the subject.

The important question is: how can a report be readable and also effective? To most people general

writing the report. The effectiveness of the report would depend upon the writer's understanding of the purpose of the report, an effective analysis of the situation and appropriate suggestions and recommendations. Good presentation skills always arouse the interest of the reader to go through the report.

Writing A Business Report

Writing a business report could be assigned to a single person or to a group of people working together with the group leader assembling and giving shape to the report. For example, the Sales Manager could ask the Sales Supervisor to write a report on the basis of information provided by the salespersons working in the territory. Each could compile the data of sales for each product, compare it with competitive products in the market, and also make suggestions about an appropriate product mix that

one section for personal suggestions.

Most of the reports are the work of a single person. All thesis and dissertations written to attain

different people and sources. Groups function when each person is working in a different location that

are the work of several persons checking, analyzing and assembling business data for the scrutiny by a chartered accountant duly recognised by the government agencies. Similarly, a business feasibility

a single person.

The effectiveness of the report would depend upon how well the person writing the report understands three important things. These are:

1. **Good knowledge of the audience.** The report could be of interest to one person who would use it as a basis for an important decision, or could be of interest to a group of people who are involved in taking the decision. It could also be for a much larger audience in some situations. The person writing the report must be aware of the audience needs.
2. **The purpose of the report.** No business report is intended to be entertainment material. A

    clearly understood by the person writing the report. The collected information, data and other facts must lead the reader to the analysis and recommendations in a logical manner to hold the interest of the reader.
3. **The presentation of the report.** The person reading the report must be immediately attracted to reading the report. This is possible only when the presentation is ideal and the reader's pur-

The Audience

The audience is the very purpose of writing the report. If the audience could do without the report there would have been no need to write it. The audience can be as varied as the people we meet

immediate audience is the professor or guide who has helped conduct a study on a particular subject.

for the person to delve in similar pursuits in the future. The study would be a matter of interest to other

The immediate audience for an exhaustive analytical sales report written by a Sales Supervisor might be the company Sales Manager, but when found meaningful the report would have a much larger audience in the Board of Directors who could use the information to develop new strategies.

price of the company.

When writing the report a person must think and consider what is really desired by the concerned individual or group in commissioning such a report. If in doubt, it would be in order to discuss this issue with the concerned person. Before writing a report one must be clear about the needs of the audience. To understand the audience better ask yourself the following questions:

> What is the current knowledge of the audience about the subject?
> What additional knowledge would the report provide them?
> Does the audience have any biases about the subject?
> What is the level of technical knowledge of the audience?
> Would I need to take special care in using non-technical terminology?

The Purpose of the Report

Next to understanding the need of the audience of a report, it is important for the writer to know the

obviously self-academic development. But that is not the real purpose of the report, as perceived by the person who has authorized the writing of the dissertation on a particular subject. His purpose would be different. He would want the person to collect information, study in detail what earlier scholars have said about the issue, analyse details, give them meaning and make recommendations on how the

the study.

The Sales Supervisor might feel that the report is an exercise in collecting information and the

purpose could also be to gradually phase out or reduce the production of products that are slow moving and promote fast selling items through brand extension. In every case the situation would be different and rather than guess the purpose of writing a report it would be better to discuss it in detail with the persons who have authorized the writing of the report. Before you write a business report you must be clear about the following:

> What is the exact purpose or goal to be attained?
> What information would have to be collected?
> Where would this information be available?
> What details should be analysed?
> What kind of suggestions or recommendations is desired?

responsibility of writing it to a person. When the purpose of writing a report is clearly understood by the person it becomes easier to write it, and also make it readable for the intended audience.

Presentation of the Report

When you visit a book shop some titles displayed on the counter are more inviting than others. Even when you open a book some books appear more attractive than others. The simple reason for these feelings is in the presentation of the cover and reading material. A report is no different. Irrespective whether a report is just a few pages, or of 50 pages put together through spiral binding, or a larger volume bound in hard cover, the way a report is presented is important for the concerned person/s to read it.

A business report is not an exercise in academic English. The purpose is not to show the extent of one's vocabulary, or writing pedantic language. It is important to follow the simple rules of writing commonly used words, writing short sentences divided into paragraphs that cover one item of the subject. Avoid the use of jargon and unnecessary adjectives. Also avoid the excessive use of "I".

audience and the purpose of writing the report. Type it out well and print on good quality paper, binding

hardbound.

Contents of the Report

A short business report would have the following sections:

Title page. This would display an appropriate title, the person/s involved in preparing the report, the name of the department, and the date of the report.

Terms of reference. This would display the details of the authority and purpose of writing the report.

Current status. It would be useful to mention the current situation to be compared with what is desired in the future.

Procedures adopted. This section would give details of methods used to collect information and other details.

Analysis of the information. The information collected could be converted to graphs or charts making it easier to make comparisons to understand the subject better.

Conclusions. What can be concluded from the analysis of the information? This would of course depend upon the perception of the person or the group writing the report.

Recommendations. Every person or group would have some recommendations to make. These must be objective and positive.

Preparing the Final Report

group, share it with the team members. Seek suggestions for improvement. If working alone, the draft could be shared with colleagues or even the person who has authorized it. Incorporate the suggestions, if you feel they would help attain the purpose of the report. Check on graphs, charts or photographs. They must facilitate an easier understanding of the information, the analysis and recommendations.

Can some of the sentences be broken to enhance readability?
Are all the spellings correct?

Is the grammar correct?
Does each paragraph convey one idea?
Do the headings and sub-headings enhance readability?
Is the report well typed on good quality paper?
Are the pages correctly numbered?
Is the binding of the report satisfactory?
What would be my reactions if I were to read a similar report?

Reports on Business Situations

Each situation in business and professional work would be different, and so would be the perception of people involved in various activities. It is the challenge of these situations that leads people to question a situation and seek answers through personal experimentation and experience. The sharing of this knowledge leads to development and progress.

The basics of a short business report along with some common writing and presentation methods have been discussed. Other situations would require elaborate inputs and techniques. They are, therefore, discussed in greater detail in the chapters that follow.

the person writes the report he or she must understand the basic structure of the report, the purpose of each section and the sequence in which the information is to be written. With the structure of the report in place, the person writing the report elaborates each section according to need and soon we have the

this in view the sooner one starts on writing the report the better it is. The collection of data, its analysis, comparison with earlier studies and a whole lot of other details require more time than most people think it would take. This fact should always be remembered.

The Report Structure

We have earlier observed that each situation would require a different treatment and it is not possible to have common rules to be followed for writing reports. The best course in this situation is to have guidelines that can be used to adapt and modify a report according to each situation. Here is a suggested report structure with comments:

Cover page. This page serves the same purpose as the cover of a book. It helps attract attention. It would have the title of the study and the name of the author on it. It is for the writer to creatively make it attractive.

Title page. This page would have the title of the report, the name of the person who has written it, and also the details of the person and department that has authorized the particular study and the report. If the report is intended to be short this page could have a brief abstract of the work.

Terms of reference. The matter on this page would give the details of the purpose of the study

Table of contents. This enables the reader to have an idea of the details and extent of study and easily open a section of personal interest.

List of illustrations
included in the report.

Glossary of terms. This page is optional and could be included when many terms not in

throughout the report.

Acknowledgements. It would be necessary to seek the support and help of several people when making a study or writing a report. The names of people could be mentioned on this page.

An abstract of the study

of the study. This section is the most popularly read section and should be written in up to 250 words.

The main body of the report. This would be written in several chapters, each with a title and beginning on a new page. Here are a few suggestions on how this section could be structured:

Introduction. This section would include a description of the purpose and scope of the study, details of limitations, assumptions made and the methods used to collect information for the report.

Background of the problem. If there were no problem there would have been no need for the study or the report. This section could explain: what is the problem? For how long has it persisted? Was any action taken earlier to control it? If so, what action was taken? What was

has it been experienced by others?

Work done by others on the problem. This section would require the person making the study read as many books and studies on the subject as are available in the library. This would require the cooperation and support of the librarian in a good library. It might be advisable to include the details of some of these studies in the report. Much of the information may not come from books, but from technical journals that publish such reports. In such a situation the details of the author and the work, the year of the study, the name of the journal and page number must be noted to be duly acknowledged in the report.

Details of data collected. This data would be based upon both quantitative and qualitative research. While the quantitative data would mean getting in touch with as many people as possible, the qualitative data would refer to their opinions, ideas, perceptions and feelings on different issues. This is an arduous process, but must be carried on objectively without

and the report authentic and authoritative. Depending upon the circumstances, the larger and more varied the targeted sample the better will be the results. For convenience of reading and understanding the data it could be represented in the form of charts and illustrations.

Interpretation of the data. This section depends entirely upon the analytical skills of the person/s doing the study and writing the report. The important thing is to look at information objectively with a positive attitude.

Conclusions. Once again it is necessary to be objective in drawing conclusions from the collected data. Brush aside all biases that you might have on the basis of past hearsay or your

way.

Recommendations. It is not easy to make recommendations. The study and the report have been assigned to you on the basis of your ability and skills. Think seriously of the factors that are involved in the study and make recommendations that would help mankind through use of

References. This would include the details of the reference material you suggest for further reading on the subject.

Bibliography. This section would give the details of books and journals you have drawn upon to discuss similar studies on the subject.

Appendices. This section includes supporting documents, illustrations, maps or questionnaires you might have used to collect and analyse data. This matter is best given in this section because if it is included in the main text it could confuse or mislead the reader from the method you might have used to discuss the different issues affecting the conclusions.

Writing the Report

You have the basic structure of a technical report before you. It does not mean that you must begin

mentioned in the beginning can be written only after the main body of the report has been written. The report would have to be written bits and pieces. As you read reference material you will need to maintain notes. The information and the data would have to be collected, also in bits and pieces. This takes a lot of time and effort. It would be best to write whatever details are available to you. You could

ready you could assemble them to comply with the formal report structure discussed above.

When writing the report you will need to remember the following:

. When is the report to be submitted? How can you be sure

getting it printed and bound.

What should be the length of the report? The person who has authorized the writing of the report is the best person to answer this question. Most reports would be 10,000 words or a little more depending upon the subject. Busy businessmen and professionals prefer shorter reports that can be read quickly.

Keep information and data securely. You can easily get into trouble if the data or information

Don't stay in doubt. You cannot write a good report when you have some doubts in your

asked you to write the report.

Be original and objective. Do not copy matter from other works on a similar subject. That might seem easy, but that would be plagiarism. Technical personnel who are avid readers easily identify copied material from the original material written by someone. When writing

through your efforts. This will ensure originality in your work.

Seek excellence. The best reports are the result of people's effort to attain excellence in whatever they do.

Chapter 62

is made to start additional branches, clinics, hospitals and factories in new areas and territories. This involves entrepreneurship. Since such activities require a huge investment, the prudent entrepreneur seeks to study the risk factors and ensures that growth is based upon a sound foundation.

The word: feasible literally means able to be done easily. Interpreting feasibility from the business angle it means whether a new project would succeed or not. There is no dearth of ideas. One could also argue that a business project that has succeeded in one city would be equally successful in another city. This is not always so. Success depends upon response from people and several other factors. Before investing one's time, money and effort it is only good sense to study the feasibility of a new project.

A feasibility study would look at several factors that contribute to success. The important ones include the following:

Technical viability. What would be the inputs, throughputs and outputs? Can these be managed satisfactorily?

Marketing viability. What is the extent of the local market? What is the status of the market at state level? The national level? Is there possibility of exports? What kind of marketing channels would have to be used? What competitor products are currently available in the market?

Financial viability. What would be the investment on land, building and equipment? How

Environmental issues. There are restrictions on many activities because of ecological concerns. Would permission be granted?

Legal considerations. Restrictions are imposed upon many activities. What restrictions are applicable to the project and how soon permission can be obtained to start working?

Economic considerations

product or service. How does the project stand from this point of view? How soon will the

Writing A Feasibility Report

First-time entrepreneurs take the help of chartered accountants or other organizations that specialize in preparing feasibility project reports for different business activities. However, companies that have been in business for a long time have managers who are well versed with the company operations and are capable of preparing a feasibility project report for expansion of business in new territories. The simple rules of writing would be applicable to writing a feasibility report. Only the subject matter

Introduction
This section would give an overview of the proposed project. This would include the purpose of the report, the need for the new activity and details of the various considerations in preparing the report.

Technical Viability
The project must be technically viable in the proposed territory. If it is not, there would be no need for further study. The technical viability depends upon three factors. Let us look at each one separately.

1. **Inputs**. As can be understood these refer to the land, building, equipment and material required for the project. If premises are hired for the project it would have to be taken on a long-term lease. One cannot look for premises on a short-term basis. The location of the premises would also be an important consideration for some projects. What is the status of the availability of equipment for the project? Is it readily available, or is to be imported? What about the maintenance and spare parts for the equipment? Can the staff for the project be hired locally, or would it be necessary to train new staff for the project? Would residences be available for the outstation staff? What about the raw material? What is the local availability? Would it have to be brought from other areas? Imported from other countries? Availability of raw material is an important consideration.

2. **Throughputs**. This refers to the material or items that pass through a system or process. This is

    be established and quality control maintained.

3. **Outputs**. This refers to the items that would be produced. Many items have to satisfy standards established by government agencies before a product can be marketed. What standards would need to be complied with and how this would be done? The report must specify these clearly -

    tion to comply with the requirements.

Marketing Viability
Returns from investment come from the sale of products or services. This would require a thorough analysis of the market at the local, state and national levels. This would depend upon several factors. Some of the important ones are:

    Local population. Most companies classify the sales territories of their products on the basis of the population. That enables them to estimate possible demand for their products.

    Consumption trends. Every area would have its own peculiar consumption trends. These depend upon the lifestyle of the people. When sales territories are created in large metro cities it has been observed that consumption trends vary in one area as compared to another. In some territories high end products sell better and in others the demand is greater for average quality products.

    Moving population. Some cities have a large moving population. This is particularly so in areas where tourists visit, or a place of pilgrimage is situated nearby. The numbers vary seasonally with higher movement during vacations, holidays and weekends. Product marketability varies periodically.

Competitor products. These are a fair indication of market trends. What competitor products are already on sale in the area? Has the product demand peaked out? Or is there scope for growth? What is the reputation of the products being sold currently? Is the pricing reasonable? Can it be matched by the new proposed products or services?

Distribution channels. What is the current distribution system used in the area? Can it be replicated for the new products or services? Can a better distribution system be introduced? Is

social standing of these parties?

Consumer attitude. All sales result from the demand by consumers. Since consumers are human beings and would have different attitudes towards products and services, it is important to know them better. How do consumers react to certain products? What motivates them to

If so, how can it be done? What would be the consequences of the change?

Elasticity of demand. In many areas the elasticity of demand for various reasons is an important factor affecting the marketing of products and services. The details must feature in the report.

Production and sales. One should look for new avenues for selling products and services only when there is production to match it. The manufacturer would like to sell wherever it is the easiest and at the least cost.

Import and export possibilities. Many products and services can be imported or exported for

Selling costs. The selling costs in all areas are not the same. It is the least near the manufacturing plant or stocking point, and as one goes further the transportation expenses increase costs.

Administrative and legal constraints. Some local bodies have imposed entry tax on goods making it more expensive. Some products cannot be sold in some areas. For example, products containing egg or non-vegetarian content cannot be sold at some Hindu pilgrim towns.

The success of any project depends upon the sale of the products and services. It is therefore essential that all aspects of marketing are thoroughly analysed and described in the project feasibility report.

Financial Viability

Projects can be small or big. The size would depend upon the money available to be invested on the project. Next to availability of the investment for the project it is important to know what would be the

viability depends upon several factors. The important ones are:

. These would include the cost of land, building and equipment and machinery. The prices of these inputs would vary with different locations because the cost of land and building vary in different places.

Alternative sites. Sometimes it is possible to get factory sheds and business premises on long-term lease, which does away with the need to buy land and building. All the possibilities must

Investment on inputs
like raw material, packaging, etc. Funds would be required from the time the raw material is

business. The faster a product moves, the better the turnover, lesser the investment and greater the returns. The movement of the products is linked with marketability of the item.

Staff expenses. At every stage work has to be done by the workforce whether it is at the

part-time help can be utilised.

Overhead expenses. Irrespective of whether production is done certain overhead expenses are inevitable in every business. These are best maintained at a low level. However, they are a

Break-even point

price. The break-even point would be where the entrepreneur knows the exact production

money received from sales should be able to pay for the raw material and other expenses

production would have to be stopped.

Financial requirements
resources to start the new project. Once the requirements are known it would be necessary to

to invest in worthwhile projects. The conditions on which they give the money, the rate of interest and the period in which the money would have to be repaid must be analysed and discussed in the project feasibility report.

. The most important part in a project would be the projected

initially for one or two years, but this should be compensated for in the following years. This aspect must be analysed thoroughly in the feasibility report.

Financial prospects

Environmental Issues

Since rapid development has affected the environment in cities, towns and villages, leading to several issues, it has become necessary to analyse the effect of the project on the environment. In several states

a new project can be operated. It is better to settle these issues before making huge investments in a project. Some of the important issues that must be considered are:

Will excessive noise be generated because of the operation of the equipment?
Will there be excessive dust that would affect others in the area?

Will there be excessive stink generated from the project area?
Will there be chemical gases emerging from the project area?
Are there high voltage electricity lines over the project land?

Will the project require the cutting down of trees in the premises?
Will there be a mobile tower that could affect nearby residential areas?

If any of these issues exist in the proposed project then appropriate measures will have to be taken before the project can be permitted to function in the area. Several pollution problems can be sorted out through equipment, but that would increase the cost of the project in terms of investment and maintenance.

Legal Considerations

In establishing any project there would be a variety of legal considerations. For example, certain kinds of projects can only be recognised when established in an industrial estate or area approved by the government. Many activities are recognised as industrial activities, but quite a few are not. Legal considerations would also include seeking permission from different government departments depending upon the activity. Medicines manufacturing or distribution would require a license from the Drugs Controller, industry registration with the Director of Industries, excise registration with the Commissioner of Excise & Customs, registration with the Commercial Tax Department and other similar registration to ensure that the laws of the land are fully adhered to. To some this can be a frustrating experience, but once all these requirements are spelt out in the project feasibility report, one can obtain the necessary permissions before one begins.

Economic Analysis

Economics is the study of the branch of knowledge concerned with the production, consumption, and

of a project. An entrepreneur is always excited about starting a new project, but it is important to do an economic analysis to understand how practical it would be to start a new project.

To understand the impact of an economic analysis just look back a few years back when we had

rooms and then converted into prints. This provided work to millions of people around the world.

photography has changed everything. This is not the end of it. Photography with mobile phones is a big challenge. This is just one example. There are many more like the changes in writing systems, hearing music or watching movies. While new activities emerge the old ones become obsolete. One needs an economic analysis periodically even after establishing a project.

aspect be given due importance in the report.

Conclusions

It would be necessary that the person writing the feasibility report must conclude the report by making appropriate remarks based upon the analysis of various factors discussed earlier. It would also be

and registrations with government departments.

Chapter 68

All self-employed persons need a business plan to begin activities at the workplace. It is often repeated: Those who fail to plan, plan to fail! A good business plan provides the foundation to attract success at the workplace. It is a road map from the beginning to the development of a project.

It is common for entrepreneurs to consider several proposals to begin with. Of these, the choice can be narrowed to three activities for which project feasibility reports can be prepared. Of these three the

be developed. The feasibility report discusses and analyses different situations, the business plan makes

plan must be a written document that describes the different elements leading to the establishment of the project.

Let us consider each element of the business plan, as it would appear in the proposed plan for implementation.

Basic Organisation

organization be a proprietorship, a partnership, a private limited company or a limited company? Each would have advantages and disadvantages. The choice would depend upon a person's circumstances.

> **Sole proprietor**. When a person has the means and the ability to manage the project single handedly, this form of organization would be all right. The proprietor would have to handle all

> later into other forms of organizations.
>
> **Partnership**. A partnership form of organization has two or more partners. Since each partner contributes his share of the capital the money for the project increases. With more working hands it also becomes possible to divide responsibilities with each person looking after one aspect of the business. In an ideal atmosphere it also becomes easier to handle business problems. However, with more people involved in the business there is the additional responsibility of maintaining cordiality and harmony among the partners. A partnership will necessarily need to

> **Private limited company**. This form of organisation is a larger version of a partnership in

> shareholders.
>
> **Public limited company**. This form of organisation is a still larger version and would have a

minimum of seven and a maximum of an unlimited number of shareholders. These companies raise large sums of money through public subscription to the shares, but are liable to many

Co-operatives. This form of organisation is owned and controlled by the people who work for it. Each has a shareholding in the organisation. These co-operatives are popular for running housing societies, purchase organizations of the kind we have in Gujarat to buy milk, or in

It is not necessary to register a proprietary form of organization, but the other forms will have to be

Obtaining Clearances and Approvals

The next step in the business plan would be to identify different kinds of clearances and approvals that are necessary to establish the project. These include approval of land use, registration with the

and safety control, and obtaining permission from appropriate authorities for different items. Some clearances have to be obtained from the village *panchayat*, the District Magistrate and authorities like

etc.) State Drug Controller (for medical industries) and from Bureau of Industries for several other

appropriate authority.

Business Premises

The premises required for the project will depend upon what is intended to be done. If the project

before starting the project. If premises are not available on a long-term lease it might be better to construct your own.

    Personal premises will need an appropriate piece of land that can be approached without hindrance 365 days of the year. It must be large enough for the project and preferably also for further development in the future. The building suitable for the kind of work intended would have to be built. This would require the services of an architect. The money spent on the building would reduce the cash in hand

against land and buildings as security.

Machinery and Equipment

If the project requires the installation of machinery and equipment it would be necessary to get in touch with manufacturers or suppliers of such equipment, obtain quotations and compare different quotations on the basis of quality of the equipment, the backup service available and also the availability of spare

upon truth it might be better to check some of the purchasers to get a feedback. When buying machinery and equipment it would be necessary to check the electricity requirements and have a backup system to ensure that no work-time is lost due to electricity failure.

Electricity and Other Utilities

Depending upon the kind of project it would be necessary to obtain an electricity connection of appropriate wattage. Rules for these connections vary from one state to another and details will have to be checked before getting ahead with the project. The premises will also need a water connection, a sewage connection, if available, and drainage of waste water. All these utilities must be mentioned as a part of the business plan.

Availability of Raw Materials

Every project would need some kind of a raw material. Is it available locally, or would it have to be brought in from outside? If it is to be brought from outside, would the cost of transport increase the overall cost to make the product uneconomical? What kind of packaging is required? Is it available locally, or would it also have to be brought from outstation? Another important consideration is the continuous availability of the raw material. Are there local agents who can make it possible, or would it be necessary to stock raw material for the period when it is not available? Will it be necessary to import certain components from other countries? If so, are they available freely, or is the supply controlled by the government. What if it is not possible to obtain these sometimes?

The business plan must analyse and state all these facts clearly and also provide the names of local suppliers and those nearby. The names of foreign suppliers must also be mentioned in the report.

Marketability of Finished Goods

kind of organization would have a different plan. A retail seller would look forward to build lasting relationships with the customers. A wholesaler would make good relationships with the retailers. Manufacturers would sell through distributors appointed at state level or for regions, depending upon the kind of product to be sold. Export products are sold through Distributors, one for each country, or through large chain stores that have big sales. There are many forms of marketing and every possibility must be considered. During the past few years e-commerce is growing in a big way and might become a very important form of selling in the future.

planned in great detail and included in the business plan.

Working Staff Requirements

kind of staff. In a new project the choice is limited, but as one gains experience and the project gains importance in the community better people are attracted to apply for positions in the organization.

wages payable, casual leave, annual leave, provident fund, health insurance and other such requirements. An entrepreneur must be clear on these issues and conform to the statutory regulations.

A person starting a project must be clear about the salary structure prevailing in the market. There

Many projects require trained personnel and these may sometimes not be available locally. Workers who are brought in from outstations would demand a higher salary not only because they have moved home, but because they would need residential quarters as close as possible to the project site. This aspect must be taken care of.

The Risk Factor

Every project has a risk factor. The real purpose of making detailed study of all the factors that would contribute to the success of a project is to understand the risks involved, and how these can be reduced. A common way of keeping the risks low is to be frugal in buying only that what is immediately necessary for the project. There should be no frills. There should be no extra staff. The purchase of the raw material must be controlled to match the production plans and the sales should be as swift as is possible.

discipline is maintained.

One way to reduce the risk factor is to keep an eye on the break-even point worked out in advance.

success and failure of the project.

Competition

to do it, soon there would be many more to follow you. Competition in business is something all of us must accept. We must live with it. In many ways it is a good thing that it keeps everyone on their toes thinking of providing better products and services making it possible for the customer to have the best at the most competitive prices.

Products and services that are better monitored enjoy a larger share in the market. To keep abreast of competition a person must always be on the lookout as to what is new in the market, what new strategies are being tried by the competitors. It is fun working with competition that works as hard as you.

An Effective Business Plan

An effective business plan must:

> **Be realistic**. When enamoured by a new activity a person tends to become idealistic rather than being realistic about analysing facts and situations. This is not the right thing to do. Do not forget that if things can go wrong, sometimes they will. This is a law of nature. You cannot do anything about it.
>
> **Provide useful products and services**. This is the real purpose of any new project. Ensure that only the best products and services are offered.

to wait until the people accept the new product or service.
Be market conscious
useful. The larger the market, the better the chances for success.
Work to goals
must be met. Gates to success are opened.
Invest money carefully
public image. It is necessary to invest wisely by maintaining a fair balance between the two. The real purpose of a project is to earn money.
Accept competition
challenge. Face it with fortitude.

Develop steadily. There is no swift road to success. It takes a lot of effort and persistence to attain one's goals. Just keep working. You will reach there.

Writing the Business Plan

Like any other report a business plan would have details on every aspect of the different factors that contribute to the success of any plan. These have been discussed earlier. A written plan makes it possible

The written report must analyse and discuss the situation under different headings or sections, with sub-sections describing one point in each paragraph. Here is a suggested layout for a business plan:

1. **Introduction**. This would include the name and address of the business and the promoters, and the nature of business.
2. **A business overview**
   summary of the whole project, and would be best written after the other sections of the report have been written.
3. **Economy survey**
   describe the past and current trends and the future prospects. It would also give details of competition, market shares and what could be expected in the future.
4. **Description of the project**. This section would include the details of the project, the products
5. **Organisation plan**. This section would give details of the promoters or partners, their past experience and ability in handling business, and also how the management would be organised along with their responsibilities.
6. **Production plan**. This section would give the details of machinery and equipment that is required, the names of possible vendors, raw material required and how and from whom it can be acquired. It would also discuss details of production, seasonal variations, if any. Alternative work or maintenance that would need to done when production is low.
7. **Marketing plan**. This section would describe methods of pricing, the kind of packaging desired, the marketing structure for selling, the suggested product-mix and what would be sales forecasts. It could include details of sales territories and possibilities of export to other countries.
8. **Perceived Risks**. This section would evaluate the possible risks of the business, and how these can be kept under control. It could also mention the new technologies that are being developed and describe contingency plans to reduce the effect of the risks.
9. **Financial Plan**. This section would describe the details of money required for the project, and

   projected over a period. It is common to prepare a balance sheet showing projected production,
10. **Appendix**. This section would include names and addresses of government agencies for seeking approvals and registrations, suppliers for machinery and equipment, raw material suppliers and details of similar information. This could also include a market survey report, copies of

Like all other kinds of reports a business plan must be well typed on good quality paper and bound

Chapter 69

A white paper is a type of business report that has a distinct purpose, audience and organisation. It is

to the problem. It is for the information of people within the government and also the public.

In business a white paper is a popular marketing tool for large corporations. It is put up on the Internet and when users seek information about products, the white paper provides the necessary information leading the readers to new products as solutions.

the decision-making of the reader and the product is indirectly promoted. The white paper could have large business houses and also the general public as its audience. The report is written authoritatively

For example, a white paper could take up the problem of drinking water, explaining how important

in our towns and cities. The supply is erratic and water must be stored for general usage. However, this stored water is not safe for drinking because it is easily infected in the storage tanks and bins. The rich use bottled water to drink but that is expensive for the general public. The alternative to bottled water is to purify the water at home by boiling it, which could also prove expensive, or use a water purifying system that is available at a nominal cost and has very low maintenance, making the availability of safe drinking water easy.

discussed it logically, and provided a solution. While it promises good health to the reader's family, it

of consumers.

A white paper is not like other business or marketing tools printed in colour on glossy paper and distributed to the potential customers directly or through post. It is prepared as an authoritative report

is superior to others. The report must be carefully drafted. For convenience it is put on the Web for

problem. Here are a few tips to write a good white paper:

Identify the problem. Describe the problem in detail. It could be lack of safe drinking water, security concerns, rising domestic costs, or something similar. The report must begin with a problem.

Identify the audience. Does the problem concern business houses? Or certain institutions and professions? It could be of general interest of the public. What is the level of knowledge and understanding of the audience? What is the level of their social status? The more the writer knows about the audience the more effective the report would be.

The length of the report. The length of the report would depend upon the problem, the education of the audience and other details. People generally prefer shorter reports. The

Choose a catchy title

on baby food could be titled "Food for Your Baby". This would draw limited attention. If it is changed to: "Don't Starve Your Baby", mothers would be immediately attracted to know if they are at fault.

Describe the problem

problem is. Why is it not getting the attention it deserves?
. Also mention the source of the information. This makes the report authoritative, a hallmark of all white papers. Describe all aspects of the problem as it affects people.

Suggest one or more solutions. If there are more than one, describe and compare the effectiveness of each proposal.

Draw conclusions. People who are short of time jump paragraphs to reach the end. The concluding remarks should begin with the problem, its effect and the solution. It should be like the punch-line of a good speech.

Suggest only a product. A white paper suggests a solution. It does not promote a company.

Chapter 20

shareholders.

Chartered Accountants. Businessmen and professionals do not need to prepare audit reports; they would need to assist the Chartered Accountant with all the information that he might require to prepare the report. They would also need to understand how these reports are prepared and how they

under the taxation laws.

Most organizations have two types of audits – internal and external. An internal audit is intended

point out lack of proper systems and controls. With the management taking note of these lapses they create systems that do not allow pilferage or leakages in the organization. An external audit analyses

are duly audited by a Chartered Accountant.

affairs of an organization. It is not an evaluation. It is an opinion stating that the information presented in the report is correct and free of material misstatements. It is for the person reading the report to evaluate the organization on the basis of the information provided in the report.

There are four common types of auditor's reports. Each presents a different situation as perceived by the auditor. These four types of reports are:

ments are correct and are in accordance with GAAP. Incorrect situations could be unavailability of the inventory details or wrong calculation of depreciation.

230   *Business English*

3. **Adverse Opinion Report**. This type of report is issued by an auditor when he is of the opinion

   given when the functioning of a branch or subsidiary is not reported in the account statements.

4. **Disclaimer of Opinion Report**

   cause of several reasons like the organization not being able to present accounts, or information explaining the transactions. The organization could be involved in legal problems or litigation.

The Audit Report

including appropriate remarks to explain some of the transactions better. After a brief introduction in

31, 2013.

stating his opinion.

statements given herewith are in accordance with generally accounting principles and represent a fair

an adverse report. The opinion paragraph would read as:

It is uncommon for an auditor to issue a Disclaimer. Such situations arise when the organisation

are paying the auditor a fee, and the income of the auditor depends upon the fees he collects from his clients, he would give a favourable report. Good auditors are known for their integrity and would refuse to give a wrong opinion. When the auditor has been appointed at a General Meeting of the company, and he is compelled to issue a report it would read as follows:

affairs of the Company.

Responsibility of Auditors
Since it is a statutory requirement
auditors take on the responsibility of guiding and correctly posting the transactions of an organization to the correct heads. To be able to do so the auditors must get appropriate support from the accountant of the organization to provide the correct information. The auditors arrive at the correct income or loss

To ensure that an organization is not faced with a situation where the statutory auditors are not able and for the partners or shareholders, it is common for the management to appoint internal auditors who check the affairs of the organization periodically, set things on the right track and gradually lead to the auditors to ensure that the systems are in place.

When preparing the audit report it is common for the auditor to include explanations on certain accounts and transactions so that the person reading the report can understand the implications of each item clearly. Some of these explanations could be on the basis of reports prepared by different auditors.

principles'.

Other Activities of Auditors

Besides auditing accounting procedures auditors are engaged in a variety of activities like preparing a

Auditors are accepted as people of integrity and their opinions are always valued by the clients.

reports on certain matters.

Beware!

cases of big scandals in the past. While much of the audit work is done by the audit clerks, and they facts before issuing a report because their reputation as a person of integrity is at stake.

Chapter 21

In any country the activities of the public including those of businessmen and professionals are regulated through laws and regulations made by the government. These rules are based upon the constitution of the nation that guarantees certain rights to all citizens. The legal profession is responsible for protecting the rights of the citizens.

understand how important it is to appreciate the value of each document.

Before we can get down to learn how to write simple legal documents it would be appropriate to must know when we can do it on our own and when to seek the support of a lawyer. Some of the most common legal documents are:

Invoices. On the purchase of any item the retailer must give us an invoice for the product, and a receipt for the payment. When we buy with cash the cash memo serves the purpose of both the documents. An invoice is not only an account of what we have bought, but it is an

a grievance, we can claim an exchange of goods or a refund on the basis of the invoice.

Receipts. Every time we pay money for a product or service we must demand a receipt
We get receipts for paying our electricity bills, water bills, municipal taxes, our children's school fees, household rent paid, salaries to the employees and for many other things. All government taxes are paid through receipts.

privileges like issue of a ration card or a passport, banks would need it to grant a loan and there

Tenancy Deed. In all businesses and professions we need to hire premises, or sometimes rent them out to others. In the interests of the landlord and the tenant it would be appropriate to write a deed that would include the details of the property and conditions of the tenancy.

Partnership Deed. When two or more people decide to work together as partners it would be necessary to write a Partnership Deed that would not only elaborate upon the conditions decided mutually, but also entitle the partners to certain legal rights and privileges.

Dissolution Deed. When a partnership is terminated it is necessary that a dissolution deed

Contracts. As a part of business many organizations demand that a contract be executed to spell out the conditions of the order clearly. Many organizations write a contract with their distributors binding them to sell their products only.

Memorandum of Incorporation. Before a company is formed it is necessary that a memorandum stating the details of the promoters, the capital, objectives, etc. be written and registered with the government. All large organizations have a MoI that serves as a guideline to investors and others.

Organisation by Laws. Since the MoI is only the founding document, the other details about the functioning of an organization are written in the form of by-laws that are used for administrative purposes. These by-laws have legal sanctity.

Sale/Purchase Deed. All properties are sold and purchased through appropriately drafted deeds that are registered with the government.

Trusts and Societies. A trust or a society must be incorporated through a legal deed describing

Record of Meetings. The proceedings of all meetings of organizations must be recorded in an appropriate way because they are liable to be scrutinized by the members and the public.

Indemnity Bonds. When a person stands assurance for another in a particular situation, it would be necessary to write an indemnity bond to make good any loss incurred because of that person.

Preparing Legal Drafts. All court cases require written drafts. A professional could handle the same, but he would not be able to give of his best unless he is provided all the details by the involved parties.

First Information Report. In certain circumstances it would be necessary to report a matter to the police. In such an eventuality it would be necessary to write a report for the police.

Serving a Notice. Many situations require that a notice be served to a party that has defaulted in some way. This could help avoid court action.

Legal Evidence. All legal evidence in the higher courts is given in the form of written statements on oath signed before an Oath Commissioner appointed by the government.

Mortgages. It is necessary to sign a mortgage deed when a person takes a loan against property. This is a legal document signed by the person taking the loan, pledging his property, and countersigned by one or more guarantors, as desired by the person giving the loan.

Writing a Will. A will is a legal document containing instructions for what will be done with one's money and property after one's death. This would be once in a lifetime document, but it would be essential for everyone who wants the best use of his money and property after death.

After going through the list of the situations when legal documents would play a crucial role in ensuring success, one can appreciate that it would be impractical to run to a lawyer for the smallest need. Even when one needs to consult and avail of the services of a legal professional it would be necessary for a person to have a written detail of the situation so that it could be transformed into a valid legal document.

Writing A Legal Document
When writing a letter can overwhelm a person, writing a legal document would appear like a distant dream. It is not really so. It is like writing a technical paper, but easier because it's about you. Who could know you and your circumstances better than you? Writing a legal document is just like any other

simpler with the frills removed. When drafting a legal document follow these simple steps:

What is the purpose? You must be clear about what you desire to achieve. Without this information, you cannot write a convincing document.

What are the facts? List all the facts. Then arrange them in order of priority. The most important ones must come in the beginning. Many times it would be necessary to write the facts in chronological order.

Plan your document. It must progress logically. Divide each point into a separate paragraph.

Avoid wordiness. Write short sentences using simple words that cannot be misinterpreted. Do not use slang.

Use numerals. Wherever necessary use numerals and not written words for numbers.

Revise the draft. Check spellings and grammar. After the draft is ready revise it to ensure that it is clear and convincing.

Use a readable font. *Times New Roman* and *Arial* are ideal for this purpose. Type leaving reasonable margins all around the document.

Professional Legal Writing
Professional legal writing falls into the realm of legal professionals, judges and sometimes the legislators who enact laws. Professional legal writing relies heavily on authority in the form of past judgments and orders of high courts and the Supreme Court. This a common practice all over the world. In professional

are used to mean something quite different from the common use of the word. Many phrases have also been borrowed from French and other languages. Together this language is referred to as legalese, or language of those practicing law. This is not for common businessman or the professional engaged in

leave the use only to the law professionals. For the average person the simple English and its use in

Writing An Invoice
An invoice is a written list that shows what products or services have been provided, the rate of each

manually but most stores now use billing machines or computers to do the needful. Law requires that the name of the seller must be printed along with the invoice number and the date of issue of the invoice.

The invoice is a legal document that ensures that the purchaser gets value for money. In the event he feels cheated he can seek relief through the Consumer's Court. The prescription that a doctor or a dentist gives is evidence of the patient having paid for services and in the event of a problem can seek relief. Law requires that a copy of the invoice must be maintained by the person issuing it.

Writing a Legal Document

Writing A Receipt
It is the responsibility of every person to write a receipt for every amount received. Since innumerable

    The number and date of receipt.
    The name and address of the person making the payment.
    The amount received.
    The purpose for which the amount is received.
    The position and signature of the person receiving the money.

information that would eventually go to the Board that would conduct the examination and mention the

Gujrada, Santnagar....Deponent
    I, Uday Shankar, depose on oath as follows:
1. That my name and address given above is correct.
2. That I have a daughter Km. Seema, who is presently studying in class IX in Nav Jyoti School,

    name is Smt. Shanti Devi.

    Signed before Notary at Santnagar on March 10, 2012:
    Deponent

Writing A Tenancy Deed
When a person gives out or takes premises on rent it is in the interests of both the landlord and the tenant to write a tenancy deed. Tenancy rules vary in different parts of the country and these should

mentioning the following:
    The name and address of the landlord.
    The name and address of the tenant.
    The details of the property to be rented out.
    The period of tenancy.
    Whether the landlord has taken any security.

The monthly rent to be paid.
Whether the tenancy can be renewed at the end of the period.
The rent at the time of renewal of tenancy.
The payment of house tax, water and electricity.
Eviction in the event of non-payment of rent.

paper. The document should progress logically on the basis of the information to be included in the deed.

Begin with the title or the type of deed being written, the date of the document and the names of the landlord and the tenant. Here is a sample beginning:

Rent Deed
A RENT DEED is written this 20th day of August 2013 between:

    inafter referred to as the Landlord, and

    050, hereinafter referred to as the Tenant.

The next obvious step would be to write the purpose of writing the document. It could be as follows:

DEED, and desires to let it out on rent.

this Deed is executed giving the details of the conditions mutually agreed upon by the two Parties.

    THIS DEED is executed on the following conditions:

The conditions that have been mutually agreed upon should be listed one by one, each sentence beginning with the word: That. It could be as follows:

1.

    Tenant.
3. *That the Tenant shall use the premises only for personal residence and would not carry out any commercial or illegal activity in the premises.*

    shall not attract any interest and would be paid back to the Tenant at the time of vacating the premises in good condition.
5. *That the Tenant shall pay Rs 10,000/- (Rupees ten thousand only) as rent for the premises by cheque at the completion of each month.*

    would be paid by the Tenant.
7. *That the Landlord and the Tenant shall review the situation one month before the expiry of this DEED whether the tenancy would continue, and if agreed a new DEED would be executed.*

The conditions described above are the usual conditions that appear in a tenancy deed. If desired, additional conditions can be listed in the same way to the satisfaction of both the parties. At the end the details of the property can be given and both the Parties could sign on the document before two witnesses, written in the deed as follows:

Details of Property:

SIGNED at Delhi before witnesses:
Witness:_____   Landlord: _____
Witness:_____   Tenant: _____

Writing A Partnership Deed

When two or more people decide to pool in their resources and do business together it becomes necessary

the event a deed is not executed and business is conducted as a group, they would be accepted as an

A partnership deed should be written on stamp paper, and written very much like a tenancy deed though the points to be agreed upon would be different. A typical partnership deed would have the following details:

The date of formation of the partnership.
The names and addresses of the partners.

interest on the capital? If so, at what rate?

be a joint responsibility or individual responsibility?

Will all partners work? Or there would be one working partner and the others would be

What salary would each partner get?
What additional compensation would be given to the working partner?
What shall be the term of the partnership?
How can the partnership be dissolved? In the event of dissolution how would the assets including the properties used for business will be divided?
Who gets the goodwill or the name of the business in the event of dissolution of the partnership

What happens in the event of death of a partner? Do his successors take over his share? Or is

entry to the business?

A partnership deed would be written like a tenancy deed as follows:

Partnership Deed

THIS DEED OF PARTNERSHIP is made this 20th day of August 2011 by:

hereinafter referred to as Party No:2

WHEREAS the above-named parties have agreed to start a business of retailing hardware items in the name and style of BHARGAVA ANAND & Co. at Fatehpuri, Delhi, and have together acquired a shop on rent for the purpose, the terms and conditions of the partnership are hereunder mentioned to avoid any misunderstanding.

The next obvious step would be to write all the conditions of the partnership so that there is no another, but would be similar to what follows:

Writing A Deed of Dissolution

Once a partnership is created by executing a Partnership Deed, it continues to be an entity liable to taxes until it is dissolved through a Deed of Dissolution, and the authorities duly informed of the dissolution. A partnership can be dissolved through mutual consent, by one member serving notice on other partners that he or she wishes to withdraw, or because of the death of one of the partners. On dissolution, the

ANAND & Co. was to be dissolved, the Deed of Dissolution would be written as follows:

The next step would be to write all the conditions of dissolution. This would be done as follows:

Writing A Contract

A contract is a written or spoken agreement between two parties intended to be enforceable morally or by law. Although a spoken moral binding can sometimes be enforced, in business and professional activities all contracts are written. A letter of employment given to an employee, a written order for goods, appointment of a dealer for a particular territory or other similar activities comes within the meaning of a contract. These involve an agreement between two parties and it is customary to have the terms and conditions written down with both signing on it and keeping a copy for future use, if the circumstances so require it.

Government organisations and large commercial establishments have standard contract forms duly drafted by professionals and are used by changing the names and the purpose of the contract. However, in smaller establishments it is customary to write a short agreement that describes the terms and conditions that are mutually agreed upon by the two parties. These contracts are written on plain paper and signed by both the parties. A typical contract must specify the following:

    The names and addresses of both the parties to the contract.

    The details of what is to be done within the terms of the contract.

The amount of money to be paid for the work to be done.
How and when the work would be done, and the money paid.

How would the parties settle a dispute?
How can a contract be terminated?

Let us take the simple example of a publisher inviting an author to write a book for him. This form of such a contract would be as follows:

This is just a sample contract form that could have conditions added or deleted from it according to each situation. In the same way a contract could be drafted for different kinds of employment or for appointment of a dealer in a particular town or city. These contracts can be written and executed without outside help. When signed by both the parties in the presence of two witnesses they become a valid document admissible by law. The more complicated contracts that involve too many conditions, and particularly include penalty clauses for non-performance of conditions are best left to be drafted by professional lawyers who might like to mention different laws in the contract form. To avoid unnecessary litigation it is necessary to have an arbitration clause in the agreement so as to sort out matters outside the court.

Writing A Memorandum of Incorporation

Whenever a new business is established it becomes necessary to write a document stating the details of the business and the people involved in it. A proprietorship business has only one proprietor, and except for getting his business registered for purposes of taxation laws he is free to run the business in

people. Therefore, it becomes necessary to have a written document in the form of a partnership, which we have already discussed, including the documents necessary to wind it up.

Establishing a company is a bigger exercise in that it involves many persons and is also subject to several laws that control the conduct of these companies in the interests of following fair practices. Laws

the details in a template and getting it registered online. In India, it requires elaborate documentation that is done by professional accountants or groups of people who help register the company for a fee, often as a package.

The memorandum of incorporation, which would also have the Articles of Association, is a document that describes the details of the promoters and sets out rules for the running of the internal affairs of the company. A company can be registered either as a private limited company or a public limited company. For establishing a company the following information must be provided:

The name of the company.
The registered address of the company.
The names and addresses of all the promoters.
The name and address of the Company secretary.
The number, names and addresses of the directors of the company.
Details of the capital and shares of the company.

Details of how the directors would be elected and the annual general meeting.

Legal provisions about conducting business through companies vary from one country to another. The laws have been enacted to protect the rights of the shareholders who have invested money in the running of the business. The promoters are free to make their own rules about how they would like to run the affairs of the company, but it is necessary that these rules should be in harmony with the suggested requirements of running an effective company.

Writing Organisation by Laws

The organization requirements of each company would be different. Therefore, each company would

items that will need the attention of the person writing these rules would normally be:

Administrative Needs

other similar items.

Human resource needs. This would include hiring policy, period of probation, responsibility schedule, staff dress, rules regarding couples working, sexual harassment and other similar concerns.

Leave rules. This would include annual leave, casual leave, sick leave and rules relating to these.

Financial rules. These would include date of salary payment, deduction of mandatory amounts like taxes, provident fund, insurance, etc., leave without pay, annual increments, special allowances, entertainment and similar issue.

Residential quarters. Organizations that offer residential quarters or allowances will need to have rules about them.

behaviour and will need regular amendments to ensure that they are not misinterpreted or misused. Write these in simple language using common everyday words that are known to all employees.

Executing Sale/Purchase Deeds

All businessmen and professionals will need to execute sale or purchase deeds. These would need to be written by a good professional lawyer and registered to make it a valid document. One would not need to write the document oneself, but it is important that the rights of both the seller and the purchaser are appropriately written in the deed. Right or wrong, once a deed is signed before the Registrar, it is

answers to the following questions:

Does the seller have the right to sell the property in question? This fact must be thoroughly

west directions along with boundaries clearly and correctly described? In the event of a doubt have a map attached to the deed.

Are the land numbers given in the description of the property correct? Have a good lawyer check these.

Does the sale deed specify the road to reach the property in question? If you cannot reach it, what good is the property?

Are all old taxes and dues on the property paid? If not, they must be paid before the deed is executed. There must also be a mention that in the event of a claim in the future the same would be paid by the seller.

Have all the amounts paid for the property clearly mentioned in the deed? The details of the amount must be clearly written.

Does the deed have a clause that the seller is passing on all the rights that are available to him at the time of sale? This is in the interest of the purchaser.

Does the deed have a clause that the seller shall indemnify the purchaser in the event of a defect in the ownership records as claimed by the seller? This protects the interests of the purchaser.

The persons executing a deed might not have personally written the deed that is being executed. However, in the event of a dispute it is presumed that it has been mutually written by them and the conditions written in it are acceptable to both of them.

Writing An Indemnity Bond

In businesses and professions many situations would arise when a person would need to make a claim that is correct, but the person who is involved in settling the claim is not certain whether the person is making a genuine claim. In that case the second person would want that the person making the claim should give him an indemnity bond that would protect him in the event someone makes a similar claim later.

To indemnify means to pay money to someone for a harm or loss caused to that person. An indemnity bond insures the person against this harm or loss from the actions of the person making the claim. It is common for the railways or transporters to ask for an indemnity bond in the event a goods receipt is lost in post or through negligence. Banks also seek an indemnity bond when making a payment in the event a person dies, or when a person stands guarantee for another person not known to the bank. Some schools ask the parents to give an indemnity bond to protect the school from any claims in the event a child gets hurt during normal school activities.

difference is that an indemnity bond would be on a stamp paper of higher value, and the person making the claim would write that he will indemnify the party in the event his claim is found to be wrong. Here is a sample bond:

Indemnity Bond

Market, Rampur, depose on oath as follows:

1. That my name and address given above is correct.
2. That M/s Trishul Traders, Mumbai, had booked a consignment of goods packed in four cases
3. That M/s Trishul Traders has informed me that the said G.R. was sent to me through Golden Courier Co., the same day but the same has not reached me as of today.

5. That it is requested that ABC Transport Co. release the consignment against this bond wherein I agree to indemnify them in the event another person makes a claim better than mine.

Signed on June 3, 2013 at Rampur before Notary Public.

Notary: _____ Deponent: _____

Writing A First Information Report (FIR)

Law requires that in the event of house-breaking, a theft, an accident or a criminal breach the matter must be reported to the nearest Police Station. In most cases a lawyer is not present to write this report. It should therefore be written by the concerned person.

A report to the police is intended to describe the facts about the crime. When writing, report who was involved, what happened, when and where it happened or why and how the crime took place. The

that cannot be misinterpreted. Do not give an opinion. Leave it to the police to investigate the matter.

might come to your knowledge later on.

Writing A Legal Notice

When things go wrong it is common to serve a legal notice to the person who has committed an offence. The larger organizations like banks hire a standing counsel who performs such duties. However, in

Writing A Legal Brief

When it becomes necessary to take a matter to the court, or to defend oneself in the court, it becomes necessary to have a professional lawyer handling the matter. However, irrespective of how brilliant or capable a lawyer might be, he does not know any bit more about the disputed matter than what you tell

about it. Were you able to speak convincingly to him? Did he understand everything as you explained it? Do not overlook that he could be thinking of something else when you were speaking to him. He could also be interpreting facts differently, as he is trained to do that.

The best way to handle legal matters through a professional lawyer is to give him all the facts in the form of a brief and only after he has read it you could verbally elaborate upon the details and he could make appropriate markings.

When writing the brief, provide all the facts. It would be appropriate to list them one by one explaining their importance. It would be better if they are listed chronologically so that the lawyer can appreciate how the situation developed and what remedial action was taken. If you have any opinions

matter that way.

When defending a case in the court it would be appropriate for you to have a copy of the plaint before you, and to reply the points one by one. If some facts stated are true, accept them as such. If they are stated in a contorted form point it out. After you have responded to all the points, you could make additional points, or state facts that have deliberately been avoided. Write and discuss them with the

In handling all legal matters for your business or profession always remember that it is not the lawyers who make you succeed in settling disputed matters. They only advise you. It is your own persistence and regular follow-up of matters in writing that carry you through to success. Rely more on a written brief than upon verbal statement.

Mortgage Loans

It is common for businessmen and professionals to secure home loans or commercial loans by pledging

documentation for these loans is done by the lender, and the person taking the loan signs on the dotted line. Regulations vary from one country to another, but it is common to have two sets of documents. One set would pertain to the loan being taken, and the second one to pledge the property to the lender.

An important aspect that every person taking a loan by pledging property must remember is that there are a lot of variables, which must be clearly understood. The common variables are the amount of the loan, the period of the loan, interest rate, method of paying off the loan and penal clauses for making early or late payments. Some lenders would want guarantors besides pledging the property and also insist that mortgage insurance be done to safeguard the interests of the lender in the event of late payment. These loans are normally repaid on a monthly basis, but there could be other conditions like not paying for a period and then paying a higher amount over a period. There could also be restriction on the development or part sale of the property.

A little care taken when handling legal affairs that pertain to one's business, profession or the home ensure that one is not cheated or made to pay more than what is due.

Writing A Will

Everyone is sentimental about one's possessions and investments in business or a profession. It is normal for a person to desire that after his or her lifetime these assets are passed on to the dear ones like one's spouse or children. But this may always not be so. Many people would want to give something to charity or to those who might have given them more love and care than one's family. To ensure that this happens, one must write a will, which is the legal way of passing on one's assets after death.

It is interesting to observe that even in developed countries only 30 to 50 per cent people write a Will. It is not that the others would not like to write a Will, but they feel that it is a complex issue to be handled only by a professional lawyer. Since they might not be in contact with a lawyer they postpone the issue for a later date and eventually leave this world without a Will. Writing a Will is not as complicated as most people imagine. Anyone can do it. There are a few simple rules that must be followed. Everyone must write a Will irrespective of what one possesses. This will ensure a happy

Everyone must have a Will. A person could have little or much. A will ensures that a person's

A Will could be handwritten or typed. A handwritten Will has lesser chances of being challenged because it is in a person's handwriting.

The Will must begin with a person's name, a statement about being in good health, and expressing the desire of writing the Will. Here is a sample beginning:

I, Ramesh Chand Sharma, aged 58 years, in good physical and emotional health, presently in government service, posted in the Secretariat at Chandigarh, residing with my wife in a rented house in sector 11, do hereby make this Will so that there is no misunderstanding about distribution of my assets

> The next paragraph of the Will should give the details of the immediate family, and also other close relationships, if any. This gives an indication about relatives who could be claimants in the event there is no Will. This paragraph could be written as follows:

My immediate family includes my wife, Pushpa, aged 56 years, a daughter Radhika, aged 30 years, married and living with her husband in New Delhi, and a son Rakesh, aged 26 years, who has recently completed his studies and taken up a job in a company in Hyderabad. My parents are living in the ancestral house at Jalandhar. They have made a provision for living on their own. I also have two brothers and a sister who are married and living with their families.

> The next step in writing the Will would be to list all the assets, both movable and immovable. When properties are owned the details must be given. It is not necessary to give the details of

> but the details need not be described. In the event a person does not mention as asset, the Will not be ineffective, but as regards the particular asset is concerned, it shall be considered that the person has died intestate (without a Will) and the asset will be distributed according to the existing family law. This section of the Will can be written as follows:

I have been in government service for over thirty years, and am entitled to a pension and to other funds to which I have also contributed. My movable and immovable assets include:

1. A house no: 123 sector 1, in Panchkula, presently given on rent. This house was built with my savings and none of my paternal family has contributed towards it or has any right on it.
2. My share in the ancestral family home in which my parents are living.
3. My pension and gratuities, when due.
4. Four life insurance policies for varied amounts. My wife is mentioned as the nominee in each of them.
5. Deposits in banks and mutual funds. I have mentioned my wife as the nominee in all of these accounts.
6. My car and a scooter both registered at Chandigarh.

details. This section of the Will can be written as follows:

I bequeath my assets as follows:

1. My Panchkula house to my wife Pushpa, with the proviso that she can live in the house or rent it out during her lifetime, but cannot sell it or pass it to anyone. After her the house will pass on to my son Rakesh, who can do whatever he likes with it.
2. My share in the ancestral home to my son Rakesh.
3. My pension and gratuities from the government to my wife Pushpa.
4. The proceeds from my insurance policies, deposits in banks and Mutual Funds shall all go to my wife, with the proviso that she shall spend appropriately out of that for the marriage of our

Rakesh and daughter Radhika.

5. My wife Pushpa can keep the car and scooter, or pass these on to our son Rakesh, as she deems

In this particular case the situation is simple in that the assets are in the control of the wife,

are many assets in the hands of different people and the family could be larger with several

left after others have received what is bequeathed to them. The person writing the Will should also appoint an Executor of the Will. The Executor would ensure that the instructions in the Will are carried out in letter and spirit. This Executor could be a trusted relative, friend or a lawyer, who could keep a copy of the Will in safe custody.
After the Executor is mentioned or any other special instructions given the person must sign

This completes the writing of the Will.
The Will can be kept in a safe place like a bank locker or even with a trusted person. Many keep a copy with a lawyer known to the family. A copy of the Will could also be kept with the

An unregistered Will is as valid as a registered Will. It is not compulsory to have the Will registered. It is easier to make changes in an unregistered Will.

In the event of complications it would be necessary to probate the Will in a court. This would have to be done by a professional lawyer.

Chapter 22

An in-house journal or newsletter is a useful tool to create good relationships within an organization. Since effective communication is the key to a successful organization, the best way is to reach out to the largest number of employees through an in-house journal or newsletter.

An in-house journal or newsletter is published by the organization for its employees, and contains matter that would interest them. There are innumerable in-house newsletters published by organizations all over the world. It does not matter whether it is a one-page newsletter or a four-page newsletter or even more, it helps keep the employees informed. It also promotes greater loyalty for the organization.

The newsletters in smaller organizations are written and compiled by the employees as part-time activity, but in larger organizations dedicated staff oversees the publication of the journal or magazine. Some publish a journal every week; others do it fortnightly, monthly or even quarterly. Some organizations have a bumper annual issue. Most of these journals are printed in black and white. A few do it in colour.

Content of the Journal

The content of the journal or newsletter would depend upon the periodicity. The contents would be different if it were published weekly, fortnightly or monthly, as compared to one published quarterly, half-yearly or annually. Whereas the content would relate more to the employees if it were published frequently, the contents would be diverse in nature if the frequency is far apart. The contents would also vary with the kind of organization and the targeted audience. A newsletter published weekly by a club would carry a lot of personal information about members as compared to a newsletter of a company that has 500 employees. If one were to pick up several newsletters published by different organizations, one would come across a lot of diverse subjects that have been included. It is for the person who is compiling the newsletter to choose the right content-mix for the journal. Here is a list of common subjects to be seen in in-house newsletters, journals and magazines:

1. **Birthdays and Wedding Anniversaries**. These can be included if the target group is small and the information for all the targeted audience is readily available with the editorial members of the newsletter. If there is 90 per cent coverage, the other 10 per cent regret that they have been ignored.
2. **Important Milestones**. There are important milestones in the lives of all employees –completing being promoted to a senior position, receiving a special honour by the public or similar situations. These deserve a mention in the newsletter
3. **Organisation News**. This is a wide subject that could include a variety of information. Care should be taken that the information must appeal to the reading audience. Everyone likes to

read about achievements where they have contributed through hard work and persistence. News about the growth and development of the organization is always well accepted.

4. **Special events**. This would include opening new branches, celebrating special occasions like a

vals in a special way. Whatever is special and of interest can be included in the newsletter.

5. **Achievements and Recognitions**. All organisations would like to share news where the organization has been recognized for special achievements. They get special coverage in the newspapers or trade magazines, awarded special prizes for safety and quality standards, or rated in comparison to business giants. The employees would want to know about these achievements.

6. **New Schemes and Launches**. Organisations continue to be innovative in trying new ideas and launching new products and services. The readers must get to know about them.

7. **Safety Rules**. A little educational information included along with entertaining reading helps send messages to the employees and their families.

8. **Motivational Quotations**. Everyone loves to read a motivation quotation, a poem or story that makes one feel inspired. These are popular in all kinds of publications. Many readers keep these clippings for future reading.

9. **Short Moral Stories**. Most people think that these are of interest only to the children. It would surprise you that the grownups enjoy these stories more than the children. These little anecdotes have much to convey.

. The employees in every organization would like to adopt new methods to

recognized with prizes.

11. **Household Hints**

comfortable for the workers' families. Everyone likes to read about them.

12. **Cooking Hints**. These are of special interest to ladies and others who love cooking. New ideas and recipes make life greater fun. Many newsletters include a recipe that would be appropriate for a situation. For example, making sweets is popular at Diwali.

13. **Jokes**. One or two jokes in every issue keep the newsletter interesting for everyone. Who doesn't like to laugh?

14. **Puzzles**. This is another thought provoking section of the newsletter. People love to be challenged. When they get the answers right it gives them a sense of achievement, which makes them look forward to the next issue.

15. **Deaths and Remembrances** -
cause these messages mean much to the bereaved family and friends. When the names and photographs are included, particularly when they are well known among the reading audience, everyone appreciates the special mention.

Putting the Newsletter Together

spread over the country, or even abroad, the publishing of a company newsletter is entrusted to a professional team within the company. They collect the information, edit it appropriately and publish the newsletter regularly.

In smaller organizations where the targeted reading audience is limited, a person within the organization takes over the responsibility to compile the newsletter and pass it on to the printers for

through a local courier.

In an ideal situation the person responsible for compiling the newsletter should build a collection of appropriate quotations, anecdotes, jokes, puzzles, household hints, cooking hints, recipes and other readily available information pertaining to the company. With a stock of this information, the only additional information that would be required is the immediate current information about the organization. This can be collected periodically at the workplace.

Just as newspapers and magazines spread out the contents in designated parts and the readers can reach out to news of their interest by opening the appropriate page, space in a newsletter should also be designated for different items. This makes it easier to replace the information in each issue with similar matter.

The structure of the newsletter would depend upon personal preferences and needs of the group for whom the newsletter is intended. Once decided the structure of the newsletter can be maintained from one issue to another. When designing the newsletter and its structure it would be advisable to keep the following aspects in view:

Have a catchy name. People and places are known by their name. So are many products known by the brand name, not by the service or needs that they provide? When the name of the newsletter is repeated thousands of times, it becomes a brand name.

Select A4 size. This is a common standard for paper. It can be easily typed and printed. When choosing another size do not overlook the convenience aspect.

Print in black and white
publishing newsletters in colour, but they can be expensive. For economy the title part of the newsletter can be printed in colour in bulk in a press, and the matter printed periodically in smaller quantities on a printer or Xerox machine.

Use two print columns. For economy of space it is ideal to have two columns. The nature of matter is such that it can be adjusted better in columns. If three columns are preferred it would be better to use A4 paper in the landscape format instead of portrait format.

Inspirational quotation. Place it under the newsletter name under the title: Thought of the Week/Month.

Organizations news
The other items can follow in later pages.

Have a place for every item. Once the space is allocated it becomes easier to replace the matter from one issue to the next.

Keep collecting items of interest
items whenever you come across interesting quotations, hints, etc.

Work to a schedule.

to ensure success.

Expressions	
No: 7 Your Monthly Newsletter July 2013	
Thought for the Month You will always rise in life to the level of responsibility that you're willing to accept. – R.W. Emerson Bonus Announced The Board has announced a bonus of	New Branch Inaugurated A new branch of the company was inaugurated at Sonepat, Haryana by Mr. Rajesh Singh, GM, Sales, on June 7. The elite gentry of the town attended the opening.

Every organization would seek to have its name in the newspaper for the good that it does. We cannot overlook that a newspaper or magazine is a commercial organization that collects revenue through advertisements published in it. Since it is not the advertisements that the public seeks to read, a

not be plain information. It must be news that interests the public.

People often ask: what is news? The answer is: news is information about recent events. Some prefer to describe news as information not previously known to the public. News is special information. For example, "dog bites man" is not news. However, "man bites dog" is news. Observe the difference between the two situations.

Every newspaper has its limitations. They have several reporters and correspondents who provide news each day. To make it easier for each other reporters get together at the Press Club or a similar place and share news that can be included in different newspapers. Since it is not possible for the reporters to visit too many places in a day, they seek press notes from organizations, particularly the government

organizations can send in press notes that can be published in the paper.

If your organisation has something of interest to the public you could prepare a press note and share

must be clear about the following:

Mind your language. Send a press note in English to an English newspaper and one in Hindi to a Hindi newspaper. Do not mix the two.

Write in newspaper style. Newspapers write to inform what happened where and who were the persons who made it happen, and also how it would affect others. The matter should require the least changes.

Keep it brief and to the point. Space is scarce for every newspaper. If the matter requires larger space it might be better to write an article, which could be published if it meets editorial requirements.

Send the press note in time. Many kinds of information are time-bound. Newspapers have their own schedules and deadlines. Press notes received in time can only be considered for printing in the newspaper.

Give details about yourself. The newspaper would want to know who has provided the news. In the event the information is wrong, or someone objects to it, they could get back to you.

Writing a Press Note

Writing A Press Note

A press note must be written keeping the abovementioned factors in mind. Let us consider a few examples.

Rotary, a service organisation with clubs all over the world decides to build 50 new schools

Here is a possible press note in this situation:

New Schools for Old

that Rotary in India has agreed to build over 50 schools in Rudraprayag and Uttarkashi districts

A committee of top leaders in Rotary in India was in Dehra Dun recently, and has signed a memorandum of understanding with the government of Uttarakhand to complete the work within a

already been initiated and the construction work would be supervised by volunteers from within the organisation.

In another situation a pharmaceutical company is experimenting with a combination of extracts of certain plants as a cure for patients with prostate cancer. They have carried out successful trials on patients and are asking the Controller of Drugs for trials at a wider level before the medicine can be marketed.

Cure for Prostate Cancer

New Delhi: Hindustan Pharmaceuticals Ltd., a leading manufacturer of drugs in the private sector, has claimed successful cure of prostate cancer with a combination of extracts of readily available plants with no ill side effects. The company has asked the Controller of Drugs for permission to carry out tests on a larger scale to verify the claims further.

The management of the company has asserted that they have the necessary facilities to manufacture and market the medicine as soon as trials are completed and permission given to market it.

good image by keeping everyone well informed.

Chapter 74

The larger business houses and organizations employ professional advertising agencies to handle all their requirements. They design the advertising, the format and placing, and all other requirements such as seeking permissions for putting up hoardings. They charge nothing for these services because they receive a commission from the newspapers and magazines for procuring advertisements for them.

But what about the common businessman or the professional who needs to advertise a special

paper on a weekly basis. People can place advertisements seeking customers, tenants, salesmen, tutors

that the advertiser will provide them the wording and design of the advertisement.

How should such advertisements be written? Those who advertise regularly to sell products could get an advertisement designed by a professional, but others could write the advertisement copy keeping a few common points in mind. These are:

Know the exact need. For example, if you want to rent out a part of your house to a family, but would not like them to have a pet dog; you should mention this when you write about the offer. If you want to hire a salesperson, you could write that both salesmen and salesgirls can apply.

Keep it brief. Describe the need in as few words as you can possibly manage to do so. Most

charged for on the basis of the size of the advertising box.

Use simple words

precise but could also be misinterpreted. That would defeat the purpose of the advertisement.

Seek the correct forum. Technical requirements are best advertised in trade journals and magazines.

Submit the matter in time. Every newspaper has a publishing schedule. The advertisement must be submitted in time to conform to the printing schedule of the publishing newspaper..

Writing the Advertisement

How does a school advertise for a new principal? Or how does an organization advertise to hire junior engineers as supervisors at worksites? Here are two sample ads:

PRINCIPAL REQUIRED
A leading co-educational school requires a Principal with a minimum 5 years' experience. Salary negotiable.
Contact: Mob: 12345 67890

REQUIRED
Two Junior Civil Engineers
For outstation supervision work
Please contact:
Anand Construction Co.
Gandhi Road, Shamnagar.
Email: anandcontruction@gmail.com

Two shops, 250 Sq.ft. each, available on sale/rent at **Shining Towers**. Contact: Mob. 12345 67890.

Godown required for MNC minimum 5000 Sq.ft where trucks can reach 24/7. Contact: 12345 67890.

communication in the past decade. Its use in business and professions has assumed special importance because of the advantages that it offers. In simple terms email is sending of electronic messages by one computer user to another through a network. Through email it is possible to send messages:

    On a one-to-one basis

    To a small group of people

    To a large group of people.

Communicating through email has many advantages. Some of them are:

when you are travelling at any time of the day or night.

The message reaches the mailbox of the recipient immediately. Of course the recipient will have access to the message only on opening the mailbox.

The message is sent by typing it on the computer. It requires no paper to write it, no envelope to hold it, or postage stamps to mail it.

It is almost free. Email requires no postage or courier charges.

A copy of the message is saved on the computer. You can retrieve it at will.

The recipient can reply it immediately at the pressing of a button and typing the response and sending it back again at the click of a button.

Since responses are noted continuously when the mail goes to and fro, one can easily go

to one or more people simultaneously.

With development of technology these messages are now being sent and received through

Communication Made Easy

Just by reading the advantages of communication through email it becomes apparent how people in

all the important personnel, and vice versa. Through this easy method a team leader keeps in touch with the team members, seeking ideas and opinions, brainstorming, providing vital information and getting back important feedback.

This way the doctors keep in touch with their colleagues, following up on important patients. Professors are keeping in touch with students and research scholars. Even at the school level the principal keeps in touch with staff members seeking progress reports on teaching and special students. Since the communication is through electronic networks it is now possible to keep in touch actively with colleagues all over the world sharing information at the click of a button immediately at almost no cost.

With the use of email meetings are becoming more effective. The agenda along with all relevant

comments. Minutes of the meeting are also sent the same way. Even for large meetings the information can be swiftly transmitted through email followed by a hard copy when necessary.

Email has become a vital tool to inform small and also very large groups. Business houses have taken advantage of this fact and are using it as an economical tool for wide-scale advertising. This can be irritating to the recipients of these messages, but nonetheless this method is being widely used for the promotion of business. Many online stores rely upon this advertising for selling the products.

Writing An E-mail Message

Though email messages are communicated through telephone networks, writing an email is not like speaking face-to-face in a conversation or on a telephone. In a direct conversation it is possible to read meanings from facial expressions and body language. In a telephone call it is possible to draw meaning from the voice tone. An email is a combination of a written letter and the speed of a telephone call. As for all other kinds of written documents there are certain ways that can make an email an effective tool of communication. It would be useful to keep the following in mind:

Remember the ABC of writing. This is especially applicable to an email message because it

Know the 'purpose' of the message. Without understanding the purpose of the message it is not possible to follow the ABC of writing.

Write an attractive 'Subject line'.
He would want to know what the email is about. If the subject is of interest he would read it, otherwise just skip it.

The subject line should be like a newspaper headline. Like a headline it must grab immediate attention and also tell the purpose of the message that follows.

Express urgency, if necessary, in the subject line. Some messages require urgent response or feedback. If so, mention it in the subject line.

Write on one subject. To be short and readable an e-mail must cover only one subject. This will get the best response. If more than one subject is covered it is likely that the reader could have different opinions about the two items and would defer the response to it for a later date that he might forget.

Cover one point in one paragraph. In the event that there are several points pertaining to one subject that you are covering in the mail, write one point in one paragraph. For convenience each paragraph could be numbered.

The message should be written like a business letter. It must be clear and to the point, and

direct and provide pertinent information.

Specify the desired response. How would you like the recipient to respond to the mail? Talk to you on the telephone? Provide you with some information? Act to do something? Whatever it be, it must be clear at the end of the message.

Close the email just as you would a letter. The recipient must have all the details of the of the email. For example:

SureshTripathi	or	Suresh Tripathi
32, Mall Road,		ASM, North Zone,
		Smart Cosmetics (Pr) Ltd.
sureshtripathi@yahoo.in		surershtripathi@yahoo.in
Mob: 12345 67890		Mob: 12345 67890

Here is an example of a well-written email:

From: Suresh Tripathi
To: N.I. Sales-team
Copy: Sales Manager

Dear Team-mates:

of activities shall be as follows:

1. Stocks shall reach the area stockists 3 days before the launch.
2. Retail store publicity material shall accompany the goods.
3. Please check that the stockists have received the goods in time.
4. Stockists should instruct their local salesmen to be ready with stocks and publicity material at 10.00 a.m. on Sept 1 to begin distribution in designated retail stores.
5. Company salesmen shall supervise the operations, reporting the progress each evening through email.
6. All designated retail stores must be covered within three days of launch.

Happy selling!
Suresh Tripathi
ASM, North Zone,
Smart Cosmetcs (Pr) Ltd.
sureshtripathi@yahoo.in
Mob: 12345 67890

Using EOM Headlines

activities are short of time to write or read messages. Like these busy persons, one could convey the whole message in the subject line only. For example:**"Meet me 10 am tomorrow – EOM"**

Sending Copies of the Mail

Like all other business mail it is possible to send carbon copies to as many people as the sender would like to send them to. It is as simple as writing the email IDs in the space: Copy to. These copies are sent without any extra effort and reach simultaneously with the original to the recipient. Since the recipient and others to whom the copies are sent receive the mail as sent by the sender, everyone gets to know to whom the mail has been sent. While it is for the person to whom the mail is sent to respond to it, it is presumed that those to whom copies have been sent is only for their information and not for response. Of course a mail could be addressed to more than one person and then each person would be expected to respond. That would depend upon the nature and purpose of the mail.

Some people like to send copies without the recipient of the mail getting to know to whom the copies have been endorsed. This is possible by sending the message through a blind carbon copy, bcc, which does not show the recipient that a copy has been endorsed to someone else.

Using Abbreviations and Emoticons

To conserve upon space and write speedily some people like to use abbreviations, which may be shortened forms of words or phrases. There are others who are more ingenious and use emoticons, which are images made by using the keyboard symbols to create the human face expressing a variety of emotions. These are included to express humour, sarcasm, excitement and other feelings and emotions. It might be all right to use abbreviations and emoticons in personal email, from one person to another as a friend. However, these are not appreciated in business and professional communications, and must be avoided at all times.

Replying E-mail

Replying email is simpler than writing an email in that all that one needs to do is to click the "Reply"

is desired to share the mail with all the recipients then instead of "Reply" button, one should press the "Reply All" button. The response would automatically go to all the recipients.

Forwarding Mail

When a message needs to be shared with another person or persons it is possible to share it by just clicking the "Forward" button, writing the email ID of the person or persons to whom the mail is to be forwarded. It is also possible to add some comments, if necessary. This is an effective way of sharing important information.

E-mail Etiquette

The wide-scale use of email in business and professional activities is fairly recent, but like all other activities it has become necessary to adopt certain basic rules when using email. Email is used by school and college students as much as by people in business and professional life, but at no stage have the users been taught to respect each other's feelings and sensitivities to avoid unpleasantness when communicating through email. It is only through experience that certain basic rules of etiquette have emerged. These must be respected by all users. These simple rules are:

Check email regularly. Just as a person checks the mailbox every day for the mail the postman may have dropped in it, email too must be checked. When you give your email ID to a person it is presumed that you check your mail every day and would respond to it just as one would respond to normal mail.

Keep the mail short and to the point. Reading a message on the computer screen is not the same as reading a letter printed on paper. When the message is long it becomes necessary to scroll down the screen making reading a bit tedious.

Mind your language. A person should write just as one would speak. But this should not mean that just because you cannot see the person you are writing to, you can use any kind of language. Be careful about the feelings and sensitivities of the people you are writing to.

Do not use only capital letters. When you use capital letters to write the message it gives the impression that you are shouting.

Do not use abbreviations and emoticons.
look at life differently, and what might be funny to someone might not be so to another person.

Do not attach too many enclosures. Many enthusiasts add a lot of attachments like written

that takes longer to transmit and also longer to receive. When a person receives too many of such mails it can clog the mailbox much to the frustration of the recipient of the mail.

Don't send everything to everyone. Many enthusiastic persons send brochures, bulletins, PowerPoint presentations and a whole lot of other material to everyone they know just because they might have liked it. Too much of such mail is not appreciated by people who do not have the time to read or see it.

Reply mail only to concerned person. It is common for people to click the "Reply all" button instead of "Reply" button, thereby sharing their response with people who are not even

Be businesslike at the workplace. When using email for business and professional work write just as you would normal business letters. All kinds of courtesies must be maintained. Do not become informal at the workplace. It can be easily misunderstood by the management.

computers to receive and send personal mail. This is not appreciated by most corporate houses. Please check on company policy about use of company computers.

Limitations of E-Mail

and photographs to keep everyone well informed of the progress, but in the best of group work there is time when it becomes necessary for everyone to sit around face-to-face and discuss things to carry them forward to attain success. Even when it comes to preparing project reports or other documents that require joint effort and action, one needs to get together to work out all the details.

Security Concerns

Despite all the freedom a person might enjoy communicating through email it is open to scrutiny

be communicated through email. Hackers have broken into highly secured computer servers to steal information. This fact must always be remembered by users.

Archiving Documents
It is obvious that everyone would like to keep a record of the information sent or received through email. This is done automatically on the computer. When necessary, the information can be printed

word processing programme in the computer.

Chapter 26

SMS is the abbreviation of short message service, a system for sending written messages from one mobile phone to another.

It is very much like the old system of sending telegrams that were short messages transmitted through a telegraph system using morse keys. It enabled an urgent transmission of a message to the recipient. That had to be done through the state run telegraph department and was expensive as compared to writing a letter. Sending a SMS is simple. A message can be sent from one mobile phone to another at the click of a button at very low cost in comparison to the cost of a phone call.

Since SMS is also transmitted through the telephone network, it can be compared to email. This is the shorter version of email and can be sent from a mobile phone.

Considering the utility of sending messages with the convenience of doing it from one's mobile to that of the recipient, it is an important means of communication in the hands of businessmen and professionals. With millions of phones in use the utility of such a service can be well appreciated.

A SMS is limited to 160 characters including the space inbetween the words. With space as a very important constraint, the need to accommodate the maximum number of words in the space has led to the development of the SMS languagereferred to as textese. It is also known as txt-speak, txtese, chatspeak, txt, txtspk, txtk, texting language, txt lingo, SMSish, txtslang or txt talk. The use of abbreviations in SMS language varies with people, places and situations. Although SMS dictionaries are offered on the Internet, SMS language is yet to be accepted for general use.

It would be useful to understand how people have adapted abbreviations of commonly used words in the English language. They are more popular amongst school and college going young people than among the businessmen and professionals. Here is a sample list of how words are expressed:

be is expressed as *b*
okay is expressed as *k* or *ok*
you is expressed as *u*
oh is expressed as *o*
to or *two* is expressed as *2*
ate is expressed as *8*

see or *sea* is expressed as *c*
are is expressed as *r*
why is expressed as *y*
won or *one* is expressed as *1*
for or *fore* is expressed as *4*

Before is written as b4, today as 2day, tomorrow as 2mro, forget as 4get, great as gr8, wait as w8, late as l8, mate as m8, your as ur, for you as 4u, easy as ez and so on.

Using SMS

Here are a few other examples of conversion of words and phrases into textese:

have a nice day	HAND	sealed with a kiss	SWAK
keep it simple, stupid		please reply	RSVP
random act of kindness		love	
so what's your problem	SWYP	parents are watching	PAW
chicks	CHX	such a laugh	SAL
at the moment	ATM	tears in my eyes	TIME
thanks	THNX	at	@
you're on your own	YOYO	oh my god	OMG
cool story, bro	CSB	as soon as possible	ASAP

It has been observed that words are abbreviated with a close relationship to the phonetics or the way they sound. SMS language uses graphones, a word derived from the combination of two words:

per cent of the users favour abbreviations. Most of these are young people in schools and colleges.

Many people complain that use of textese is a sure method of corrupting the language and would lead to poor written English. They also point out that some people are already using abbreviations in normal written work in English. We should look at it only as a point of view of some people. It is not completely true or universally accepted. People are welcome to hold their own opinions. The fact is that people would do what they think best. Businessmen and professionals are not different. If they can

It is best for businessmen and professionals to use the conventional language, writing the SMS just as telegrams were written in earlier years. If they are tempted to use textese, which most people would like to do, it should be restricted to messages to people who are known informally. One would need to be conservative with the people who are known only professionally.

Just like the use of email there are certain commonsense rules that must be remembered when communicating through SMS. One would do well to remember the following:

> **Be sure of what you do.** Communicate through SMS only when you are convinced that your contacts are not averse to it.
>
> **Use it only when it promotes business.** The communications must promote better relationships and productivity at the workplace.
>
> **Make it clear and simple.** This would not offend the sensitivities of people and would still convey the message.
>
> **Make the message complete.**
> the use of only 160 characters. Choose words correctly, describe the purpose and the action required. Close with your name.
>
> Do not take the liberty of forwarding jokes and funny stories you receive from friends to business contacts. Just because you like them would not mean that they would like it too.

Using Sms As A Marketing Tool

It is becoming common for many corporate houses to use SMS to promote their products and services. However, this is not as popular as the use of email messages that are elaborate and also carry illustrations to make them descriptive and useful. Since receiving SMS messages on the mobile can sometimes be very irritating, government agencies have restricted their use within limitations.

While it is true that a SMS reaches a person directly it does not mean that all marketing messages or service through SMS? If so, who would be the ideal audience? Also, what would be an ideal message?

To use SMS as a marketing tool it might be preferable to have the message prepared professionally it at an appropriate time. It is generally felt that late afternoon is a good time to send such messages.

Using Sms As Alerts

With the rapid liberalization and use of Internet for banking operations it has become necessary to keep the customers well-informed not only as a promotion activity, but also to avoid banking frauds by the staff and mischief mongers. To make this possible most of the progressive banks now send transaction alerts to customers when amounts are debited or credited to their accounts. A SMS message conveys the details of the transaction. Here are a few examples:

Avl bal as on 08-Aug-2013 in your A/c No.XX0761 is INR 5,141 (including linked deposits and limit)	Your A/c No.XX0761 has been debited with INR 2,000 thru Internet Banking Avl bal INR 3,141-

SMS alerts are also used to draw the attention of customers to bills that are waiting to be paid, or subscriptions that require to be renewed. Here are a few examples:

Payment of Tata Sky ID xxx381is due tomorrow. Monthy charge for ID is Rs 325. Recharge with this amount.	Your BSNL Wireline account XXX7608 has been billed with Rs 483 on Aug-1-13. Pay by Aug-27-2013.

Section 4

Effective business and professional activities require a lot of information. This is particularly so when

English is a vast language. Over a long period of use special meanings have been given to certain words, terms and phrases. When a person consults a dictionary, with several meanings for each word, the meaning of a word can easily be misinterpreted. There are many words that are not generally used, but one comes across them at the workplace. For convenience a glossary of such business terms has

and accountancy. The subject is mentioned along with the common meaning. Where a term has dual meanings the same are described appropriately.

Learning these popular terms would increase a person's vocabulary substantially, making it easier to understand business conversations and written documents. One would do well to go through them repeatedly to learn these words and phrases.

computer terms. Therefore, a glossary of computer terms is also included. A knowledge of these terms

equipment.

With many business houses transacting business at the international level, it is common to use foreign terms used in Business English. An effort has been made to list the most popular ones along with the meaning.

Since different countries use a variety of currencies it becomes necessary for businessmen and professionals to know them. It also becomes necessary to know about the variations in time around the world so that one can communicate nutually at convenient timings. Therefore the details of currencies

Many abbreviations are used by businessmen and professionals. Many people are not acquainted with them. The popular ones are listed for convenience.

interpret the same in terms of those used by them. For convenience the weights, measures, lengths and areas used all over the world are listed comparing one to the other. Conversion tables are also given.

Reference Section

English Improvement/Self-Help

Career & Business Management

visit our online bookstore: www.vspublishers.com

Student Development

visit our online bookstore: www.vspublishers.com

www.ingramcontent.com/pod-product-compliance
Lightning Source LLC
Chambersburg PA
CBHW080246030426
42334CB00023BA/2719